Pisistratus Caxton

What will he do with it?

Pisistratus Caxton

What will he do with it?

ISBN/EAN: 9783742808721

Manufactured in Europe, USA, Canada, Australia, Japa

Cover: Foto ©Klaus-Uwe Gerhardt /pixelio.de

Manufactured and distributed by brebook publishing software (www.brebook.com)

Pisistratus Caxton

What will he do with it?

WHAT WILL HE DO WITH IT?

BOOK I.—CHAPTER I.

In which the History opens with a description of the Social Manners, Habits, and Amusements of the English People, as exhibited in an immemorial National Festivity.—Characters to be commemorated in the History, introduced and graphically portrayed, with a naeological illustration.—Original suggestions as to the idiosyncrasies engendered by trades and callings, with other matters worthy of note, conveyed in artless dialogue after the manner of Herodotus, Father of History (Mother unknown).

It was a summer fair in one of the prettiest villages in Surrey. The main street was lined with booths, abounding in toys, gleaming crockery, gay ribbons, and gilded gingerbread. Farther on, where the street widened into the ample village-green, rose the more pretending fabrics which lodged the attractive forms of the Mermaid, the Norfolk Giant, the Pig-faced Lady, the Spotted Boy, and the Calf with Two Heads; while high over even these edifices, and occupying the most conspicuous vantage-ground, a lofty stage promised to rural playgoers the "Grand Melodramatic Performance of The Remorseless Baron and the Bandit's Child." Music, lively if artless, resounded on every side;—drums, fifes, penny-whistles, cat-calls, and a hand-organ played by a dark foreigner, from the height of whose shoulder a cynical but observant monkey eyed the hubbub and cracked his nuts.

It was now sunset—the throng at the fullest—an animated joyous scene. The day had been sultry; no clouds were to be seen, except low on the western horizon, where they stretched, in lengthened ridges of gold and purple, like the borderland between earth and sky. The tall elms on the green were still, save, near the great stage, one or two, upon which had climbed young urchins, whose laughing faces peered forth, here and there, from the foliage trembling under their restless movements.

Amidst the crowd, as it streamed saunteringly along, were two spectators—strangers to the place, as was notably proved by the attention they excited, and the broad jokes their dress and appearance provoked from the rustic wits,—jokes which they took with amused good-humour and sometimes retaliated with a zest which had already made them very popular personages; indeed, there was that about them which propitiated liking. They were young, and the freshness of enjoyment was so visible in their faces, that it begot a sympathy, and wherever they went, other faces brightened round them.

One of the two whom we have thus individualised was of that enviable age, ranging from five-and-twenty to

B

or two younger than himself. "Found in the act, sentenced, punished," cried he, snatching a kiss, and receiving a gentle slap. "And now, good for evil, here's a ribbon for you—choose."

The girl slunk back shyly, but her companions pushed her forward, and she ended by selecting a cherry-coloured ribbon, for which the boy paid carelessly, while his elder and wiser friend looked at him with grave compassionate rebuke, and grumbled out,—"Dr. Franklin tells us that once in his life he paid too dear for a whistle; but then he was only seven years old, and a whistle has its uses. But to pay such a price for a scratchback!—Prodigal! Come along."

As the friends strolled on, naturally enough all the young girls who wished for ribbons, and were possessed of scratchbacks, followed in their wake. Scratch went the instruments, but in vain.

"Lasses," said the elder, turning sharply upon them his nose in the air, "ribbons are plentiful—shillings scarce; and kisses, though pleasant in private, are insipid in public. What, still! Beware! know that, innocent as we seem, we are women-eaters; and if you follow us farther, you are devoured!" So saying, he expanded his jaws to a width so preternaturally large, and exhibited a row of grinders so formidable, that the girls fell back in consternation. The friends turned down a narrow alley between the booths, and though still pursued by some adventurous and mercenary spirits, were comparatively undisturbed as they threaded their way along the back of the booths, and arrived at last on the village-green, and in front of the Great Stage.

"Oho, Lionel!" quoth the elder friend; "Thespian and classical—worth seeing, no doubt." Then turning to a grave cobbler in leathern apron, who was regarding with saturnine interest the motley figures ranged in front of the curtain as the "*Dramatis Personæ*," he said, "You seem attracted, sir; you have probably already witnessed the performance."

"Yes," returned the Cobbler; "this is the third day, and to-morrow's the last. I arn't missed once yet, and I shan't miss; but it arn't what it was awhile back."

"That is sad; but then the same thing is said of everything by everybody who has reached your respectable age, friend. Summers, and suns, stupid old watering-places, and pretty young women, 'arn't what they were awhile back.' If men and things go on degenerating in this way, our grandchildren will have a dull time of it."

The Cobbler eyed the young man, and nodded approvingly. He had sense enough to comprehend the ironical philosophy of the reply—and our Cobbler loved talk out of the common way. "You speaks truly and cleverly, sir. But if old folks do always say that things are worse than they were, ben't there always summat in what is always said? I'm for the old times; my neighbour, Joe Spruce, is for the new, and says we are all a-progressing. But he's a pink—I'm a blue."

"You are a blue!" said the boy Lionel—"I don't understand."

"Young 'un, I'm a Tory—that's blue; and Spruce is a Rad—that's pink! And, what is more to the purpose, he is a tailor, and I'm a cobbler."

"Aha!" said the elder, with much interest; "more to the purpose is it? How so?"

The Cobbler put the forefinger of the right hand on the forefinger of the left; it is the gesture of a man about to ratiocinate or demonstrate

he's broke down now, anyhow. But she takes care of him, little darling —God bless thee!" and the Cobbler here exchanged a smile and a nod with the little girl, whose face brightened when she saw him amidst the crowd.

"By the brush and pallet of Raffaelle!" cried the elder of the young men, "before I am many hours older I must have that child's head!"

"Her head, man!" cried the Cobbler, aghast.

"In my sketch-book. You are a poet—I a painter. You know the little girl?"

"Don't I! She and her grandfather lodge with me—her grandfather—that's Waife—marvellous man! But they ill-uses him; and if it warn't for her, he'd starve. He fed them all once; he can feed them no longer—he'd starve. That's the world; they use up a genus, and when it falls on the road, push on; that's what Joe Spruce calls a-progressing. But there's the drum! they're a-going to act; won't you look in, gents?"

"Of course," cried Lionel—"of course. And, hark ye, Vance, we'll toss up which shall be the first to take that little girl's head."

"Murderer in either sense of the word!" said Vance, with a smile that would have become Correggio if a tyro had offered to toss up which should be the first to paint a cherub.

CHAPTER II.

The Historian takes a view of the British Stage as represented by the Irregular Drama, the Regular having (ere the date of the events to which this narrative is restricted) disappeared from the Vestiges of Creation.

THEY entered the little theatre, and the Cobbler with them; but the last retired modestly to the threepenny row. The young gentlemen were favoured with reserved seats, price one shilling. "Very dear," murmured Vance, as he carefully buttoned the pocket to which he restored a purse woven from links of steel, after the fashion of chain mail. Ah, *Messieurs* and *Confrères*, the Dramatic Authors, do not flatter yourselves that we are about to give you a complacent triumph over the Grand Melodrame of "The Remorseless Baron and the Bandit's Child." We grant it was horrible rubbish, regarded in an æsthetic point of view, but it was mightily affective in the theatrical. Nobody yawned; you did not even hear a cough, nor the cry of that omnipresent baby, who is always sure to set up an unappeasable wail in the midmost interest of a classical fiveact piece, represented for the first time on the metropolitan boards. Here the story rushed on, *per fas aut nefas*, and the audience went with it. Cartes, some men who understood the stage must have put the incidents together, and then left it to each illiterate histrio to find the words—words, my dear *confrères*, signify so little in an acting play. The movement is the thing. Grand secret! Analyse, practise it, and restore to grateful stars that lost Pleiad the British Acting Drama.

Of course the Bandit was an ill-

the title-deeds, filched from the Baron, and by her side the King's Lieutenant, who proclaims the Bandit's pardon, with due restoration to his honours and estates, and consigns, to the astounded Sheriff, the august person of the Remorseless Baron. Then the affecting scene, father and child in each other's arms; and then an exclamation, which had been long hovering about the lips of many of the audience, broke out, "Waife, Waife!" Yes, the Bandit, who appeared but in the last scene, and even then uttered not a word, was the once great actor on that itinerant Thespian stage, known through many a fair for his exuberant humour, his impromptu jokes, his arch eye, his redundant life of drollery, and the strange pathos or dignity with which he could suddenly exalt a jester's part, and call forth tears in the startled hush of laughter; he whom the Cobbler had rightly said, "might have made a fortune at Covent Garden." There was the remnant of the old popular mime!—all his attributes of eloquence reduced to dumb show! Masterly touch of nature and of art in this representation of him—touch which all, who had ever in former years seen and heard him on that stage, felt simultaneously. He came in for his personal portion of dramatic tears.

"Waife, Waife!" cried many a village voice, as the little girl led him to the front of the stage. He hobbled; there was a bandage round his eyes. The plot, in describing his accident that had befallen the Bandit, idealised the genuine infirmities of the man—infirmities that had befallen him since last seen in that village. He was blind of one eye; he had become crippled; some malady of the trachea or larynx had seemingly broken up the once joyous key of the old pleasant voice. He did not trust himself to speak, even on that stage, but silently bent his head to the rustic audience; and Vance, who was an habitual play-goer, saw in that simple salutation that the man was an artistic actor. All was over, the audience streamed out, much affected, and talking one to the other. It had not been at all like the ordinary stage-exhibitions at a village fair. Vance and Lionel exchanged looks of surprise, and then, by a common impulse, moved towards the stage, pushed aside the curtain, which had fallen, and were in that strange world which has so many reduplications, fragments of one broken mirror, whether in the proudest theatre, or the lowliest barn—nay, whether in the palace of kings, the cabinet of statesmen, the home of domestic life—the world we call "Behind the Scenes."

WHAT WILL HE DO WITH IT?

arm hastily, pulled me down to her own height, and whispered, 'How much will he give?' Confused by a question so point-blank, I answered at random, 'I don't know; ten shillings perhaps.' You should have seen her face!"

"See her face! radiant—I should think so. Too much by half!" exclaimed Vance. "Ten shillings! Spendthrift!"

"Too much—she looked as you might look if one offered you ten shillings for your picture of 'Julius Cæsar considering whether he should cross the Rubicon.' But when the manager had declared her to be his property, and appointed you to call to-morrow—implying that he was to be paid for allowing her to sit—her countenance became overcast, and she muttered sullenly, 'I'll not sit —I'll not!' Then she turned to her grandfather, and something very quick and close was whispered between the two; and she pulled me by the sleeve, and said in my ear— oh, but so eagerly!—'I want three pounds, sir,—three pounds!—if he would give three pounds;—And come to our lodgings—Mr. Merle, Willow Lane. Three pounds— three!" And with those words hissing in my ear, and coming from that fairy mouth, which ought to drop pearls and diamonds, I left her," added Lionel, as gravely as if he were sixty, "and lost an illusion!"

"Three pounds!" cried Vance, raising his eyebrows to the highest arch of astonishment, and lifting his nose in the air towards the majestic moon,—three pounds!—a fabulous sum! Who has three pounds to throw away? Dukes, with a hundred thousand a-year in acres, have not three pounds to draw out of their pockets in that reckless profligate manner. Three pounds!—what could I not buy for three pounds! I could buy the Dramatic Library, bound in calf, for three pounds; I could buy a dress coat for three pounds (silk lining not included); I could be lodged for a month for three pounds! And a jade in tinsel, just entering on her teens, to ask three pounds for what? for becoming immortal on the canvass of Francis Vance?—bother!"

Here Vance felt a touch on his shoulder. He turned round quickly, as a man out of temper does under similar circumstances, and beheld the swart face of the Cobbler.

"Well, master, did not she act fine? —how d'ye like her?"

"Not much in her natural character; but she sets a mighty high value on herself."

"Anan, I don't take you."

"She'll not catch me taking her! Three pounds!—three kingdoms!"

"Stay," cried Lionel to the Cobbler; "did not you say she lodged with you? Are you Mr. Merle?"

"Merle's my name, and she do lodge with me—Willow Lane."

"Come this way, then, a few yards down the road—more quiet. Tell me what the child means, if you can?" and Lionel related the offer of his friend, the reply of the manager, and the grasping avarice of Miss Juliet Araminta.

The Cobbler made no answer; and when the young friends, surprised at his silence, turned to look at him, they saw he was wiping his eyes with his sleeve.

"Poor little thing!" he said at last, and still more pathetically than he had uttered the same words at her appearance in front of the stage; "'tis all for her grandfather; I guess —I guess."

"Oh," cried Lionel, joyfully, "I am so glad to think that. It alters the whole case, you see, Vance."

"It don't alter the case of the three pounds," grumbled Vance. "What's her grandfather to me,

wi' catching cold, and lost his voice, and became the sad object you have gazed on, young happy things that ye are."

"But he got some compensation from the railway, I suppose?" said Vance, with the unfeeling equanimity of a stoical demon.

"He did, and spent it. I suppose the gentleman broke out in him as soon as he had money, and ill though he was, the money went. Then it seems he had no help for it but to try and get back to Mr. Rugge. But Mr. Rugge was sore and spiteful at his leaving; for Rugge counted on him, and had even thought of taking the huge theatre at York, and bringing out Gentleman Waife as his trump card. But it warn't fated, and Rugge thought himself ill-used, and so at first he would have nothing more to say to Waife. And truth is, what could the poor man do for Rugge? But then Waife produces little Sophy."

"You mean Juliet Araminta?" said Vance.

"Same—in private life she be Sophy. And Waife taught her to act, and put together the plays for her. And Rugge caught at her; and she supports Waife with what she gets; for Rugge only gives him four shillings a-week, and that goes on 'baccy and suchlike."

"Suchlike—drink, I presume!" said Vance.

"No—he don't drink. But he do smoke; and he has little genteel ways with him, and four shillings goes on 'em. And they have been about the country this spring, and done well, and now they be here. But Rugge behaves shocking hard to both on 'em: and I don't believe he has any right to her in law, as he pretends—only a sort of understanding which she and her grandfather could break if they pleased; and that's what they wish to do, and that's why little Sophy wants the three pounds."

"How?" cried Lionel, eagerly. "If they had three pounds could they get away? and if they did, how could they live? Where could they go?"

"That's their secret. But I heard Waife say—the first night they came here—'that if he could get three pounds, he had hit on a plan to be independent like.' I tell you what put his back up: it was Rugge insisting on his coming on the stage agin, for he did not like to be seen such a wreck. But he was forced to give in; and so he contrived to cut up that play-story, and appear hisself at the last without speaking."

"My good friend," cried young Lionel, "we are greatly obliged to you for your story—and we should much like to see little Sophy and her grandfather at your house to-morrow—can we?"

"Certain sure you can — after the play's over; to-night, if you like."

"No, to-morrow; you see my friend is impatient to get back now —we will call to-morrow."

"'Tis the last day of their stay," said the Cobbler. "But you can't be sure to see them safely at my house afore ten o'clock at night—and not a word to Rugge! mum!"

"Not a word to Rugge," returned Lionel; "good-night to you."

The young men left the Cobbler still seated on the milestone, gazing on the stars, and ruminating. They walked briskly down the road.

"It is I who have had the talk now," said Lionel, in his softest tone. He was bent on coaxing three pounds out of his richer friend, and that might require some management. For amongst the wild youngsters in Mr. Vance's profession, there ran many a joke at the

prosaic one—we'll blink it. Yes; I am glad to be a painter. But you must not catch the fever of my calling. Your poor mother would never forgive me if she thought I had made you a dauber by my example."

LIONEL (gloomily).—"No, I shall not be a painter! But what can I be? How shall I ever build on the earth one of the castles I have built in the air? Fame looks so far—Fortune so impossible. But one thing I am bent upon" (speaking with knit brow and clenched teeth) —"I will gain an independence somehow, and support my mother."

VANCE.—"Your mother is supported—she has the pension—"

LIONEL.—"Of a captain's widow; and" (he added with a flushed cheek) "a first floor that she lets to lodgers."

VANCE.—"No shame in that! Peers let houses; and on the Continent, princes let not only first floors, but fifth and sixth floors, to say nothing of attics and cellars. In beginning the world, friend Lionel, if you don't wish to get chafed at every turn, fold up your pride carefully, put it under lock and key, and only let it out to air upon grand occasions. Pride is a garment all stiff brocade outside, all grating sackcloth on the side next to the skin. Even kings don't wear the dalmaticum except at a coronation. Independence you desire; good. But are you dependent now? Your mother has given you an excellent education, and you have already put it to profit. My dear boy," added Vance, with unusual warmth, "I honour you; at your age, on leaving school, to have shut yourself up, translated Greek and Latin per sheet for a bookseller, at less than a valet's wages, and all for the purpose of buying comforts for your mother; and having a few pounds in your own pockets, to rove your little holiday with me, and pay your share of the costs! Ah, there are energy and spirit and life in all that, Lionel, which will found upon rock some castle as fine as any you have built in air. Your hand, my boy."

This burst was so unlike the practical dryness, or even the more unctuous humour, of Frank Vance, that it took Lionel by surprise, and his voice faltered as he pressed the hand held out to him. He answered, "I don't deserve your praise, Vance, and I fear the pride you tell me to put under lock and key, has the larger share of the merit you ascribe to better motives. Independent? No! I have never been so."

VANCE.—"Well, you depend on a parent,—who, at seventeen, does not?"

LIONEL.—"I did not mean my mother; of course, I could not be too proud to take benefits from her. But the truth is simply this: my father had a relation, not very near, indeed—a cousin, at about as distant a remove, I fancy, as a cousin well can be. To this gentleman my mother wrote when my poor father died—and he was generous, for it is he who paid for my schooling. I did not know this till very lately. I had a vague impression, indeed, that I had a powerful and wealthy kinsman who took interest in me, but whom I had never seen."

VANCE.—"Never seen?"

LIONEL.—"No. And here comes the sting. On leaving school last Christmas, my mother, for the first time, told me the extent of my obligations to this benefactor, and informed me that he wished to know my own choice as to a profession—that if I preferred Church or Bar, he would maintain me at College."

VANCE.—"Body o' me! where's the sting in that? Help yourself to toddy, my boy, and take more genial views of life."

spite of the ability and promise that had been so vaunted, the dulness of a college and the labour of learned professions were so distasteful to me, he had no desire to dictate to my choice, but that as he did not wish one who was, however remotely, of his blood, and bore the name of Haughton, to turn shoeblack or pickpocket—Vance—Vance!"

VANCE.—" Lock up your pride—the sackcloth frets you—and go on; and that therefore he—"

LIONEL.—" Would buy me a commission in the army, or get me an appointment in India."

VANCE.—" Which did you take?"

LIONEL (passionately).—" Which! so offered—which?—of course neither! But distrusting the tone of my mother's reply, I sate down, the evening before I left home, and wrote myself to this cruel man. I did not show my letter to my mother—did not tell her of it. I wrote shortly—that if he would not accept my gratitude, I would not accept his benefits; that shoeblack I might be —pickpocket, no! that he need not fear I should disgrace his blood or my name; and that I would not rest till, sooner or later, I had paid him back all that I had cost him, and felt relieved from the burthens of an obligation which—which—" The boy paused, covered his face with his hands, and sobbed.

Vance, though much moved, pretended to scold his friend, but finding that ineffectual, fairly rose, wound his arm brother-like round him, and drew him from the arbour to the shelving margin of the river. "Comfort," then said the Artist, almost solemnly, as here, from the inner depths of his character the true genius of the man came forth and spoke—" Comfort, and look round; see where the islet interrupts the tide, and how smilingly the stream flows on. See, just where we stand, how the slight pebbles are fretting the wave—would the wave, if not fretted, make that pleasant music? A few miles farther on, and the river is spanned by a bridge, which busy feet now are crossing; by the side of that bridge now is rising a palace;—all the men who rule England have room in that palace. At the rear of the palace soars up the old Abbey where kings have their tombs in right of the names they inherit; men, lowly as we, have found tombs there, in right of the names which they made. Think, now, that you stand on that bridge with a boy's lofty hope, with a man's steadfast courage; then turn again to that stream, calm with starlight, flowing on towards the bridge—spite of islet and pebbles."

Lionel made no audible answer, though his lips murmured, but he pressed closer and closer to his friend's side; and the tears were already dried on his cheek—though their dew still glistened in his eyes.

LIONEL (joyously).—"My dear Vance, you are the best fellow in the world."

VANCE.—"Small compliment to humankind. Take the oars—it is your turn now."

Lionel obeyed; the boat once more danced along the tide—thoro' reeds —thoro' waves, skirting the grassy islet—out into pale moonlight. They talked but by fits and starts. What of? —a thousand things! Bright young hearts, eloquent young tongues! No sins in the past; hopes gleaming through the future. O summer nights, on the glass of starry waves! O Youth, Youth!

CHAPTER VI.

Wherein the Historian tracks the Public Characters that fret their hour on the stage, into the bosom of private life.—The reader is invited to arrive at a conclusion which may often, in periods of perplexity, restore ease to his mind: viz., that if man will reflect on all the hopes he has nourished, all the fears he has admitted, all the projects he has formed, the wisest thing he can do, nine times out of ten, with hope, fear, and project, is to let them end with the chapter—in smoke.

IT was past nine o'clock in the evening of the following day. The exhibition at Mr Rugge's theatre had closed for the season in that village, for it was the conclusion of the fair. The final performance had been begun and ended somewhat earlier than on former nights. The theatre was to be cleared from the ground by daybreak, and the whole company to proceed onward betimes in the morning. Another fair awaited them in an adjoining county, and they had a long journey before them.

Gentleman Waife and his Juliet Araminta had gone to their lodgings over the Cobbler's stall. Their rooms were homely enough, but had an air not only of the comfortable, but the picturesque. The little sitting-room was very old-fashioned—panelled in wood that had once been painted blue—with a quaint chimney-piece that reached to the ceiling. That part of the house spoke of the time of Charles I. It might have been tenanted by a religious Roundhead; and, framed in over the low door, there was a grim faded portrait of a pinched-faced saturnine man, with long lank hair, starched band, and a length of upper-lip that betokened relentless obstinacy of character, and might have curled in sullen glee at the monarch's scaffold, or preached an interminable sermon to the stout Protector. On a table, under the deep-sunk window, were neatly arrayed a few sober-looking old books; you would find amongst them *Colley's Astrology, Owen Feltham's Resolves, Glanville on Witches, the Pilgrim's Progress,* an early edition of *Paradise Lost,* and an old Bible; also two flower-pots of clay brightly reddened, and containing stocks; also two small worsted rugs, on one of which rested a carved cocoa-nut, on the other an egg-shaped ball of crystal,—that last the pride and joy of the Cobbler's visionary soul. A door left wide open communicated with an inner room (very low was its ceiling), in which the Bandit

c

under-tone,—"if I were alone in the world."

"O! Grandy."

"'I know a spot on which a bed-post grows,
And do remember where a roper lives.'

Delightful prospect, not to be indulged; for if I were in peace at one end of the rope, what would chance to my Sophy, left forlorn at the other?"

"Don't talk so, or I shall think you are sorry to have taken care of me."

"Care of thee, O child! and what care? It is thou who takest care of me. Put thy hands from my mouth; sit down, darling, there, opposite, and let us talk. Now, Sophy, thou hast often said that thou wouldst be glad to be out of this mode of life, even for one humbler and harder: think well—is it so?"

"Oh! yes, indeed, grandfather."

"No more tinsel dresses and flowery wreaths; no more applause; no more of the dear divine stage-excitement; the heroine and fairy vanished; only a little commonplace child in dingy gingham, with a purblind cripple for thy sole charge and playmate; Juliet Araminta evaporated evermore into little Sophy!"

"It would be so nice!" answered little Sophy, laughing merrily.

"What would make it nice?" asked the Comedian, turning on her his solitary piercing eye, with curious interest in his gaze.

Sophy left her seat, and placed herself on a stool at her grandfather's knee; on that knee she clasped her tiny hands, and shaking aside her curls, looked into his face with confident fondness. Evidently these two were much more than grandfather and grandchild—they were *friends*, they were equals, they were in the habit of consulting and prattling with each other. She got at his meaning, however covert his humour; and he to the core of her heart, through its careless babble. Between you and me, Reader, I suspect that, in spite of the comedian's sagacious wrinkles, the one was as much a child as the other.

"Well," said Sophy, "I will tell you, Grandy, what would make it nice—no one would vex and affront you, we should be all by ourselves; and then, instead of those nasty lamps, and those dreadful painted creatures, we could go out and play in the fields, and gather daisies; and I could run after butterflies, and when I am tired I should come here, where I am now, any time of the day, and you would tell me stories, and pretty verses, and teach me to write a little better than I do now, and make such a wise little woman of me; and if I wore gingham, but it need not be dingy, Grandy, it would be all mine, and you would be all mine too, and we'd keep a bird, and you'd teach it to sing; and oh, would it not be nice!"

"But still, Sophy, we should have to live, and we could not live upon daisies and butterflies. And I can't work now—for the matter of that, I never could work—more shame for me, but so it is. Merle says the fault is in the stars—with all my heart. But the stars will not go to the jail or the workhouse instead of me. And though they want nothing to eat, we do."

"Dat, Grandy, you have said every day since the first walk you took after coming here, that if you had three pounds, we could get away and live by ourselves, and make a fortune!"

"A fortune!—that's a strong word; let it stand. A fortune! But still, Sophy, though we should be free of this thrice execrable Rugge, the scheme I have in my head lies

c 2

CHAPTER VII.

The Historian, in pursuance of his stern duties, reveals to the scorn of future ages some of the occult practices which discredit the March of Light in the Nineteenth Century.

"MAY I come in?" asked the Cobbler outside the door.

"Certainly come in," said Gentleman Waife. Sophy looked wistfully at the aperture, and sighed to see that Merle was alone. She crept up to him.

"Will they not come?" she whispered.

"I hope so, pretty one; it ben't ten yet."

"Take a pipe, Merle," said Gentleman Waife, with a Grand Comedian air.

"No, thank you kindly; I just looked in to ask if I could do anything for ye, in case—in case ye must go to-morrow."

"Nothing; our luggage is small, and soon packed. Sophy has the money to discharge the meaner part of our debt to you."

"I don't value that," said the Cobbler, colouring.

"But we value your esteem," said Mr. Waife, with a smile that would have become a field-marshal. "And so, Merle, you think, if I am a broken-down vagrant, it must be put to the long account of the celestial bodies!"

"Not a doubt of it," returned the Cobbler, solemnly. "I wish you would give me date and place of Sophy's birth—that's what I want —I'd take her horryscope. I'm sure she'd be lucky."

"I'd rather not, please," said Sophy, timidly.

"Rather not?—very odd. Why?"

"I don't want to know the future."

"That is odder and odder," quoth the Cobbler, staring; "I never heard a girl say that afore."

"Wait till she's older, Mr. Merle," said Waife; "girls don't want to know the future till they want to be married."

"Summat in that," said the Cobbler. He took up the crystal. "Have you looked into this ball, pretty one, as I bade ye?"

"Yes, two or three times."

"Ha! and what did you see?"

"My own face made very long," said Sophy—"as long as *that*"— stretching out her hands.

The Cobbler shook his head dolefully, and screwing up one eye, applied the other to the mystic ball.

MR. WAIFE.—"Perhaps you will see if those two gentlemen are coming."

SOPHY.—"Do, do! and if they will give us three pounds!"

The COBBLER (triumphantly).— "Then you do care to know tho future, after all?"

SOPHY.—"Yes so far as that goes; but don't look any farther, pray."

The COBBLER (intent upon the ball, and speaking slowly, and in jerks).—"A mist now. Ha! an arm with a besom—sweeps all before it."

SOPHY (frightened).—"Send it away, please."

COBBLER.—It is gone. Ha! there's Ruggo—looks very angry— savage, indeed."

WAIFE.—"Good sign that I proceed."

COBBLER.—"Shakes his fist; gone. Ha! a young man, boyish, dark hair."

CHAPTER VIII.

Showing the arts by which a man, however high in the air Nature may have formed his nose, may be led by that nose, and in directions perversely opposite to those which, in following his nose, he might be supposed to take; and therefore, that nations the most liberally endowed with practical good sense, and in conceit thereof, carrying their noses the most horizontally aloof, when they come into conference with nations more skilled in diplomacy, and more practised in "stage play," end by the surrender of the precise object which it was intended they should surrender before they laid their noses together.

We all know that Demosthenes said, Everything in oratory was acting— stage-play. Is it in oratory alone that the saying holds good? Apply it to all circumstances of life,—" stage-play, stage-play, stage-play!"—only *ars est celare artem*, conceal the art. Gleesome in soul to behold his visitors, calculating already on the three pounds to be extracted from them, seeing in that hope the crisis in his own chequered existence, Mr. Waife rose from his seat in superb *apocrisia* or stage-play, and asked, with mild dignity,—" To what am I indebted, gentlemen, for the honour of your visit?"

In spite of his nose, even Vance was taken aback. Pope says that Lord Bolingbroke had "the nobleman air." A great comedian Lord Bolingbroke surely was. But, ah, had Pope seen Gentleman Waife! Taking advantage of the impression he had created, the actor added, with the finest imaginable breeding, — "But pray be seated;" and, once seeing them seated, resumed his easy-chair, and felt himself master of the situation.

"Hum!" said Vance, recovering his self-possession, after a pause— "hum!"

"Hem!" re-echoed Gentleman Waife; and the two men eyed each other much in the same way as Admiral Napier might have eyed the fort of Cronstadt, and the fort of Cronstadt have eyed Admiral Napier.

Lionel struck in with that youthful boldness which plays the deuce with all dignified strategical science. "You must be aware why we come, sir; Mr. Merle will have explained. My friend, a distinguished artist, wished to make a sketch, if you do not object, of this young lady's very"——" Pretty little face," quoth Vance, taking up the discourse. "Mr. Rugge, this morning, was willing,—I understand that your grandchild refused. We are come here to see if she will be more complaisant under your own roof, or under Mr. Merle's, which, I take it, is the same thing for the present." —Sophy had sidled up to Lionel. He might not have been flattered if he knew why she preferred him to Vance. She looked on him as a boy —a fellow-child—and an instinct, moreover, told her, that more easily through him than his shrewd-looking bearded guest could she attain the object of her cupidity—" three pounds!"

"Three pounds!" whispered Sophy, with the tones of an angel, into Lionel's thrilling ear.

Mr. Waife.—"Sir, I will be frank with you." At that ominous commencement, Mr. Vance recoiled, and mechanically buttoned his trousers

bestow on us the sum you say, we shall not leave the village till you have completed your picture. It is Mr. Rugge and his company we will leave."

VANCE.—" And may I venture to ask what you propose to do, towards a new livelihood for yourself and your grandchild, by the help of a sum which is certainly much for me to pay—enormous, I might say, quoad me—but small for a capital whereon to set up a business?"

WAIFE.—" Excuse me if I do not answer that very natural question at present. Let me assure you that that precise sum is wanted for an investment which promises her and myself an easy existence. But to insure my scheme, I must keep it secret. Do you believe me?"

"I do!" cried Lionel; and Sophy, whom, by this time, he had drawn upon his lap, put her arm gratefully round his neck.

"There is your money, sir, beforehand," said Vance, declining downward his betrayed and resentful nose, and depositing three sovereigns on the table.

"And how do you know," said Waife, smiling, "that I may not be off to-night with your money and your model?"

"Well," said Vance, curtly, "I think it is on the cards. Still, as John Kemble said when rebuked for too large an alms,

'It is not often that I do these things,
But when I do, I do them handsomely.'"

"Well applied, and well delivered, sir," said the Comedian, "only you should put a little more emphasis on the word do."

"Did I not put enough? I am sure I felt it strongly; no one can feel the do more!"

Waife's pliant face relaxed into a genial brightness—the équivoque charmed him. However, not affecting to comprehend it, he thrust back the money, and said, "No, sir, —not a shilling till the picture is completed. Nay, to relieve your mind, I will own that, had I no scruple more delicate, I would rather receive nothing till Mr. Rugge is gone. True, he has no right to any share in it. But you see before you a man who, when it comes to arguing, could never take a wrangler's degree—never get over the Ass's Bridge, sir. Plucked at it scores of times clean as a feather. But do not go yet. You came to give us money—give us what, were I rich, I should value more highly,—a little of your time. You, sir, are an artist; and you, young gentleman?" addressing Lionel.

LIONEL (colouring).—" I — am nothing as yet."

WAIFE.—" You are fond of the drama, I presume, both of you? Apropos of John Kemble, you, sir, said that you have never heard him. Allow me, so far as this cracked voice can do it, to give you a faint idea of him."

"I shall be delighted," said Vance, drawing nearer to the table, and feeling more at his ease. "But since I see you smoke, may I take the liberty to light my cigar?"

"Make yourself at home," said Gentleman Waife, with the good-humour of a fatherly host. And, all the while, Lionel and Sophy were babbling together, she still upon his lap.

Waife began his imitation of John Kemble. Despite the cracked voice, it was admirable. One imitation drew on another; then succeeded anecdotes of the Stage, of the Senate, of the Bar. Waife had heard great orators, whom every one still admires for the speeches which nobody, nowadays, ever reads; he gave a lively idea of each. And then came sayings of dry humour,

That act over, her thoughts took a more comely aspect than had been worn by the preceding phantasies, reflected Lionel's kind looks, and repeated his gentle words. "Heaven bless him!" she said with emphasis, as a supplement to the habitual prayers; and then tears gathered to her grateful eyelids, for she was one of those beings whose tears come slow from sorrow, quick from affection. And so the grey dawn found her still wakeful, and she rose, bathed her cheeks in the cold fresh water, and drew them forth with a glow like Hebe's. Dressing herself with the quiet activity which characterised all her movements, she then opened the casement and inhaled the air. All was still in the narrow lane, the shops yet unclosed. But on the still trees behind the shops the birds were beginning to stir and chirp. Chanticleer, from some neighbouring yard, rung out his brisk *reveillée*. Pleasant English summer dawn in the pleasant English country village. She stretched her graceful neck far from the casement, trying to catch a glimpse of the blue river. She had seen its majestic flow on the day they had arrived at the fair, and longed to gain its banks; then her servitude to the stage forbade her. Now she was to be free! O joy! Now she might have her careless hours of holiday; and, forgetful of Waife's warning that their vocation must be plied in towns, she let her fancy run riot amidst visions of green fields and laughing waters, and in fond delusion gathered the daisies and chased the butterflies. Changeling transferred into that lowest world of Art from the cradle of civil Nature, her human child's heart yearned for the human child-like delights. All children love the country, the flowers, the sward, the birds, the butterflies; or if some do not, despair, O Philanthropy, of their after-lives!

She closed the window, smiling to herself; stole through the adjoining doorway, and saw that her grandfather was still asleep. Then she busied herself in putting the little sitting-room to rights, reset the table for the morning meal, watered the stocks, and finally took up the crystal and looked into it with awe, wondering why the Cobbler could see so much, and she only the distorted reflection of her own face. So interested, however, for once, did she become in the inspection of this mystic globe, that she did not notice the dawn pass into broad daylight, nor hear a voice at the door below —nor, in short, take into cognition the external world, till a heavy tread shook the floor, and then, starting, she beheld the Remorseless Baron, with a face black enough to have darkened the crystal of Dr. Dee himself.

"Ho, ho," said Mr. Rugge, in hissing accents, which had often thrilled the threepenny gallery with anticipative horror. "Rebellious, eh?— won't come? Where's your grandfather, baggage?"

Sophy let fall the crystal—a mercy it was not broken—and gazed vacantly on the Baron.

"Your vile scamp of a grandfather?"

SOPHY (with spirit).—"He is not vile. You ought to be ashamed of yourself speaking so, Mr. Rugge!"

Here, simultaneously, Mr. Waife, hastily endued in his grey dressing-gown, presented himself at the aperture of the bedroom door, and the Cobbler on the threshold of the sitting-room. The Comedian stood mute, trusting, perhaps, to the imposing effect of his attitude. The Cobbler, yielding to the impulse of untheatric man, put his head dog-

I said I was free to dismiss you both, if the child did not suit. You, poor helpless creature, could be of no use. But I never heard you say you were to be free too. Stands to reason not! Put my engagements at a Waife's mercy! I, Lorenzo Rugge!—stuff! But I'm a just man, and a liberal man, and if you think you ought to have a higher salary, if this ungrateful proceeding is only, as I take it, a strike for wages, I will meet you. Juliet Araminta does play better than I could have supposed; and I'll conclude an engagement on good terms, as we were to have done if the experiment answered, for three years."

Waife shook his head. "You are very good, Mr. Rugge, but it is not a strike. My little girl does not like the life at any price; and since she supports me, I am bound to please her. Besides," said the actor, with a stiffer manner, "you have broken faith with me. It was fully understood that I was to appear no more on your stage; all my task was to advise with you in the performances, remodel the plays, help in the stage-management; and you took advantage of my penury, and, when I asked for a small advance, insisted on forcing these relics of what I was upon the public pity. Enough—we part. I bear no malice."

RUGGE.—"Oh, don't you? No more do I. But I am a Briton, and I have the spirit of one. You had better not make an enemy of me."

WAIFE.—"I am above the necessity of making enemies. I have an enemy ready made in myself."

Rugge placed a strong bony hand upon the cripple's arm. "I dare say you have! A bad conscience, sir. How would you like your past life looked into, and blabbed out?"

GENTLEMAN WAIFE (mournfully).—"The last four years of it have been spent in your service, Mr. Rugge.—If their record had been blabbed out for my benefit, there would not have been a dry eye in the house."

RUGGE.—"I disdain your sneer. When a scorpion nursed at my bosom sneers at me—I leave it to its own reflections. But I don't speak of the years in which that scorpion has been enjoying a salary and smoking canaster at my expense. I refer to an earlier dodge in its checkered existence. Ha, sir, you wince! I suspect I can find out something about you which would—"

WAIFE (fiercely).—"Would what?"

RUGGE.—"Oh, lower your tone, sir; no bullying me. I suspect! I have good reason for suspicion; and if you sneak off in this way, and cheat me out of my property in Juliet Araminta, I will leave no stone unturned to prove what I suspect—look to it, slight man! Come, I don't wish to quarrel; make it up, and" (drawing out his pocket-book) "if you want cash down, and will have an engagement in black and white for three years for Juliet Araminta, you may squeeze a good sum out of me, and go yourself where you please; you'll never be troubled by me. What I want is the girl."

All the actor laid aside, Waife growled out, "And hang me, sir, if you shall have the girl!"

At this moment Sophy opened the door wide, and entered boldly. She had heard her grandfather's voice raised, though its hoarse tones did not allow her to distinguish his words. She was alarmed for him. She came in, his guardian fairy, to protect him from the oppressor of six feet high. Rugge's arm was raised, not indeed to strike, but rather to declaim. Sophy slid between him and her grandfather, and, clinging round the latter, flung out her own

colour faded from the old man's face. Exhausted by the excitement he had gone through, he sank on a chair, and, with one quick gasp as for breath, fainted away.

CHAPTER XI.

Progress of the Fine Arts.—Biographical Anecdotes.—Fluctuations in the Value of Money.—Speculative Tendencies of the Time.

WHATEVER the shock which the brutality of the Remorseless Baron inflicted on the nervous system of the persecuted but triumphant Bandit, it had certainly subsided by the time Vance and Lionel entered Waife's apartment, for they found grandfather and grandchild seated near the open window, at the corner of the table (on which they had made room for their operations by the removal of the carved cocoa-nut, the crystal egg, and the two flowerpots), eagerly engaged, with many a silvery laugh from the lips of Sophy, in the game of dominoes.

Mr. Waife had been devoting himself, for the last hour and more, to the instruction of Sophy in the mysteries of that intellectual amusement; and such pains did he take, and so impressive were his exhortations, that his happy pupil could not help thinking to herself that *this* was the new art upon which Waife depended for their future livelihood. She sprang up, however, at the entrance of the visitors, her face beaming with grateful smiles; and, running to Lionel, and taking him by the hand, while she curtsied with more respect to Vance, she exclaimed,— "We are free! thanks to you—thanks to you both! He is gone! Mr. Rugge is gone."

"So I saw on passing the green; stage and all," said Vance, while Lionel kissed the child and pressed her to his side. It is astonishing how paternal he felt—how much she had crept into his heart.

"Pray, sir," asked Sophy, timidly, glancing to Vance, "has the Norfolk Giant gone too?"

VANCE.—"I fancy so—all the shows were either gone or going."

SOPHY.—"The Calf with Two Heads?"

VANCE.—"Do you regret it?"

SOPHY.—"Oh, dear, no."

Waife, who, after a profound bow, and a cheery "Good day, gentlemen," had hitherto remained silent, putting away the dominoes, now said—"I suppose, sir, you would like at once to begin your sketch?"

VANCE.—"Yes; I have brought all my tools—see, even the canvas. I wish it were larger, but it is all I have with me of that material—'tis already stretched—just let me arrange the light."

WAIFE.—"If you don't want me, gentlemen, I will take the air for half an hour or so. In fact, I may now feel free to look after my investment."

SOPHY (whispering Lionel).— "You are *sure* the Calf has gone as well as the Norfolk Giant?"

Lionel wonderingly replied that he thought so; and Waife disappeared into his room, whence he soon emerged, having doffed his

WHAT WILL HE DO WITH IT? 33

was silent for about half an hour, when he said, "You may get up, Lionel; I have done with you for the present."

SOPHY.—"And me, too—may I ace?"

VANCE.—"No; but you may talk now. So you had a doll? What has become of it?"

SOPHY.—"I left it behind, sir. Grandfather thought it would distract me from attending to his lessons, and learning my part."

VANCE.—"You love your grandfather more than the doll?"

SOPHY.—"Oh! a thousand million million times more."

VANCE.—"He brought you up, I suppose? Have you no father—no mother?"

SOPHY.—"I have only grandfather."

LIONEL. — "Have you always lived with him?"

SOPHY.—"Dear me, no; I was with Mrs. Crane till grandfather came from abroad, and took me away, and put me with some very kind people; and then, when grandfather had that bad accident, I came to stay with him, and we have been together ever since."

LIONEL.—"Was Mrs. Crane no relation of yours?"

SOPHY.—"No, I suppose not, for she was not kind—I was so miserable; but don't talk of it—I forget that now. I only wish to remember from the time grandfather took me in his lap, and told me to be a good child, and love him; and I have been happy ever since."

"You *are* a dear good child," said Lionel, emphatically, "and I wish I had you for my sister."

VANCE. — "When your grandfather has received from me that exorbitant—not that I grudge it—sum, I should like to ask, What will he do with it? As he said it was a secret, I must not pump you."

SOPHY.—"What will he do with it? I should like to know too, sir; but whatever it is, I don't care, so long as I and grandfather are together."

Here Waife re-entered. "Well, how goes on the picture?"

VANCE.—"Tolerably for the first sitting; I require two more."

WAIFE.—Certainly; only—only" (he drew aside Vance, and whispered), "only the day after to-morrow, I fear I *shall* want the money. It is an occasion that never will occur again—I would seize it."

VANCE.—"Take the money now."

WAIFE.—"Well, thank you, sir; you are sure now that we shall not run away; and I accept your kindness; it will make all safe."

Vance, with surprising alacrity, slipped the sovereigns into the old man's hand; for, truth to say, though thrifty, the Artist was really generous. His organ of caution was large, but that of acquisitiveness moderate. Moreover, in those moments when his soul expanded with his art, he was insensibly less alive to the value of money. And strange it is that, though states strive to fix for that commodity the most abiding standards, yet the value of money to the individual who regards it, shifts and fluctuates, goes up and down half-a-dozen times a-day. For my part, I honestly declare that there are hours in the twenty-four—such, for instance, as that just before breakfast, or that succeeding a page of this History in which I have been put out of temper with my performance and myself, when any one in want of five shillings at my disposal would find my value of that sum put it quite out of his reach; while at other times—just after dinner, for instance, or when I have effected what seems to me a happy stroke, or a good bit of

D

mourist, with high animal spirits; and, withal, an infantine simplicity at times, like the clever man who never learns the world, and is always taken in.

A circumstance, trifling in itself, but suggestive of speculation either as to the character or antecedent circumstances of Gentleman Waife, did not escape Vance's observation. Since his rupture with Mr. Rugge, there was a considerable amelioration in that affection of the trachea, which, while his engagement with Rugge lasted, had rendered the comedian's dramatic talents unavailable on the stage. He now expressed himself without the pathetic hoarseness or cavernous wheeze which had previously thrown a wet blanket over his efforts at discourse. But Vance put no very stern construction on the dissimulation which this change seemed to denote. Since Waife was still one-eyed and a cripple, he might very excusably shrink from reappearance on the stage, and affect a third infirmity to save his pride from the exhibition of the two infirmities that were genuine.

That which most puzzled Vance was that which had most puzzled the Cobbler,—What could the man once have been?—how fallen so low?—for fall it was, that was clear. The painter, though not himself of patrician extraction, had been much in the best society. He had been a petted favourite in great houses. He had travelled. He had seen the world. He had the habits and instincts of good society.

Now, in what the French term the *beau monde*, there are little traits that reveal those who have entered it,—certain tricks of phrase, certain modes of expression—even the pronunciation of familiar words, even the modulation of an accent. A man of the most refined bearing may not have these peculiarities; a man, otherwise coarse and brusque in his manner, may. The slang of the *beau monde* is quite apart from the code of high-breeding. Now and then, something in Waife's talk seemed to show that he had lighted on that beau-world; now and then, that something wholly vanished. So that Vance might have said, "He has been admitted there, not inhabited it."

Yet Vance could not feel sure, after all; comedians are such takes in. But was the man, by the profession of his earlier life, a comedian? Vance asked the question adroitly.

"You must have taken to the stage young?" said he.

"The stage!" said Waife; "if you mean the public stage—no. I have acted pretty often in youth, even in childhood, to amuse others, never professionally to support myself, till Mr. Rugge civilly engaged me four years ago."

"Is it possible—with your excellent education! But pardon me; I have hinted my surprise at your late vocation before, and it displeased you."

"Displeased me!" said Waife, with an abject, depressed manner; "I hope I said nothing that would have misbecome a poor broken vagabond like me. I am no prince in disguise —a good-for-nothing varlet who should be too grateful to have something to keep himself from a dunghill."

LIONEL.—" Don't talk so. And but for your accident you might now be the great attraction on the Metropolitan Stage. Who does not respect a really fine actor?"

WAIFE (gloomily).—" The Metropolitan Stage! I was talked into it; I am glad even of the accident that saved me—say no more of that, no more of that. But I have spoiled

CHAPTER XIII.

Inspiring effect of the Fine Arts: the Vulgar are moved by their exhibition into generous impulses and flights of fancy, checked by the ungracious severities of their superiors, as exemplified in the instance of Cobbler Merle and his Servant-of-All-Work.

THE next day, perhaps with the idea of removing all scruple from Sophy's mind, Waife had already gone after his investment when the friends arrived. Sophy at first was dull and dispirited, but by degrees she brightened up; and when, the sitting over and the picture done (save such final touches as Vance reserved for solitary study), she was permitted to gaze at her own effigy, she burst into exclamations of frank delight. "Am I like that! is it possible? Oh, how beautiful! Mr. Merle, Mr. Merle, Mr. Merle!" and running out of the room before Vance could stop her, she returned with the Cobbler, followed, too, by a thin gaunt girl, whom he pompously called his housekeeper, but who, in sober-truth, was servant-of-all-work. Wife he had none—his horoscope, he said, having Saturn in square to the Seventh House, forbade him to venture upon matrimony. All gathered round the picture; all admired, and with justice—it was a *chef d'œuvre*. Vance in his maturest day never painted more charmingly. The three pounds proved to be the best outlay of capital he had ever made. Pleased with his work, he was pleased even with that unsophisticated applause.

"You must have Mercury and Venus very strongly aspected," quoth the Cobbler; "and if you have the Dragon's Head in the Tenth House, you may count on being much talked of after you are dead."

"After I am dead!—sinister omen!" said Vance, discomposed. "I have no faith in artists who count of being talked of after they are dead. Never knew a dauber who did not! But stand back—time flies—tie up your hair—put on your bonnet, Titania. You have a shawl?—not tinsel, I hope!—quieter the better. You stay and see to her, Lionel."

Said the gaunt servant-of-all-work to Mr. Merle—"I'd let the gentleman paint me, if he likes it—shall I tell him, master?"

"Go back to the bacon, foolish woman. Why, he gave £3 for her likeness, 'cause of her Benefics! But you'd have to give him three years' wages afore he'd look you straight in the face, 'cause, you see, your Aspects are crooked. And," added the Cobbler, philosophising, "when the Malefics are dead agin a girl's mug, man is so constituted by natur that he can't take to that mug unless it has a gold handle. Don't fret, 'tis not your fault: born under Scorpio—coarse-limbed—dull complexion—and the Head of the Dragon, aspected of Infortunes in all your Angles."

And I don't know why he refused you." The young men exchanged compassionate glances.

Lionel then sought to make her talk of her past life—tell him more of Mrs. Crane. Who and what was she?

Sophy could not, or would not, tell. The remembrances were painful; she had evidently tried to forget them. And the people with whom Waife had placed her, and who had been kind?

The Misses Burton — and they kept a day-school, and taught Sophy to read, write, and cipher. They lived near London, in a lane opening on a great common, with a green rail before the house, and had a good many pupils, and kept a tortoise-shell cat and a canary. Not much to enlighten her listener did Sophy impart here.

And now they neared that stately palace, rich in associations of storm and splendour. The grand Cardinal —the iron-clad Protector; Dutch William of the immortal memory, whom we try so hard to like, and, in spite of the great Whig historian, that Titian of English prose, can only frigidly respect. Hard task for us Britons to like a Dutchman who dethrones his father-in-law, and drinks schnaps. Prejudice certainly; but so it is. Harder still to like Dutch William's unfilial Frau! Like Queen Mary! I could as soon like Queen Goneril! Romance flies from the prosperous phlegmatic Æneas; flies from his plump Lavinia, his "fidus Achates," Bentinck; flies to follow the poor deserted fugitive Stuart, with all his sins upon his head. Kings have no rights divine, except when deposed and fallen; they are then invested with the awe that belongs to each solemn image of mortal vicissitude—Vicissitude that startles the Epicurean, "*insanientis sapientia consultus,*"

and strikes from his careless lyre the notes that attest a God! Some proud shadow chases another from the throne of Cyrus, and Horace hears in the thunder the rush of Diespiter, and identifies Providence with the Fortune that snatches off the diadem in her whirring swoop.* But fronts discrowned take a new majesty to generous natures;—in all sleek prosperity there is something commonplace—in all grand adversity, something royal.

The boat shot to the shore; the young people landed, and entered the arch of the desolate palace. They gazed on the great hall and the presence-chamber, and the long suite of rooms, with faded portraits— Vance as an artist, Lionel as an enthusiastic well-read boy, Sophy as a wondering, bewildered, ignorant child. And then they emerged into the noble garden, with its regal trees. Groups were there of well-dressed persons. Vance heard himself called by name. He had forgotten the London world—forgotten, amidst his madsummer ramblings, that the London season was still ablaze—and there, stragglers from the great Focus, fine people, with languid tones and artificial jaded smiles, caught him in his wanderer's dress, and walking side by side with the infant wonder of Mr. Rugge's show, exquisitely neat indeed, but still in

* "———— Valet ima summis
Mutare, et insignem attenuat Deus,
Obscura promens; hinc apicem rapax
Fortuna cum stridore acuto
Sustulit,—hic posuisse gaudet."
—Horat. Carm., lib. I. xxxiv.
The concluding allusion is evidently to the Parthian revolutions, and the changeful fate of Phraates IV.; and I do not feel sure that the preceding lines upon the phenomenon of the thunder in a serene sky have not a latent and half-allegorical meaning, dimly applicable, throughout, to the historical reference at the close.

tracting you from—what I hate to think you ever stooped to perform."

As Lionel, his crest erect, and nostril dilated, and holding Sophy firmly by the hand, took his way out from the gardens, he was obliged to pass the patrician party, of whom Vance now made one.

His countenance and air, as he swept by, struck them all, especially Lady Selina. "A very distinguished-looking boy," said she. "What a fine face! Who did you say he was, Mr. Vance?"

VANCE.—"His name is Haughton—Lionel Haughton."

LADY SELINA. — "Haughton! Haughton! Any relation to poor dear Captain Haughton — Charlie Haughton, as he was generally called?"

Vance, knowing little more of his young friend's parentage than that his mother let lodgings, at which, once domiciliated himself, he had made the boy's acquaintance, and that she enjoyed the pension of a captain's widow, replied carelessly—

"His father was a captain, but I don't know whether he was a Charlie."

MR. CRAMPE (the Wit).—"Charlies are extinct! I have the last in a fossil,—box and all?"

General laugh. Wit shut up again.

LADY SELINA.—"He has a great look of Charlie Haughton. Do you know if he is connected with that extraordinary man, Mr. Darrell?"

VANCE.—"Upon my word, I do not. What Mr. Darrell do you mean?"

Lady Selina, with one of those sublime looks of celestial pity with which personages in the great world forgive ignorance of names and genealogies in those not born within its orbit, replied, "Oh, to be sure; it is not exactly in the way of your delightful art to know Mr. Darrell, one of the first men in Parliament, a connection of mine."

LADY FROST (nippingly).—"You mean Guy Darrell, the lawyer."

LADY SELINA.—"Lawyer—true, now I think of it; he was a lawyer. But his chief fame was in the House of Commons. All parties agreed that he might have commanded any station; but he was too rich, perhaps, to care sufficiently about office. At all events, Parliament was dissolved when he was at the height of his reputation, and he refused to be re-elected."

One SIR GREGORY STOLLHEAD (a member of the House of Commons, young, wealthy, a constant attendant, of great promise, with speeches that were filled with facts, and emptied the benches).—"I have heard of him. Before my time; lawyers not much weight in the House now."

LADY SELINA.—"I am told that Mr. Darrell did not speak like a lawyer. But his career is over—lives in the country, and sees nobody—a thousand pities—a connection of mine, too—great loss to the country. Ask your young friend, Mr. Vance, if Mr. Darrell is not his relation. I hope so, for his sake. Now that our party is in power, Mr. Darrell could command anything for others, though he has ceased to act with us. Our party is not forgetful of talent."

LADY FROST (with icy crispness).—"I should think not; it has so little of that kind to remember."

SIR GREGORY.—"Talent is not wanted in the House of Commons now—don't go down, in fact. Business assembly."

LADY SELINA (suppressing a yawn).—"Beautiful day! We had better think of going back to Richmond."

General assent, and slow retreat.

and cherries were temptingly fresh—the sun still very powerful. At the back of the fruiterer's was a small garden, or rather orchard, smiling cool through the open door—little tables laid out there. The good woman who kept the shop was accustomed to the wants and tastes of humble metropolitan visitors. But the garden was luckily now empty—it was before the usual hour for tea-parties; so the young folks had the pleasantest table under an apple-tree, and the choice of the freshest fruit. Milk and cakes were added to the fare. It was a banquet, in Sophy's eyes, worthy that happy day. And when Lionel had finished his share of the feast, eating fast, as spirited, impatient boys formed to push on in life and spoil their digestion are apt to do; and while Sophy was still lingering over the last of the strawberries, he threw himself back on his chair, and drew forth his letter. Lionel was extremely fond of his mother, but her letters were not often those which a boy is over eager to read. It is not all mothers who understand what boys are—their quick susceptibilities, their precocious manliness, all their mystical ways and oddities. A letter from Mrs. Haughton generally somewhat fretted and irritated Lionel's high-strung nerves, and he had instinctively put off the task of reading the one he held, till satisfied hunger and cool-breathing shadows, and rest from the dusty road, had lent their soothing aid to his undeveloped philosophy.

He broke the seal slowly; another letter was enclosed within. At the first few words his countenance changed; he uttered a slight exclamation, read on eagerly; then, before concluding his mother's epistle, hastily tore open that which it had contained, ran his eye over its contents, and, dropping both letters on the turf below, rested his face on his hand in agitated thought. Thus ran his mother's letter:—

"MY DEAR BOY,

"How could you! Do it slyly!! Unknown to your own mother!!! I could not believe it of you!!!! Take advantage of my confidence in showing you the letters of your father's cousin, to write to himself—*clandestinely !*—you, who I thought had such an open character, and who ought to appreciate mine. Every one who knows me says I am a woman in ten thousand—not for beauty and talent (though I have had my admirers for them too), but for GOODNESS! As a wife and mother, I may say I have been exemplary. I had sore trials with the dear captain—and IMMENSE temptations. But he said on his deathbed, 'Jessica, you are an angel.' And I have had offers since—IMMENSE offers—but I devoted myself to my child, as you know. And what I have put up with, letting the first floor, nobody can tell; and only a widow's pension—going before a magistrate to get it paid! And to think my own child, for whom I have borne so much, should behave so cruelly to me! Clandestine! 'tis *that* which stabs me. Mrs. Inman found me crying, and said, 'What is the matter?—you, who are such an angel, crying like a baby!' And I could not help saying, '*Tis* the serpent's tooth, Mrs. I.' What you wrote to your benefactor (and I *had* hoped patron) I don't care to guess; something very rude and imprudent it must be, judging by the few lines he addressed to me. I don't mind copying them for you to read. All my acts are above board—as often and often Captain H. used to say, 'Your heart is in a glass case, Jessica;' and so it is! *but my son keeps his under lock and key.*

he read Mr. Darrell's blunt but not offensive lines. His pride was soothed—why should he not now love his father's friend? He rose briskly, paid for the fruit, and went his way back to the boat with Sophy. As his oars cut the wave he talked gaily, but he ceased to interrogate Sophy on her past. Energetic, sanguine, ambitious, his own future entered now into his thoughts. Still, when the sun sunk as the inn came partially into view from the winding of the banks and the fringe of the willows, his mind again settled on the patient quiet little girl, who had not ventured to ask him one question in return for all he had put so unceremoniously to her. Indeed, she was silently musing over words he had inconsiderately let fall — "What I hate to think you had ever stooped to perform." Little could Lionel guess the unquiet thoughts which those words might hereafter call forth from the brooding deepening meditations of lonely childhood! At length said the boy abruptly, as he had said once before—

"I wish, Sophy, you were my sister." He added in a saddened tone, "I never had a sister—I have so longed for one! However, surely we shall meet again. You go tomorrow—so must I."

Sophy's tears flowed softly, noiselessly.

"Cheer up, ladybird, I wish you liked me half as much as I like you!"

"I do like you—oh, so much!" cried Sophy, passionately.

"Well, then, you can write, you say?"

"A little."

"You shall write to me now and then, and I to you. I'll talk to your grandfather about it. Ah, there he is, surely!"

The boat now ran into the shelving creek, and by the honeysuckle arbour stood Gentleman Waife, leaning on his stick.

"You are late," said the actor, as they landed, and Sophy sprang into his arms. "I began to be uneasy, and came here to inquire after you. You have not caught cold, child?"

SOPHY.—"Oh, no."

LIONEL.—"She is the best of children. Pray, come into the inn, Mr. Waife; no toddy, but some refreshment."

WAIFE.—"I thank you — no, sir; I wish to get home at once. I walk slowly; it will be dark soon."

Lionel tried in vain to detain him. There was a certain change in Mr. Waife's manner to him; it was much more distant—it was even pettish, if not surly. Lionel could not account for it—thought it mere whim at first, but as he walked part of the way back with them towards the village, this asperity continued, nay increased. Lionel was hurt; he arrested his steps.

"I see you wish to have your grandchild to yourself now. May I call early to-morrow? Sophy will tell you that I hope we may not altogether lose sight of each other. I will give you my address when I call."

"What time to-morrow, sir?"

"About nine."

Waife bowed his head and walked on, but Sophy looked back towards her boy friend, sorrowfully, gratefully—twilight in the skies that had been so sunny—twilight in her face that had been so glad! She looked back once, twice, thrice, as Lionel halted on the road and kissed his hand. The third time Waife said, with unwonted crossness—

"Enough of that, Sophy; looking after young men is not proper! What does he mean about 'seeing

across the country—two hours by
the railway. There is a station at
the town which bears the post-mark
of the letter. I shall make for that,
if you advise it."

"You knew I should advise it, or
you would not have tortured your
intellect by those researches into
Bradshaw."

"Shrewdly said," answered Lionel,
laughing; "but I wished for your
sanction of my crude impressions."

"You never told me your cousin's
name was Darrell — not that I
should have been much wiser if you
had, but, thunder and lightning,
Lionel, do you know that your
cousin Darrell is a famous man?"

LIONEL.—" Famous!—Nonsense.
I suppose he was a good lawyer, for
I have heard my mother say, with a
sort of contempt, that he had made
a great fortune at the bar!"

VANCE.—" But he was in Parliament."

LIONEL.—" Was he? I did not
know."

VANCE.—" And this is senatorial
fame! You never heard your
schoolfellows talk of Mr. Darrell?
—they would not have known his
name if you had boasted of it."

LIONEL.—" Certainly not."

VANCE.—" Would your schoolfellows have known the names of
Wilkie, of Landseer, of Turner.
Maclise—I speak of Painters!"

LIONEL.—" I should think so,
indeed."

VANCE (soliloquising). — " And
yet Her Serene Sublimityship, Lady
Salina Vipont, says to me with
divine compassion, 'Not in the way
of your delightful art to know such
men as Mr. Darrell!' Oh, as if I
did not see through it too when she
said, apropos of my jean cap and
velveteen jacket, 'What matters
how you dress? Every one knows
who you are!' Would she have
said that to the Earl of Dunder, or
even to Sir Gregory Stollhead? No,
I am the painter Frank Vance—
nothing more nor less; and if I
stood on my head in a check shirt
and a sky-coloured apron, Lady
Salina Vipont would kindly murmur, 'Only Frank Vance the
painter — what does it signify?'
Aha!—and they think to put me to
use!—puppets and lay figures!—it
is I who put them to use! Harkye,
Lionel, you are nearer akin to these
fine folks than I knew of. Promise
me one thing: you may become of
their set, by right of your famous
Mr. Darrell; if ever you hear an
artist, musician, scribbler, no matter
what, ridiculed as a tuft-hunter—
seeking the great—and so forth—
before you join in the laugh, ask
some great man's son, with a pedigree that dates from the Ark, 'Are
you not a toad-eater too! Do you
want political influence?—do you
stand contested elections?—do you
curry and fawn upon greasy Sam
the butcher and grimy Tom the
blacksmith for a vote? Why?
useful to your career—necessary to
your ambition? Aha! is it meaner
to curry and fawn upon white-
handed women and elegant coxcombs? Tut, tut! useful to a career
—necessary to ambition." Vance
paused, out of breath. The spoiled
darling of the circles—he—to talk
such republican rubbish! Certainly
he must have taken his two guineas'
worth out of those light wines.
Nothing so treacherous! they inflame the brain like fire, while
melting on the palate like ice. All
inhabitants of light-wine countries
are quarrelsome and democratic.

LIONEL (astounded).—"No one,
I am sure, could have meant to call
you a tuft-hunter—of course, every
one knows that a great painter—"

VANCE.—" Dates from Michael
Angelo, if not from Zeuxis! Common
individuals trace their pedigree from

the faces?" A poet has said, "Eternity itself cannot restore the loss struck from the minute." Are you happy in the spot on which you tarry with the persons, whose voices are now melodious to your ear?—beware of parting; or, if part you must, say not in insolent defiance to Time and Destiny, " What matters! —we shall soon meet again."

Alas, and alas! when we think of the lips which murmured, "Soon meet again," and remember how, in heart, soul, and thought, we stood for ever divided the one from the other, when, once more face to face, we each inly exclaimed,—"Met again!"

The air that we breathe makes the medium through which sound is conveyed; be the instrument unchanged, be the force which is applied to it the same, still, the air that thou seest not, *the air* to thy ear gives the music.

Ring a bell underneath an exhausted receiver, thou wilt scarce hear the sound; give the bell due vibration by free air in warm daylight, or sink it down to the heart of the ocean, where the air, all compressed, fills the vessel around it,* and the chime, heard afar, starts thy soul, checks thy footstep,—unto deep calls the deep,—a voice from the heart is borne to thy soul.

Where, then, the change, when thou sayest, " Lo, the same metal—why so faint-heard the ringing?" Ask the air that thou seest not, or above thee in sky, or below thee in ocean. Art thou sure that the bell, so faint-heard, is not struck underneath an exhausted receiver?

CHAPTER XIX.

The wandering inclinations of Nomad Tribes not to be accounted for on the principles of action peculiar to civilised men, who are accustomed to live in good houses and able to pay the income-tax.—When the money that once belonged to a man civilised, vanishes into the pockets of a nomad, neither lawful art nor occult science can, with certainty, discover what he will do with it.—Mr. Vance narrowly escapes well-merited punishment from the nails of the British Fair.—Lionel Haughton, in the temerity of youth, braves the dangers of a British Railway.

THE morning was dull and overcast, rain gathering in the air, when Vance and Lionel walked to Waife's lodging. As Lionel placed his hand on the knocker of the private door, the Cobbler, at his place by the window in the stall beside, glanced towards him, and shook his head.

"No use knocking, gentlemen. Will you kindly step in?—this way."

"Do you mean that your lodgers are out?" asked Vance.

"Gone!" said the Cobbler, thrusting his awl with great vehemence through the leather destined to the repair of a ploughman's boot.

"Gone—for good!" cried Lionel; "you cannot mean it. I call by appointment."

"Sorry, sir, for your trouble. Stop

* The bell in a sunk diving-bell, where the air is compressed, sounds with increased power. Sound travels four times quicker in water than in the upper air.

and the poor little girl will come back again?"

COBBLER.—"Praps; I know he was looking hard into the county map at the stationer's over the way; that seems as if he did not mean to go very far. P'raps he may come back."

VANCE.—"Did he take all his goods with him?"

COBBLER.—"Barrin' an old box—nothing in it, I expect, but theatre rubbish—play-books, paints, an old wig, and sichlike. He has good clothes—always had; and so has she, but they don't make more than a bundle."

VANCE.—"But surely you must know what the old fellow's project is. He has got from me a great sum —what will he do with it?"

COBBLER.—"Just what has been a-bothering me. What will he do with it? I cast a figure to know—could not make it out. Strange signs in Twelfth House. Enemies and Big Animals. Well, well, he's a marbellous man, and if he warn't a misbeliever in the crystal, I should say he was under Herschell; for you see, sir" (laying hold of Vance's button, as he saw that gentleman turning to escape)—"yon see Herschell, though he be a sinister chap eno', specially in affairs connected with t'other sex, disposes the native to dive into the mysteries of natur. I'm a Herschell man, out and outer! Born in March, and—"

"As mad as its hares," muttered Vance, wrenching his button from the Cobbler's grasp, and impatiently striding off. But he did not effect his escape so easily, for, close at hand, just at the corner of the lane, a female group, headed by Merle's gaunt housekeeper, had been silently collecting from the moment the two friends had paused at the Cobbler's door. And this petticoated divan suddenly closing round the painter, one pulled him by the sleeve, another by the jacket, and a third, with a nose upon which somebody had sat in early infancy, whispered, "Please, sir, take my picter fust."

Vance stared aghast—"Your picture, you drab!" Here another model of rustic charms, who might have furnished an ideal for the fat scullion in *Tristram Shandy*, bobbing a curtsy, put in her rival claim.

"Sir, if you don't objex to coming in to the kitching, after the family has gone to bed, I don't care if I lets you make a minnytur of me for two pounds."

"Miniature of you, porpoise!"

"Polly, sir, not Porpus—ax pardon. I shall clean myself, and I have a butyful new cap—Honeytun, and—"

"Let the gentleman go, will you?" said a third; "I am surprised at ye, Polly. The kitching unbeknown! Sir, I'm in the nussery—yes, sir—and missus says you may take me any time, purvided you'll take the babby, in the back parlour—yes, sir. Number 5 in the High Street. Mrs. Spratt,—yes, sir. Babby has had the smallpox—in case you're a married gentleman with a family—quite safe there—yes, sir."

Vance could endure no more, and, forgetful of that gallantry which should never desert the male sex, burst through the phalanx with an anathema, blackening alike the beauty and the virtue of those on whom it fell—that would have justified a cry of shame from every manly bosom, and which at once changed into shrill wrath the supplicatory tones with which he had been hitherto addressed. Down the street he hurried, and down the street followed the insulted fair. "Hiss—hiss—no gentleman, no gentleman! Aha—skulk off—do—low blaggurd!" shrieked Polly. From their counters shop-folks rushed to their doors. Stray dogs, excited by

musingly towards the station for of man." Therefore taking into
starting, where the smoke-cloud now account the poor cousin's vigilant
curled from the wheel-track of iron, pride on the *qui vive* for offence, and
—truth to say, the anxious doubt the rich cousin's temper (as judged
which disturbed him was not that by his letters) rude enough to pre-
which his friends might have felt on sent it, we must own that if Lionel
his behalf. In words, it would have Haughton has at this moment what
shaped itself thus—"Where *is* that is commonly called "a chance," the
poor little Sophy! and what will question as yet is not, what is that
become of her—what?" But when, chance, but *what will he do with it?*
launched on the journey, hurried on And as the reader advances in this
to its goal, the thought of the ordeal history, he will acknowledge that
before him forced itself on his mind, there are few questions in this world
he muttered inly to himself—"Done so frequently agitated, to which the
with each other; let it be as he solution is more important to each
pleases, so that I do not fawn on his puzzled mortal, than that upon
pleasure. Better a million times which starts every sage's discovery,
enter life as a penniless gentleman, every novelist's plot — that which
who must work his way up like a applies to MAN'S LIFE, from its first
man, than as one who creeps on his sleep in the cradle, "WHAT WILL
knees into fortune, shaming birth- HE DO WITH IT?"
right of gentleman, or soiling honour

BOOK II.—CHAPTER I.

Primitive character of the country in certain districts of Great Britain.—Connection between the features of surrounding scenery and the mental and moral inclinations of man, after the fashion of all sound Ethnological Historians.—A charioteer, to whom an experience of British Laws suggests an ingenious mode of arresting the progress of Roman Papacy, carries Lionel Haughton and his fortunes to a place which allows of description and invites repose.

In safety, but with naught else rare enough, in a railway train, to deserve commemoration, Lionel reached the station to which he was bound. He there inquired the distance to Fawley Manor House; it was five miles. He ordered a fly, and was soon wheeled briskly along a rough parish-road, through a country strongly contrasting the gay River Scenery he had so lately quitted. Quite as English, but rather the England of a former race than that which spreads round our own generation like one vast suburb of garden-ground and villas—Here, nor village, nor spire, nor porter's lodge came in sight. Rare even were the cornfields—wide spaces of unenclosed common opened, solitary and primitive, on the road, bordered by large woods, chiefly of beech, closing the horizon with ridges of undulating green. In such an England, Knights Templars might have wended their way to scattered monasteries, or fugitive partisans in the bloody Wars of the Roses have found shelter under leafy coverts.

The scene had its romance, its beauty—half savage, half gentle—leading perforce the mind of any cultivated and imaginative gazer far back from the present day—waking up long-forgotten passages from old poets. The stillness of such wastes of sward—such deeps of woodland—induced the nurture of reverie, gravely soft and lulling. There, Ambition might give rest to the wheel of Ixion, Avarice to the sieve of the Danaïds; there, disappointed Love might muse on the brevity of all human passions, and count over the tortured hearts that have found peace in holy meditation, or are now stilled under grassy knolls. See where, at the crossing of three roads upon the waste, the landscape suddenly unfolds—an upland in the distance, and on the upland a building, the first sign of social man. What is the building? only a silenced windmill—the sails dark and sharp against the dull leaden sky.

Lionel touched the driver—"Are we yet on Mr. Darrell's property?" Of the extent of that property he had involuntarily conceived a vast idea.

"Lord, sir, no; we be two miles from Squire Darrell's. He han't much property to speak of hereabouts. But he bought a good bit

masonry, so thick its walls—and thus abruptly left to moulder—a palace constructed for the reception of crowding guests—the pomp of stately revels—abandoned to owl and bat. And the homely old house beside it, which that lordly hall was doubtless designed to replace, looking so safe and tranquil at the baffled presumption of its spectral neighbour.

The driver had rung the bell, and now turning back to the chaise, met Lionel's inquiring eye, and said—"Yes; Squire Darrell began to build that—many years ago—when I was a boy. I heerd say it was to be the show-house of the whole county. Been stopped these ten or a dozen years."

"Why?—do you know?"

"No one knows. Squire was a lawyer, I b'leve—perhaps he put it into Chancery. My wife's grandfather was put into Chancery just as he was growing up, and never grew afterwards—never got out o' it—nout ever does. There's our churchwarden comes to me with a petition to sign agin the Pope. Says I, 'that old Pope is always in trouble—what's he bin doin now?' Says he, 'Spreading! He's agot into Parlyment, and he's now got a colledge, and we pays for it. I doesn't know how to stop him.' Says I, 'Put the Pope into Chancery, along with wife's grandfather, and he'll never spread agin.'"

The driver had thus just disposed of the Papacy, when an elderly servant, out of livery, opened the door. Lionel sprung from the chaise, and paused in some confusion—for then, for the first time, there darted across him the idea that he had never written to announce his acceptance of Mr. Darrell's invitation—that he ought to have done so—that he might not be expected. Meanwhile the servant surveyed him with some surprise. "Mr. Darrell?" hesitated Lionel, inquiringly.

"Not at home, sir," replied the man, as if Lionel's business was over, and he had only to re-enter his chaise. The boy was naturally rather bold than shy, and he said, with a certain assured air, "My name is Haughton. I come here on Mr. Darrell's invitation."

The servant's face changed in a moment—he bowed respectfully. "I beg pardon, sir. I will look for my master—he is somewhere on the grounds." The servant then approached the fly, took out the knapsack, and observing Lionel had his purse in his hand, said, "Allow me to save you that trouble, sir. Driver, round to the stable-yard." Stepping back into the house, the servant threw open a door to the left, on entrance, and advanced a chair—"If you will wait here a moment, sir, I will see for my master."

WHAT WILL HE DO WITH IT? 59

fall of light. We hear it, indeed, familiarly said that such an one is like an old picture. Never could it be more appositely said than of the face on which the young visitor gazed, much startled and somewhat awed. Not such as inferior limners had painted in the portraits there, though it had something in common with those family lineaments, but such as might have looked tranquil power out of the canvass of Titian.

The man stepped forward, and the illusion passed. "I thank you," he said, holding out his hand, "for taking me at my word, and answering me thus in person." He paused a moment, surveying Lionel's countenance with a keen but not unkindly eye, and added softly, "Very like your father."

At these words Lionel involuntarily pressed the hand which he had taken. That hand did not return the pressure. It lay an instant in Lionel's warm clasp—not repelling, not responding—and was then very gently withdrawn.

"Did you come from London?"

"No, sir; I found your letter yesterday at Hampton Court. I had been staying some days in that neighbourhood. I came on, this morning,—I was afraid too unceremoniously; your kind welcome reassures me there."

The words were well chosen and frankly said. Probably they pleased the host, for the expression of his countenance was, on the whole, propitious; but he merely inclined his head with a kind of lofty indifference, then, glancing at his watch, he rang the bell. The servant entered promptly. "Let dinner be served within an hour."

"Pray, sir," said Lionel, "do not change your hours on my account."

Mr. Darrell's brow slightly contracted. Lionel's tact was in fault there; but the great man answered quietly, "All hours are the same to me; and it were strange if a host could be deranged by consideration to his guest—on the first day too. Are you tired? Would you like to go to your room, or look out for half an hour? The sky is clearing."

"I should so like to look out, sir."

"This way then."

Mr. Darrell, crossing the hall, threw open a door opposite to that by which Lionel entered, and the lake (we will so call it) lay before them,—separated from the house only by a shelving gradual declivity, on which were a few beds of flowers —not tho most in vogue nowadays —and disposed in rambling old-fashioned parterres. At one angle, a quaint and dilapidated sun-dial; at the other, a long bowling-alley, terminated by one of those summer-houses which the Dutch taste, following the Revolution of 1688, brought into fashion. Mr. Darrell passed down this alley (no bowls there now), and observing that Lionel looked curiously towards the summer-house, of which the doors stood open, entered it. A lofty room with coved ceiling, painted with Roman trophies of helms and fasces, alternated with crossed fifes and fiddles, painted also.

"Amsterdam manners," said Mr. Darrell, slightly shrugging his shoulders. "Here a former race heard music, sung glees, and smoked from clay pipes. That age soon passed, unsuited to English energies, which are not to be united with Holland phlegm! But the view from the window—look out there. I wonder whether men in whigs and women in hoops enjoyed *that*. It is a mercy they did not clip those banks into a straight canal!"

The view was indeed lovely—the water looked so blue and so large

and without waiting for permission, ran indoors to find some one whom he could ask for the bread.

"Sonless, childless, hopeless, objectless!" said Darrell, murmuringly to himself, and sunk again into reverie.

By the time Lionel returned with the bread, another petted friend had joined the master. A tame doe had caught sight of him from her covert far away, came in light bounds to his side, and was pushing her delicate nostril into his drooping hand. At the sound of Lionel's hurried step, she took flight, trotted off a few paces, then turned, looking wistfully.

"I did not know you had deer here."

"Deer!—in this little paddock!— of course not; only that doe. Fairthorn introduced her here. By the by," continued Darrell, who was now throwing the bread to the swans, and had resumed his careless unmeditative manner, "you were not aware that I have a brother hermit —a companion besides the swans and the doe. Dick Fairthorn is a year or two younger than myself, the son of my father's bailiff. He was the cleverest boy at his grammar-school. Unluckily he took to the flute, and unfitted himself for the present century. He condescends, however, to act as my secretary—a fair classical scholar—plays chess—is useful to me—I am useful to him. We have an affection for each other. I never forgive any one who laughs at him. The half-hour bell, and you will meet him at dinner. Shall we come in and dress?"

They entered the house—the same man-servant was in attendance in the hall. "Show Mr. Haughton to his room." Darrell inclined his head —I use that phrase, for the gesture was neither bow nor nod—turned down a narrow passage and disappeared.

Led up an uneven staircase of oak, black as ebony, with huge balustrades, and newel-posts supporting clumsy balls, Lionel was conducted to a small chamber, modernised a century ago by a faded Chinese paper, and a mahogany bedstead, which took up three-fourths of the space, and was crested with dingy plumes, that gave it the cheerful look of a hearse; and there the attendant said, "Have you the key of your knapsack, sir? shall I put out your things to dress?" Dress! Then for the first time the boy remembered that he had brought with him no evening dress — nay, evening dress, properly so called, he possessed not at all in any corner of the world. It had never yet entered into his modes of existence. Call to mind when you were a boy of seventeen, "betwixt two ages hovering like a star," and imagine Lionel's sensations. He felt his cheek burn as if he had been detected in a crime. "I have no dress things," he said, piteously; "only a change of linen, and this," glancing at the summer jacket. The servant was evidently a most gentlemanlike man — his native sphere that of groom of the chambers. "I will mention it to Mr. Darrell; and if you will favour me with your address in London, I will send to telegraph for what you want against to-morrow."

"Many thanks," answered Lionel, recovering his presence of mind; "I will speak to Mr. Darrell myself."

"There is the hot water, sir; that is the bell. I have the honour to be placed at your commands." The door closed, and Lionel unlocked his knapsack—other trousers, other waistcoat had he—those worn at the fair, and once white. Alas! they had not since then passed to the care of the laundress. Other shoes —doubled-soled for walking. There was no help for it but to appear at

"You mean, perhaps, that you like reading, if you may choose your own books."

"Or rather, if I may choose my own time to read them, and that would not be on bright summer days."

"Without sacrificing bright summer days, one finds one has made little progress when the long winter nights come."

"Yes, sir. But must the sacrifice be paid in books? I fancy I learned as much in the playground as I did in the schoolroom, and for the last few months, in much my own master, reading hard, in the forenoon, it is true, for many hours at a stretch, and yet again for a few hours at evening, but rambling also through the streets, or listening to a few friends whom I have contrived to make—I think, if I can boast of any progress at all, the books have the smaller share in it."

"You would, then, prefer an active life to a studious one."

"Oh, yes—yes."

"Dinner is served," said the decorous Mr. Mills, throwing open the door.

CHAPTER III.

In our happy country every man's house is his castle. But however stoutly he fortify it, Care enters, as surely as she did in Horace's time, through the porticoes of a Roman's villa. Nor, whether ceilings be fretted with gold and ivory, or whether only coloured with whitewash, does it matter to Care any more than it does to a house-fly. But every tree, be it cedar or blackthorn, can harbour its singing-bird; and few are the homes in which, from nooks least suspected, there starts not a music. Is it quite true that, "non avium citharæque cantus somnum reducent?" Would not even Damocles himself have forgotten the sword, if the lute-player had changed on the notes that lull?

The dinner was simple enough, but well dressed and well served. One footman, in plain livery, assisted Mr. Mills. Darrell ate sparingly, and drank only water, which was placed by his side iced, with a single glass of wine at the close of the repast, which he drank on bending his head to Lionel, with a certain knightly grace, and the prefatory words of "Welcome here to a Haughton." Mr. Fairthorn was less abstemious —tasted of every dish, after examining it long through a pair of tortoise-shell spectacles, and drank leisurely through a bottle of port, holding up every glass to the light. Darrell talked with his usual cold but not uncourteous indifference. A remark of Lionel's on the portraits in the room turned the conversation chiefly upon pictures, and the host showed himself thoroughly accomplished in the attributes of the various schools and masters. Lionel, who was very fond of the art, and indeed painted well for a youthful amateur, listened with great delight.

"Surely, sir," said he, struck much with a very subtle observation upon the causes why the Italian masters admit of copyists with greater facility than the Flemish—" surely, sir, you yourself must have practised the art of painting?"

quick good night, and disappeared through a side-door which led to his own rooms.

Lionel looked round for Fairthorn, who now emerged *ab angulo*—from his nook.

"Oh, Mr. Fairthorn, how you have enchanted me! I never believed the flute could have been capable of such effects!"

Mr. Fairthorn's grotesque face lighted up. He took off his spectacles, as if the better to contemplate the face of his eulogist. "So you were pleased! really?" he said, chuckling a strange grim chuckle, deep in his inmost self.

"Pleased! it is a cold word! Who would not be more than pleased?"

"You should hear me in the open air."

"Let me do so—to-morrow."

"My dear young sir, with all my heart. Hist!"—gazing round as if haunted—"I like you. I wish him to like you. Answer all his questions as if you did not care how he turned you inside out. Never ask him a question, as if you sought to know what he did not himself confide. So there is something, you think, in a flute, after all? There are people who prefer the fiddle."

"Then they never heard your flute, Mr. Fairthorn." The musician again emitted his discordant chuckle, and, nodding his head nervously and cordially, shambled away without lighting a candle, and was engulfed in the shadows of some mysterious corner.

CHAPTER IV.

The Old World and the New.

IT was long before Lionel could sleep. What with the strange house and the strange master—what with the magic flute and the musician's admonitory caution — what with tender and regretful reminiscences of Sophy, his brain had enough to work on. When he slept at last, his slumber was deep and heavy, and he did not wake till gently shaken by the well-bred arm of Mr. Mills. "I humbly beg pardon—nine o'clock, sir, and the breakfast-bell going to ring." Lionel's toilet was soon hurried over; Mr. Darrell and Fairthorn were talking together as he entered the breakfast-room—the same room as that in which they had dined.

"Good morning, Lionel," said the host. "No leave-taking to-day, as you threatened. I find you have made an appointment with Mr. Fairthorn, and I shall place you under his care. You may like to look over the old house, and make yourself"— Darrell paused—"At home," jerked out Mr. Fairthorn, filling up the *hiatus*. Darrell turned his eye towards the speaker, who evidently became much frightened, and, after looking in vain for a corner, sidled away to the window, and poked himself behind the curtain. "Mr. Fairthorn, in the capacity of my secretary, has learned to find me thoughts, and put them in his own words," said Darrell, with

aspect that accompanies the upright carriage. His figure was inclined to be slender, though broad of shoulder and deep of chest; it was the figure of a young man, and probably little changed from what it might have been at five-and-twenty. A certain youthfulness still lingered even on the countenance—strange, for sorrow is supposed to expedite the work of age; and Darrell had known sorrow of a kind most adapted to harrow his peculiar nature, as great in its degree as ever left man's heart in ruins. No grey was visible in the dark brown hair, that, worn short behind, still retained in front the large Jove-like curl. No wrinkle, save at the corner of the eyes, marred the pale bronze of the firm cheek; the forehead was smooth as marble, and as massive. It was that forehead which chiefly contributed to the superb expression of his whole aspect. It was high to a fault; the perceptive organs, over a dark, strongly-marked, arched eyebrow, powerfully developed, as they are with most eminent lawyers; it did not want for breadth at the temples; yet, on the whole, it bespoke more of intellectual vigour and dauntless will than of serene philosophy or all-embracing benevolence. It was the forehead of a man formed to command and awe the passions and intellect of others by the strength of passions in himself, rather concentred than chastised, and by an intellect forceful from the weight of its mass rather than the niceness of its balance. The other features harmonised with that brow; they were of the noblest order of aquiline, at once high and delicate. The lip had a rare combination of exquisite refinement and inflexible resolve. The eye, in repose, was cold, bright, unrevealing, with a certain absent, musing, self-absorbed expression, that often made the man's words appear as if spoken mechanically, and assisted towards that seeming of listless indifference to those whom he addressed, by which he wounded vanity, without, perhaps, any malice prepense. But it was an eye in which the pupil could suddenly expand, the hue change from grey to dark, and the cold still brightness flash into vivid fire. It could not have occurred to any one, even to the most commonplace woman, to have described Darrell's as a handsome face; the expression would have seemed trivial and derogatory; the words that would have occurred to all, would have been somewhat to this effect:— "What a magnificent countenance! What a noble head!" Yet an experienced physiognomist might have noted that the same lineaments which bespoke a virtue bespoke also its neighbouring vice; that with so much will there went stubborn obstinacy; that with that power of grasp there would be the tenacity in adherence which narrows, in astringing, the intellect; that a prejudice once conceived, a passion once cherished, would resist all rational argument for relinquishment. When men of this mould do relinquish prejudice or passion, it is by their own impulse, their own sure conviction that what they hold is worthless: then they do not yield it graciously; they fling it from them in scorn, but not a scorn that consoles. That which they thus wrench away had grown a living part of themselves; their own flesh bleeds —the wound seldom or never heals. Such men rarely fail in the achievement of what they covet, if the gods are neutral; but, adamant against the world, they are vulnerable through their affections. Their love is intense, but undemonstrative; their hatred implacable, but unrevengeful. Too proud to revenge too galled to pardon.

F 3

joined the gallery, and which the host had fitted up for the purpose of scientific experiments in chemistry, or other branches of practical philosophy. These more private rooms Lionel was not permitted to enter.

Altogether the house was one of those cruel tenements which it would be a sin to pull down, or even materially to alter, but which it would be an hourly inconvenience for a modern family to inhabit. It was out of all character with Mr. Darrell's former position in life, or with the fortune which Lionel vaguely supposed him to possess, and considerably underrated. Like Sir Nicholas Bacon, the man had grown too large for his habitation.

"I don't wonder," said Lionel, as their wanderings over, he and Fairthorn found themselves in the library, "that Mr. Darrell began to build a new house. But it would have been a great pity to pull down this for it."

"Pull down this! Don't hint at such an idea to Mr. Darrell. He would as soon have pulled down the British Monarchy! Nay, I suspect, sooner."

"But the new building must surely have swallowed up the old one?"

"Oh, no; Mr. Darrell had a plan by which he would have enclosed this separately in a kind of court, with an open screen-work or cloister; and it was his intention to appropriate it entirely to mediæval antiquities, of which he has a wonderful collection. He had a notion of illustrating every earlier reign in which his ancestors flourished — different apartments in correspondence with different dates. It would have been a chronicle of national manners."

"But, if it be not an impertinent question, where is this collection? In London?"

"Hush! hush! I will give you a peep of some of the treasures, only don't betray me."

Fairthorn here, with singular rapidity, considering that he never moved in a straightforward direction, undulated into the open air in front of the house, described a rhomboid towards a side-buttress in the new building, near to which was a postern-door; unlocked that door from a key in his pocket, and, motioning Lionel to follow him, entered within the ribs of the stony skeleton. Lionel followed in a sort of supernatural awe, and beheld, with more substantial alarm, Mr. Fairthorn winding up an inclined plank which he embraced with both arms, and by which he ultimately ascended to a timber joist in what should have been an upper floor, only flooring there was none. Perched there, Fairthorn glared down on Lionel through his spectacles. "Dangerous," he said, whisperingly; "but one gets used to everything! If you feel afraid, don't venture!"

Lionel, animated by that doubt of his courage, sprang up the plank, balancing himself, schoolboy fashion, with outstretched arms, and gained the side of his guide.

"Don't touch me!" exclaimed Mr. Fairthorn, shrinking, "or we shall both be over. Now observe and imitate." Dropping himself then carefully and gradually, till he dropped on the timber joist as if it were a velocipede, his long legs dangling down, he, with thigh and hand, impelled himself onward till he gained the ridge of a wall, on which he delivered his person, and wiped his spectacles.

Lionel was not long before he stood in the same place. "Here we are," said Fairthorn.

"I don't see the collection," an-

means fond of fishing, laid his rod on the bank, and strolled across the long grass to his companion.

"It will rain soon," said he. "Let me take advantage of the present time, and hear the flute, while we can yet enjoy the open air. No, not by the margin, or you will be always looking after the trout. On the rising ground, see that old thoroughfare—let us go and sit under it. The new building looks well from it. What a pile it would have been! I may not ask you, I suppose, why it is left uncompleted. Perhaps it would have cost too much, or would have been disproportionate to the estate."

"To the present estate it would have been disproportioned, but not to the estate Mr. Darrell intended to add to it. As to cost, you don't know him. He would never have undertaken what he could not afford to complete; and what he once undertook, no thoughts of the cost would have scared him from finishing. Prodigious mind—granite! And so rich!" added Fairthorn, with an air of great pride. "I ought to know; I write all his letters on money matters. How much do you think he has, without counting land?"

"I cannot guess."

"Nearly half a million; in two years it will be more than half a million. And he had not three hundred a-year when he began life; for Fawley was sadly mortgaged."

"Is it possible! Could any lawyer make half a million at the bar?"

"If any man could, Mr. Darrell would. When he sets his mind on a thing—the thing is done; no help for it. But his fortune was not all made at the bar, though a great part of it was. An old East Indian bachelor of the same name, but who had never been heard of hereabouts till he wrote from Calcutta to Mr. Darrell (inquiring if they were any relations—and Mr. Darrell referred him to the College-at-Arms, which proved that they came from the same stock, ages ago)—left him all his money. Mr. Darrell was not dependent on his profession when he stood up in Parliament. And since we have been here, such savings! Not that Mr. Darrell is avaricious, but how can he spend money in this place? You should have seen the establishment we kept in Carlton Gardens. Such a cook too—a French gentleman—looked like a marquess. Those were happy days, and proud ones! It is true that I order the dinner here, but it can't be the same thing. Do you like fillet of veal?—we have one to-day."

"We used to have fillet of veal at school on Sundays. I thought it good then."

"It makes a nice mince," said Mr. Fairthorn, with a sensual movement of his lips. "One must think of dinner when one lives in the country—so little else to think of! Not that Mr. Darrell does, but then *he is*—granite!"

"Still," said Lionel, smiling, "I do not get my answer. Why was the house uncompleted? and why did Mr. Darrell retire from public life?"

"He took both into his head; and when a thing once gets there, it is no use asking why. But," added Fairthorn, and his innocent ugly face changed into an expression of earnest sadness—"but no doubt he had his reasons. He has reasons for all he does, only they lie far far away from what appears on the surface—far as that rivulet lies from its source! My dear young sir, Mr. Darrell has known griefs on which it does not become you and me to talk. He never talks of them. The least I can do for my benefactor is

WHAT WILL HE DO WITH IT? 73

some land in this county, in which the ancestral possessions had once been large, and built the present house, of a size suited to the altered fortunes of a race that, in a former age, had manned castles with retainers. The baptismal name of the soldier who thus partially refounded the old line in England was that now borne by your cousin, Guy—a name always favoured by Fortune in the family annals; for in Elizabeth's time, from the rank of small gentry, to which their fortune alone lifted them since their return to their native land, the Darrells rose once more into wealth and eminence under a handsome young Sir Guy —we have his picture in black flowered velvet—who married the heiress of the Haughtons, a family that had grown rich under the Tudors, and was in high favour with the Maiden-Queen. This Sir Guy was befriended by Essex, and knighted by Elizabeth herself. Their old house was then abandoned for the larger mansion of the Haughtons, which had also the advantage of being nearer to the Court. The renewed prosperity of the Darrells was of short duration. The Civil Wars came on, and Sir John Darrell took the losing side. He escaped to France with his only son. He is said to have been an accomplished, melancholy man; and my belief is, that he composed that air which you justly admire for its mournful sweetness. He turned Roman Catholic, and died in a convent. But the son, Ralph, was brought up in France with Charles II. and other gay roisterers. On the return of the Stuart, Ralph ran off with the daughter of the Roundhead to whom his estates had been given, and, after getting them back, left his wife in the country, and made love to other men's wives in town. Shocking profligate! no fruit could thrive upon such a branch. He squandered all he could squander, and would have left his children beggars, but that he was providentially slain in a tavern brawl for boasting of a lady's favours to her husband's face. The husband suddenly stabbed him —no fair duello—for Sir Ralph was invincible with the small-sword. Still the family fortune was much dilapidated, yet still the Darrells lived in the fine house of the Haughtons, and left Fawley to the owls. But Sir Ralph's son, in his old age, married a second time, a young lady of high rank, an earl's daughter. He must have been very much in love with her, despite his age, for to win her consent or her father's he agreed to settle all the Haughton estates on her and the children she might bear to him. The smaller Darrell property had already been entailed on his son by his first marriage. This is how the family came to a split. Old Darrell had children by his second wife; the eldest of those children took the Haughton name, and inherited the Haughton property. The son by the first marriage had nothing but Fawley, and the scanty domain round it. You descend from the second marriage, Mr. Darrell from the first. You understand now, my dear young sir?"

"Yes, a little; but I should very much like to know where those fine Haughton estates are now?"

"Where they are now? I can't say. They were once in Middlesex. Probably much of the land, as it was sold piecemeal, fell into small allotments, constantly changing hands. But the last relics of the property were, I know, bought on speculation by Cox the distiller; for, when we were in London, by Mr. Darrell's desire I went to look after them, and inquire if they could be repurchased. And I found that so rapid in a few years has been the pro-

Carlton Gardens. Our Mr. Darrell's mother was very pretty, even as I remember her: she died when he was about ten years old. And she too was a relation of yours—a Haughton by blood; but perhaps you will be ashamed of her, when I say she was a governess in a rich mercantile family. She had been left an orphan. I believe old Mr. Darrell (not that he was old then) married her because the Haughtons could or would do nothing for her, and because she was much snubbed and put upon, as I am told governesses usually are—married her because, poor as he was, he was still the head of both families, and bound to do what he could for decayed scions! The first governess a Darrell ever married, but no true Darrell would have called *that* a *mésalliance*, since she was still a Haughton and 'Fors non mutat genus'—Chance does not change race."

"But how comes it that the Haughtons, my grandfather Haughton, I suppose, would do nothing for his own kinswoman?"

"It was not your grandfather, Robert Haughton, who was a generous man—he was then a mere youngster, hiding himself for debt—but your great-grandfather, who was a hard man, and on the turf. He never had money to give—only money for betting. He left the Haughton estates sadly dipped. But when Robert succeeded, he came forward, was godfather to our Mr. Darrell, insisted on sharing the expense of sending him to Eton, where he became greatly distinguished; thence to Oxford, where he increased his reputation; and would probably have done more for him, only Mr. Darrell, once his foot on the ladder, wanted no help to climb to the top."

"Then my grandfather, Robert, still had the Haughton estates? Their last relics had not been yet transmuted by Mr. Cox into squares and a paragon?"

"No; the grand old mansion, though much dilapidated, with its park, though stripped of saleable timber, was still left with a rental from farms that still appertained to the residence, which would have sufficed a prudent man for the luxuries of life, and allowed a reserve fund to clear off the mortgages gradually. Abstinence and self-denial for one or two generations would have made a property, daily rising in value as the metropolis advanced to its outskirts, a princely estate for a third. But Robert Haughton, though not on the turf, had a grand way of living; and while Guy Darrell went into the law to make a small patrimony a large fortune, your father, my dear young sir, was put into the Guards to reduce a large patrimony—into Mr. Cox's distillery."

Lionel coloured, but remained silent.

Fairthorn, who was as unconscious, in his zest of narrator, that he was giving pain as an entomologist in his zest for collecting, when he pins a live moth into his cabinet, resumed: "Your father and Guy Darrell were warm friends as boys and youths. Guy was the elder of the two, and Charlie Haughton (I beg your pardon, he was always called Charlie) looked up to him as to an elder brother. Many's the scrape Guy got him out of; and many a pound, I believe, when Guy had some funds of his own, did Guy lend to Charlie."

"I am very sorry to hear that," said Lionel, sharply.

Fairthorn looked frightened. "I'm afraid I have made a blunder. Don't tell Mr. Darrell."

"Certainly not; I promise. But how came my father to need this aid, and how came they at last to quarrel?"

out of the county jail! It was those cutting words, "Sold even your name." His face, before very crimson, became livid; his head sunk on his breast. He walked towards the old gloomy house by Fairthorn's side, as one who, for the first time in life, feels on his heart the leaden weight of an hereditary shame.

CHAPTER VI.

Showing how sinful it is in a man who does not care for his honour to beget children.

WHEN Lionel saw Mr. Fairthorn devoting his intellectual being to the contents of a cold chicken-pie, he silently stepped out of the room and slunk away into a thick copse at the farthest end of the paddock. He longed to be alone. The rain descended, not heavily, but in penetrating drizzle; he did not feel it, or rather he felt glad that there was no gaudy mocking sunlight. He sate down forlorn in the hollows of a glen which the copse covered, and buried his face in his clasped hands.

Lionel Haughton, as the reader may have noticed, was no premature man—a manly boy, but still a habitant of the twilight, dreamy, shadow-land of boyhood. Noble elements were stirring fitfully within him, but their agencies were crude and undeveloped. Sometimes, through the native acuteness of his intellect, he apprehended truths quickly and truly as a man—then, again, through the warm haze of undisciplined tenderness, or the raw mists of that sensitive pride in which objects, small in themselves, loom large with undetected outlines, he fell back into the passionate dimness of a child's reasoning. He was intensely ambitious; Quixotic in the point of honour; dauntless in peril, but morbidly trembling at the very shadow of disgrace, as a foal, destined to be the war-horse, and trample down levelled steel, starts in its tranquil pastures at the rustling of a leaf. Glowingly romantic, but not inclined to vent romance in literary creations, his feelings were the more high-wrought and enthusiastic because they had no outlet in poetic channels. Most boys of great ability and strong passion write verses—it is nature's relief to brain and heart at the critical turning-age. Most boys thus gifted do so; a few do not, and out of those few Fate selects the great men of action—those large luminous characters that stamp poetry on the world's prosaic surface. Lionel had in him the pith and substance of Fortune's grand nobodies, who become Fame's abrupt somebodies when the chances of life throw suddenly in their way a noble something, to be ardently coveted and boldly won. But I repeat, as yet he was a boy—so he sate there, his hands before his face, an unreasoning self-torturer. He knew now why this haughty Darrell had written with so little tenderness and respect to his beloved mother. Darrell looked on her as the cause of his ignoble kinsman's "sale of name;" nay, most probably ascribed

instant, and replied in a voice involuntarily more kind than usual—
"Some one very commonplace, but since the Picts went out of fashion, very necessary to mortals the most sublime. I ought to apologise for his coming. You threatened to leave me yesterday because of a defect in your wardrobe. Mr. Fairthorn wrote to my tailor to hasten hither and repair it. He is here. I commend him to your custom! Don't despise him because he makes' for a man of my remote generation. Tailors are keen observers, and do not grow out of date so quickly as politicians."

The words were said with a playful good-humour very uncommon to Mr. Darrell. The intention was obviously kind and kinsmanlike. Lionel sprang to his feet; his lip curled, his eye flashed, and his crest rose.

"No, sir; I will not stoop to this! I will not be clothed by your charity —yours! I will not submit to an implied taunt upon my poor mother's ignorance of the manners of a rank to which she was not born! You said we might not like each other, and if so, we should part for ever. I do not like you, and I will go!" He turned abruptly, and walked to the house—magnanimous. If Mr. Darrell had not been the most singular of men, he might well have been offended. As it was, though few were less accessible to surprise, he was surprised. But offended? Judge for yourself. "I declare," muttered Guy Darrell, gazing on the boy's receding figure,—"I declare that I almost feel as if I could once again be capable of an emotion! I hope I am not going to like that boy! The old Darrell blood in his veins, surely. I might have spoken as he did at his age, but I must have had some better reason for it. What did I say to justify such an explosion! *Quid feci?—ubi lapsus.'* Gone, no doubt, to pack up his knapsack, and take the Road to Ruin! Shall I let him go? Better for me, if I am really in danger of liking him; and so be at his mercy to sting—what? my heart! I defy him; it is dead. No; he shall not go thus. I am the head of our joint houses. Houses! I wish he had a house, poor boy! And his grandfather loved me. Let him go! I will beg his pardon first; and he may dine in his drawers if that will settle the matter!".

Thus, no less magnanimous than Lionel, did this misanthropical man follow his ungracious cousin. "Ha!" cried Darrell, suddenly, as approaching the threshold, he saw Mr. Fairthorn at the dining-room window occupied in nibbing a pen upon an ivory thumb-stall—"I have hit it! That abominable Fairthorn has been shedding its prickles! How could I trust flesh and blood to such a bramble? I'll know what it was this instant!" Vain menace! No sooner did Mr. Fairthorn catch glimpse of Darrell's countenance within ten yards of the porch, than, his conscience taking alarm, he rushed incontinent from the window—the apartment—and, ere Darrell could fling open the door, was lost in some lair—"nullis penetrabilis astris"—in that sponge-like and cavernous abode, wherewith benignant Providence had suited the locality to the creature.

CHAPTER IX.

Darrell: mystery in his past life. What has he done with it?

SOME days passed—each day varying little from the other. It was the habit of Darrell, if he went late to rest, to rise early. He never allowed himself more than five hours' sleep. A man greater than Guy Darrell— Sir Walter Raleigh—carved from the solid day no larger a slice for Morpheus. And it was this habit perhaps, yet more than temperance in diet, which preserved to Darrell his remarkable youthfulness of aspect and frame, so that at fifty-two he looked, and really was, younger than many a strong man of thirty-five. For, certain it is, that on entering middle life, he who would keep his brain clear, his step elastic, his muscles from fleshiness, his nerves from tremor—in a word, retain his youth in spite of the register —should beware of long slumbers. Nothing ages like laziness. The hours before breakfast Darrell devoted first to exercise, whatever the weather—next to his calm scientific pursuits. At ten o'clock punctually he rode out alone, and seldom returned till late in the afternoon. Then he would stroll forth with Lionel into devious woodlands, or lounge with him along the margin of the lake, or lie down on the tedded grass, call the boy's attention to the insect populace which sports out its happy life in the summer months, and treat of the ways and habits of each varying species, with a quaint learning, half humorous, half grave. He was a minute observer, and an accomplished naturalist. His range of knowledge was, indeed, amazingly large for a man who has had to pass his best years in a dry and absorbing study: necessarily not so profound in each section as that of a special professor, but if the science was, often on the surface, the thoughts he deduced from what he knew were as often original and deep. A maxim of his, which he dropped out one day to Lionel in his careless manner, but pointed diction, may perhaps illustrate his own practice and its results: "Never think it enough to have solved the problem started by another mind, till you have deduced from it a corollary of your own."

After dinner, which was not over till past eight o'clock, they always adjourned to the library, Fairthorn vanishing into a recess, Darrell and Lionel each with his several book, then an air on the flute, and each to his own room before eleven. No life could be more methodical; yet to Lionel it had an animating charm, for his interest in his host daily increased, and varied his thoughts with perpetual occupation. Darrell, on the contrary, while more kind and cordial, more cautiously on his guard not to wound his young guest's susceptibilities than he had been before the quarrel and its reconciliation, did not seem to feel for Lionel the active interest which Lionel felt for him. He did not, as most clever men are apt to do in their intercourse with youth, attempt to draw him out, plumb his intellect, or guide his tastes. If he was at times instructive, it was because talk fell on subjects on which it pleased himself to touch, and in which he could

G

arms, stand upon the petty and steep cragstone, which alone looms out of the Measureless Sea, and say to ourselves, looking neither backward nor beyond, "Let us bear what is;" and so for the moment the eye can lighten and the lip can smile.

Lionel could no longer glean from Mr. Fairthorn any stray hints upon the family records. That gentleman had evidently been reprimanded for indiscretion, or warned against its repetition, and he became as reserved and mum as if he had just emerged from the cave of Trophonius. Indeed he shunned trusting himself again alone to Lionel, and affecting a long arrear of correspondence on behalf of his employer, left the lad during the forenoons to solitary angling, or social intercourse with the swans and the tame doe. But from some mystic concealment within doors would often float far into the open air the melodies of that magic flute; and the boy would glide back, along the dark-red mournful walls of the old house, or the futile pomp of pilastered arcades in the uncompleted new one, to listen to the sound: listening, as, blissful boy, forgot the present; he seized the unchallenged royalty of his years. For him no rebels in the past conspired with poison to the wine-cup, murder to the sleep. No deserts in the future, arresting the march of ambition, said—"Here are sands for a pilgrim, not fields for a conqueror."

CHAPTER X.

In which chapter the History quietly moves on to the next.

THUS nearly a week had gone, and Lionel began to feel perplexed as to the duration of his visit. Should he be the first to suggest departure? Mr. Darrell rescued him from that embarrassment. On the seventh day, Lionel met his host in a lane near the house, returning from his habitual ride. The boy walked home by the side of the horseman, patting the steed, admiring its shape, and praising the beauty of another saddle-horse, smaller and slighter, which he had seen in the paddock exercised by a groom. "Do you ever ride that chestnut? I think it even handsomer than this."

"Half our preferences are due to the vanity they flatter. Few can ride this horse—any one, perhaps, that."

"There speaks the Dare-all!" said Lionel, laughing.

The host did not look displeased. "Where no difficulty, there no pleasure," said he in his curt laconic diction. "I was in Spain two years ago. I had not an English horse there, so I bought that Andalusian jennet. What has served him at need, no preux chevalier would leave to the chance of ill-usage. So the jennet came with me to England. You have not been much accustomed to ride, I suppose?"

"Not much; but my dear mother thought I ought to learn. She pinched for a whole year to have me

powerful and wealthy man had felt that interest, he had thrust it from him. That he meant to be generous was indeed certain, and this he had typically shown in a very trite matter-of-fact way. The tailor, whose visit had led to such perturbation, had received instructions beyond the mere supply of the raiment for which he had been summoned; and a large patent portmanteau, containing all that might constitute the liberal outfit of a young man in the rank of gentleman, had arrived at Fawley, and amazed and moved Lionel, whom Darrell had by this time thoroughly reconciled to the acceptance of benefits. The gift denoted this: "In recognising you as kinsman, I shall henceforth provide for you as gentleman." Darrell indeed meditated applying for an appointment in one of the public offices, the settlement of a liberal allowance, and a parting shake of the hand, which should imply, "I have now behaved as becomes me; the rest belongs to you. We may never meet again. There is no reason why this good-by may not be for ever."

But in the course of that ride, Darrell's intentions changed. Wherefore? You will never guess! Nothing so remote as the distance between cause and effect, and the cause for the effect here was—poor little Sophy.

The day was fresh, with a lovely breeze, as the two riders rode briskly over the turf of rolling commons, with the feathery boughs of neighbouring woodlands tossed joyously to and fro by the sportive summer wind. The exhilarating exercise and air raised Lionel's spirits, and released his tongue from all trammels; and when a boy is in high spirits, ten to one but he grows a frank egotist, feels the teeming life of his individuality, and talks about himself.

Quite unconsciously, Lionel rattled out gay anecdotes of his school-days; his quarrel with a demoniacal usher; how he ran away; what befell him; how the doctor went after, and brought him back; how splendidly the doctor behaved—neither flogged nor expelled him, but after patient listening, while he rebuked the pupil, dismissed the usher, to the joy of the whole academy; how he fought the head boy in the school for calling the doctor a sneak; how, licked twice, he yet fought that head boy a third time, and licked him; how, when head boy himself, he had roused the whole school into a civil war, dividing the boys into Cavaliers and Roundheads; how clay was rolled out into cannon-balls and pistol-shot, sticks shaped into swords; the play-ground disturfed to construct fortifications; how a slovenly stout boy enacted Cromwell; how he himself was elevated into Prince Rupert; and how, reversing all history, and infamously degrading Cromwell, Rupert would not consent to be beaten; and Cromwell at the last, disabled by an untoward blow across the knuckles, ignominiously yielded himself prisoner, was tried by a court-martial, and sentenced to be shot! To all this rubbish did Darrell incline his patient ear—not encouraging, not interrupting, but sometimes stifling a sigh at the sound of Lionel's merry laugh, or the sight of his fair face, with heightened glow on its cheeks, and his long silky hair, worthy the name of lovelocks, blown by the wind from the open loyal features, which might well have graced the portrait of some youthful Cavalier. On bounded the Spanish jennet, on rattled the boy rider. He had left school now, in his headlong talk; he was describing his first friendship with Frank Vance, as a lodger at his mother's; how example fired him, and he took

penury and hardships of such a life! If you could but have seen and heard her! She could never have been born to it! You look away— I offend you! I have no right to tax your benevolence for others; but, instead of showering favours upon me, so little would suffice for her!—if she were but above positive want, with that old man (she would not be happy without him), safe in such a cottage as you give to your own peasants! I am a man, or shall be one soon; I can wrestle with the world, and force my way somehow; but that delicate child, a village show, or a beggar on the high-road!—no mother, no brother, no one but that broken-down cripple, leaning upon her arm as his crutch. I cannot bear to think of it. I am sure I shall meet her again somewhere; and when I do, may I not write to you, and will you not come to her help? Do speak—do say 'Yes,' Mr. Darrell."

The rich man's breast heaved slightly; he closed his eyes, but for a moment. There was a short and sharp struggle with his better self, and the better self conquered.

"Let go my reins—see, my horse puts down his ears—he may do you a mischief. Now canter on—you shall be satisfied. Give me a moment to—to unbutton my coat—it is too tight for me."

CHAPTER XII.

Guy Darrell gives way to an impulse, and quickly decides what he will do with it.

"LIONEL HAUGHTON," said Guy Darrell, regaining his young cousin's side, and speaking in a firm and measured voice, "I have to thank you for one very happy minute; the sight of a heart so fresh in the limpid purity of goodness is a luxury you cannot comprehend till you have come to my age; journeyed, like me, from Dan to Beersheba, and found all barren. Heed me: if you had been half-a-dozen years older, and this child for whom you plead had been a fair young woman, perhaps just as innocent, just as charming—more in peril—my benevolence would have lain as dormant as a stone. A young man's foolish sentiment for a pretty girl. As your true friend, I should have shrugged my shoulders and said, 'Beware!' Had I been your father, I should have taken alarm, and frowned. I should have seen the sickly romance, which ends in dupes or deceivers. But at your age, you, hearty, genial, and open-hearted boy—you, caught but by the chivalrous compassion for helpless female childhood—oh that you *were* my son—oh that my dear father's blood were in those knightly veins! I had a son once! God took him;" the strong man's lips quivered — he hurried on. "I felt there was manhood in you, when you wrote to fling my churlish favours in my teeth — when you would have left my roof-tree in a burst of passion which might be foolish, but was nobler than the wisdom of calculating submission—manhood, but only perhaps man's pride as man—man's heart not less

and had a woman who loved him been by to listen, she would have heard the short slight sigh which came and went too quickly for the duller sense of man's friendship to recognise it as the sound of sorrow.

In Darrell himself, thus insensibly altered, Lionel daily discovered more to charm his interest and deepen his affection. In this man's nature there were, indeed, such wondrous under-currents of sweetness, so suddenly gushing forth, so suddenly vanishing again! And exquisite in him were the traits of that sympathetic tact which the world calls fine breeding, but which comes only from a heart at once chivalrous and tender, the more bewitching in Darrell from their contrast with a manner usually cold, and a bearing so stamped with masculine, self-willed, haughty power. Thus days went on as if Lionel had become a very child of the house. But his sojourn was in truth drawing near to a close not less abrupt and unexpected than the turn in his host's humours to which he owed the delay of his departure.

One bright afternoon, as Darrell was standing at the window of his private study, Fairthorn, who had crept in on some matter of business, looked at his countenance long and wistfully, and then, shambling up to his side, put one hand on his shoulder with a light timid touch, and, pointing with the other to Lionel, who was lying on the grass in front of the casement reading the *Faerie Queen*, said, "Why do you take him to your heart if he does not comfort it?"

Darrell winced, and answered gently, "I did not know you were in the room. Poor Fairthorn; thank you!"

"Thank me!—what for?"

"For a kind thought. So, then, you like the boy?"

"Mayn't I like him?" asked Fairthorn, looking rather frightened; "surely you do!"

"Yes, I *like* him much; I am trying my best to *love* him. But, but"—Darrell turned quickly, and the portrait of his father over the mantelpiece came full upon his sight—an impressive, a haunting face—sweet and gentle, yet with the high narrow brow and arched nostril of pride, with restless melancholy eyes, and an expression that revealed the delicacy of intellect, but not its power. There was something forlorn, but imposing, in the whole effigy. As you continued to look at the countenance, the mournful attraction grew upon you. Truly a touching and a most lovable aspect. Darrell's eyes moistened.

"Yes, my father, it is so!" he said softly. "All my sacrifices were in vain. The race is not to be rebuilt! No grandchild of yours will succeed me—me, the last of the old line! Fairthorn, how *can* I love that boy? He may be my heir, and in his veins not a drop of my father's blood!"

"But he has the blood of your father's ancestors; and why must you think of him as your heir?— you, who, if you would but go again into the world, might yet find a fair wi—"

With such a stamp came Darrell's foot upon the floor, that the holy and conjugal monosyllable dropping from Fairthorn's lips was as much cut in two as if a shark had snapt it. Unspeakably frightened, the poor man sidled away, thrust himself behind a tall reading-desk, and, peering aslant from that covert, whimpered out, "Don't, don't now, don't be so awful; I did not mean to offend, but I'm always saying

waste land before them; and Lionel said merrily,

"But this is the very scene! Here the young knight, leaving his father's hall, would have checked his *destrier*, glancing wistfully now over that green wild which seems so boundless, now to the 'umbrageous horror' of those breathless woodlands, and questioned himself which way to take for adventure."

"Yes," said Darrell, coming out from his long reserve on all that concerned his past life—"Yes, and the gold of the gorse-blossoms tempted me; and I took the waste land." He paused a moment, and renewed: "And then, when I had known cities and men, and snatched romance from dull matter-of-fact, then I would have done as civilization does with romance itself—I would have enclosed the waste land for my own aggrandisement. Look," he continued, with a sweep of the hand round the width of prospect, "all that you see to the verge of the horizon, some fourteen years ago, was to have been thrown into the petty paddock we have just quitted, and serve as park round the house I was then building. Vanity of human wishes! What but the several proportions of their common folly distinguishes the baffled squire from the arrested conqueror? Man's characteristic cerebral organ must certainly be acquisitiveness."

"Was it his organ of acquisitiveness that moved Themistocles to boast that 'he could make a small state great?'"

"Well remembered—ingeniously quoted," returned Darrell, with the polite bend of his stately head. "Yes, I suspect that the coveting organ had much to do with the boast. To build a name was the earliest dream of Themistocles, if we are to accept the anecdote that makes him say, 'The trophies of Miltiades would not suffer him to sleep.' To build a name, or to create a fortune, are but varying applications of one human passion. The desire of something we have not is the first of our childish remembrances; it matters not what form it takes, what object it longs for; still it is to acquire; it never deserts us while we live."

"And yet, if I might, I should like to ask, what you now desire that you do not possess?"

"I—nothing; but I spoke of the living! I am dead. Only," added Darrell, with his silvery laugh, "I say, as poor Chesterfield said before me, 'it is a secret—keep it.'"

Lionel made no reply; the melancholy of the words saddened him: but Darrell's manner repelled the expression of sympathy or of interest; and the boy fell into conjecture—what had killed to the world this man's intellectual life?

And thus silently they continued to wander on till the sound of the flute had long been lost to their ears. Was the musician playing still?

At length they came round to the other end of Fawley village, and Darrell again became animated.

"Perhaps," said he, returning to the subject of talk that had been abruptly suspended—"Perhaps the love of power is at the origin of each restless courtship of Fortune; yet, after all, who has power with less alloy than the village thane! With so little effort, so little thought, the man in the manor-house can make men in the cottage happier here below, and more fit for a hereafter yonder. In leaving the world I come from contest and pilgrimage, like our sires the Crusaders, to reign at home."

As he spoke, he entered one of the cottages. An old paralytic man was seated by the fire, hot though the July sun was out of doors; and his wife, of the same age, and almost as

Turning then to the hostess, who was standing somewhat within the threshold, a glass of brandy-and-water in her hand (the third glass that stranger had called for during his half-hour's rest in the hostelry), quoth the man—

"The taller gentleman yonder is surely your squire, is he not? but who is the shorter and younger person?"

The landlady put forth her head. "Oh! that is a relation of the squire's down on a visit, sir. I heard coachman say that the squire's taken to him hugely; and they do think at the hall that the young gentleman will be his heir."

"Aha!—indeed—his heir! What is the lad's name? What relation can he be to Mr. Darrell?"

"I don't know what relation exactly, sir; but he is one of the Haughtons, and they've been kin to the Fawley folks time out of mind."

"Haughton?—aha! Thank you, ma'am. Change, if you please."

The stranger tossed off his dram, and stretched his hand for his change.

"Beg pardon, sir, but this must be forring money," said the landlady, turning a five-franc piece on her palm with suspicious curiosity.

"Foreign! Is it possible?" The stranger dived again into his pocket, and apparently with some difficulty hunted out half-a-crown.

"Sixpence more, if you please, sir; three brandies, and bread-and-cheese, and the ale too, sir."

"How stupid I am! I thought that French coin was a five-shilling piece. I fear I have no English money about me but this half-crown; and I can't ask you to trust me, as you don't know me."

"Oh, sir, 'tis all one if you know the squire. You may be passing this way again."

"I shall not forget my debt when I do, you may be sure," said the stranger; and, with a nod, he walked away in the same direction as Darrell and Lionel had already taken—through a turnstile by a public path that, skirting the churchyard and the neighbouring parsonage, led along a cornfield to the demesnes of Fawley.

The path was narrow, the corn rising on either side, so that two persons could not well walk abreast. Lionel was some paces in advance, Darrell walking slow. The stranger followed at a distance; once or twice he quickened his pace, as if resolved to overtake Darrell; then, apparently, his mind misgave him, and he again fell back.

There was something furtive and sinister about the man. Little could be seen of his face, for he wore a large hat of foreign make, slouched deep over his brow, and his lips and jaw were concealed by a dark and full mustache and beard. As much of the general outline of the countenance as remained distinguishable was, nevertheless, decidedly handsome; but a complexion naturally rich in colour, seemed to have gained the heated look which comes with the earlier habits of intemperance, before it fades into the leaden hues of the later.

His dress bespoke pretension to a certain rank; but its component parts were strangely ill-assorted, out of date, and out of repair: pearl-coloured trousers, with silk braids down their sides; brodequins to match—Parisian fashion three years back, but the trousers shabby, the braiding discoloured, the brodequins in holes. The coat—once a black evening-dress coat—of a cut a year or two anterior to that of the trousers; satin facings—cloth napless, satin stained. Over all, a sort of summer travelling-cloak, or rather large cape of a waterproof silk, once

you are standing upon the land of my fathers. If you would speak with me, this way;" and, brushing through the corn, Darrell strode towards a patch of waste land that adjoined the field: the man followed him, and both passed from Lionel's eyes. The doe had come to the gate to greet her master; she now rested her nostrils on the bar, with a look disappointed and plaintive.

"Come," said Lionel, "come." The doe would not stir.

So the boy walked on alone, not much occupied with what had just passed. "Doubtless," thought he, "some person in the neighbourhood upon country business."

He skirted the lake, and seated himself on a garden bench near the house. What did he there think of?—who knows? Perhaps of the Great World; perhaps of little Sophy! Time fled on: the sun was receding in the west, when Darrell hurried past him without speaking, and entered the house.

The host did not appear at dinner, nor all that evening. Mr. Mills made an excuse—Mr. Darrell did not feel very well.

Fairthorn had Lionel all to himself, and having within the last few days reindulged in open cordiality to the young guest, he was especially communicative that evening. He talked much on Darrell, and with all the affection that, in spite of his fear, the poor flute-player felt for his ungracious patron. He told many anecdotes of the stern man's tender kindness to all that came within its sphere. He told also anecdotes more striking of the kind man's sternness where some obstinate prejudice, some ruling passion, made him "granite."

"Lord, my dear young sir," said Fairthorn, "be his most bitter open enemy, and fall down in the mire, the first hand to help you would be Guy Darrell's; but be his professed friend, and betray him to the worth of a straw, and never try to see his face again if you are wise—the most forgiving and the least forgiving of human beings. But—"

The study door noiselessly opened, and Darrell's voice called out,

"Fairthorn, let me speak with you."

CHAPTER XV.

Every street has two sides, the shady side and the sunny. When two men shake hands and part, mark which of the two takes the sunny side; he will be the younger man of the two.

THE next morning, neither Darrell nor Fairthorn appeared at breakfast; but as soon as Lionel had concluded that meal, Mr. Mills informed him, with customary politeness, that Mr. Darrell wished to speak with him in the study. Study, across the threshold of which Lionel had never yet set footstep! He entered it now with a sentiment of mingled curiosity and awe. Nothing in it remarkable, save the portrait of the host's father over the mantelpiece. Books strewed tables, chairs, and floors in the disorder loved by habitual students. Near the window was a glass bowl containing goldfish, and close by, in its cage, a sing-

Darrell's brows met. "I don't know," said he, curtly. "Adieu." He opened the door as he spoke.

Lionel looked at him with wistful yearning, filial affection, through his swimming eyes. "God bless you, sir," he murmured, simply, and passed away.

"That blessing should have come from me!" said Darrell to himself, as he turned back, and stood on his solitary hearth. "But they on whose heads I once poured a blessing, where are they—where? And that man's tale, reviving the audacious fable which the other, and I verily believe the less guilty knave of the two, sought to palm on me years ago!

Stop; let me weigh well what he said. If it were true! Oh, shame, shame!"

Folding his arms tightly on his breast, Darrell paced the room with slow, measured strides, pondering deeply. He was, indeed, seeking to suppress feeling, and to exercise only judgment; and his reasoning process seemed at length fully to satisfy him, for his countenance gradually cleared, and a triumphant smile passed across it. "A lie—certainly a palpable and gross lie; lie it must and shall be. Never will I accept it as truth. Father" (looking full at the portrait over the mantel-shelf), "father, fear not—never—never!"

thinking of him, and the Thames and the butterflies, and find hard life still more irksome. Of all this, and much more, in the general way of consolers who set out on the principle that grief is a matter of logic, did Gentleman Waife deliver himself with a vigour of ratiocination which admitted of no reply, and conveyed not a particle of comfort. And feeling this, that great Actor—not that he was acting then—suddenly stopped, clasped the child in his arms, and murmured in broken accents—"But if I see you thus cast down, I shall have no strength left to hobble on through the world; and the sooner I lie down, and the dust is shovelled over me, why, the better for you; for it seems that Heaven sends you friends, and I tear you from them."

And then Sophy fairly gave way to her sobs: she twined her little arms round the old man's neck convulsively, kissed his rough face with imploring pathetic fondness, and forced out through her tears, "Don't talk so! I've been ungrateful and wicked. I don't care for any one but my own dear, dear Grandy."

After this little scene, they both composed themselves, and felt much lighter of heart. They pursued their journey, no longer apart, but side by side, and the old man leaning, though very lightly, on the child's arm. But there was no immediate reaction from gloom to gaiety. Waife began talking in softened undertones, and vaguely, of his own past afflictions; and partial as was the reference, how vast did the old man's sorrows seem beside the child's regrets; and yet he commented on them as if rather in pitying her state than grieving for his own.

"Ah, at your age, my darling, I had not your troubles and hardships. I had not to trudge these dusty roads on foot with a broken-down good-for-nothing scatterling. I trod rich carpets, and slept under silken curtains. I took the air in gay carriages—I such a scapegrace—and you little child—you so good! All gone, all melted away from me, and not able now to be sure that you will have a crust of bread this day week."

"Oh, yes! I shall have bread, and you too, Grandy," cried Sophy, with cheerful voice. "It was you who taught me to pray to God, and said that in all your troubles God had been good to you; and He has been so good to me since I prayed to Him; for I have no dreadful Mrs. Crane to beat me now, and say things more hard to bear than beating—and you have taken me to yourself. How I prayed for that. And I take care of you too, Grandy, —don't I? I prayed for that too; and as to carriages," added Sophy, with superb air, "I don't care if I am never in a carriage as long as I live; and you know I have been in a van, which is bigger than a carriage, and I didn't like that at all. But how came people to behave so ill to you, Grandy?"

"I never said people behaved ill to me, Sophy."

"Did not they take away the carpets and silk curtains, and all the fine things you had as a little boy?"

"I don't know," replied Waife, with a puzzled look, "that people actually took them away—but they melted away. However, I had much still to be thankful for—I was so strong, and had such high spirits, Sophy, and found people not behaving ill to me—quite the contrary —so kind. I found no Crane (she monster) as you did, my little angel. Such prospects before me, if I had walked straight towards them. But I followed my own fancy, which led me zigzag; and now that I would stray back into the high-road, you

you, body and soul, than the worst that has happened to you with me. And so we have been thrown together; and so you have supported me; and so, when we could exist without Mr. Rugge, Providence got rid of him for us. And so we are now walking along the high-road; and through yonder trees you can catch a peep of the roof under which we are about to rest for a while; and there you will learn what I have done with the Three Pounds!"

"It is not the Spotted Boy, Grandy?"

"No," said Waife, sighing; "the Spotted Boy is a handsome income; but let us only trust in Providence, and I should not wonder if our new acquisition proved a monstrous—"

"Monstrous!"

"Piece of good fortune."

CHAPTER II.

The Investment revealed.

GENTLEMAN WAIFE passed through a turnstile, down a narrow lane, and reached a solitary cottage. He knocked at the door; an old peasant-woman opened it, and dropped him a civil curtsy. "Indeed, sir, I am glad you are come. I'se most afeared he be dead."

"Dead!" exclaimed Waife. "Oh, Sophy, if he should be dead."

"Who?"

Waife did not heed the question. "What makes you think him dead?" said he, fumbling in his pockets, from which he at last produced a key. "You have not been disobeying my strict orders, and tampering with the door?"

"Lor' love ye, no, sir. But he made such a noise a fust—awful! And now he's as still as a corpse. And I did peep through the keyhole, and he was stretched stark."

"Hunger, perhaps," said the Comedian; "'tis his way when he has been kept fasting much over his usual hours. Follow me, Sophy." He put aside the woman, entered the sanded kitchen, ascended a stair that led from it; and Sophy following, stopped at a door and listened: not a sound. Timidly he unlocked the portals and crept in, when, suddenly, such a rush—such a spring, and a mass of something vehement yet soft, dingy yet whitish, whirled past the actor, and came pounce against Sophy, who therewith uttered a shriek. "Stop him, stop him, for heaven's sake," cried Waife. "Shut the door below—seize him." Down-stairs, however, went the mass, and down-stairs after it hobbled Waife, returning in a few moments with the re-captured and mysterious fugitive.

"There," he cried triumphantly to Sophy, who, standing against the wall with her face buried in her frock, long refused to look up—"there—tame as a lamb, and knows me. See"—he seated himself on the floor, and Sophy, hesitatingly opening her eyes, beheld gravely gazing at her from under a profusion of shaggy locks an enormous—

He lifted himself on his hind-legs, and laid his missive on the counter. The shopwoman—you know her, Mrs. Traill—unfolded the paper and read the order. 'Clever dog that, sir,' said she. 'To fetch and carry?' said I, indifferently. 'More than that, sir; you shall see. The order is for two penn'orth of snuff. The dog knows he is to take back fourpence. I will give him a penny short.' So she took the sixpence and gave the dog threepence out of it. The dog shook his head and looked gravely into her face. 'That's all you'll get,' said she. The dog shook his head again, and tapped his paw once on the counter, as much as to say, 'I'm not to be done—a penny more, if you please.' 'If you'll not take that, you shall have nothing,' said Mrs. Traill, and she took back the threepence."

"Dear! and what did the dog do then—snarl or bite?"

"Not so; he knew he was in his rights, and did not lower himself by showing bad temper. The dog looked quietly round, saw a basket which contained two or three pounds of candles lying in a corner for the shopboy to take to some customer; took up the basket in his mouth, and turned tail, as much as to say, 'Tit for tat then.' He understood, you see, what is called 'the law of reprisals.' 'Come back this moment,' cried Mrs. Traill. The dog walked out of the shop; then she ran after him, and counted the fourpence before him, on which he dropped the basket, picked up the rightchange, and went off demurely. 'To whom does that poodle belong?' said I. 'To a poor drunken man,' said Mrs. Trail; 'I wish it was in better hands.' 'So do I, ma'am,' answered I;—'did he teach it?' 'No, it was taught by his brother, who was an old soldier, and died in his house two weeks ago. It knows a great many tricks, and is quite young. It might make a fortune as a show, sir.' So I was thinking. I inquired the owner's address, called on him, and found him disposed to sell the dog. But he asked £3, a sum that seemed out of the question then. Still I kept the dog in my eye; called every day to make friends with it, and ascertain its capacities. And at last, thanks to you, Sophy, I bought the dog; and what is more, as soon as I had two golden sovereigns to show, I got him for that sum, and we have still £1 left (besides small savings from our last salaries) to go to the completion of his education, and the advertisement of his merits. I kept this a secret from Merle—from all. I would not even let the drunken owner know where I took the dog to yesterday. I brought him here, where, I learned in the village, there were two rooms to let—locked him up—and my story is told."

"But why keep it such a secret?"

"Because I don't want Rugge to trace us. He might do one a mischief; because I have a grand project of genteel position and high prices for the exhibition of that dog. And why should it be known where we come from, or what we were? And because, if the owner knew where to find the dog, he might decoy it back from us. Luckily he had not made the dog so fond of him, but what, unless it be decoyed, it will accustom itself to us. And now I propose that we should stay a week or so here, and devote ourselves exclusively to developing the native powers of this gifted creature. Get out the dominoes."

"What is his name?"

"Ha! that is the first consideration. What shall be his name?"

"Has he not one already?"

"Yes—trivial and unattractive—

about the Brazen Head, Friar Bacon! He must have been very wise."

WAIFE.—"Not bad; mysterious, but not recondite; historical, yet familiar. What does Mop say to it? Friar, Friar, Friar Bacon, sir,—Friar."

SOPHY (coaxingly).—"Friar."

Mop, evidently conceiving that appeal is made to some other personage, canine or human, not present, rouses up, walks to the door, smells at the chink, returns, shakes his head, and rests on his haunches, eyeing his two friends superciliously.

SOPHY.—"He does not take to that name."

WAIFE.—"He has his reasons for it; and indeed there are many worthy persons who disapprove of anything that savours of magical practices. Mop intimates that, on entering public life, one should beware of offending the respectable prejudices of a class."

Mr. Waife then, once more resorting to the recesses of scholastic memory, plucked therefrom, somewhat by the head and shoulders, sundry names reverenced in a bygone age. He thought of the seven wise men of Greece, but could only recall the nomenclature of two out of the seven—a sad proof of the distinction between collegiate fame and popular renown. He called Thales; he called Dion. Mop made no response. "Wonderful intelligence!" said Waife; "he knows that Thales and Dion would not draw!—obsolete."

Mop was equally mute to Aristotle. He pricked up his ears at Plato, perhaps because the sound was not wholly dissimilar from that of Ponto—a name of which he might have had vague reminiscences. The Romans, not having cultivated an original philosophy, though they contrived to produce great men without it, Waife passed by that perished people. He crossed to China, and tried Confucius. Mop had evidently never heard of him.

"I am at the end of my list, so far as the wise men are concerned," said Waife, wiping his forehead. "If Mop were to distinguish himself by valour, one would find heroes by the dozen—Achilles, and Hector, and Julius Cæsar, and Pompey, and Bonaparte, and Alexander the Great, and the Duke of Marlborough. Or, if he wrote poetry, we could fit him to a hair. But wise men certainly are scarce, and when one has hit on a wise man's name, it is so little known to the vulgar that it would carry no more weight with it than Spot or Toby. But necessarily some name the dog must have, and take to, sympathetically."

Sophy meanwhile had extracted the dominoes from Waife's bundle, and with the dominoes an alphabet and a multiplication-table in printed capitals. As the Comedian's one eye rested upon the last, he exclaimed, "But after all, Mop's great strength will probably be in arithmetic, and the science of numbers is the root of all wisdom. Besides, every man, high and low, wants to make a fortune, and associations connected with addition and multiplication are always pleasing. Who, then, is the sage at computation most universally known? Unquestionably Cocker! He must take to that — Cocker, Cocker" (commandingly)—"C-o-c-k-e-r" (with persuasive sweetness).

Mop looked puzzled; he put his head first on one side, then the other.

SOPHY (with mellifluous endearment).—"Cocker, good Cocker; Cocker dear."

cast up a simple sum in addition. Nothing brought him to the end of his majestic tether like dot and carry one. Notable type of our human incompleteness, where men might deem our studies had made us most complete! Notable type, too, of that grandest order of all human genius which seems to arrive at results by intuition;—which a child might pose by a row of figures on a slate—while it is solving the laws that link the stars to infinity! But *revenons à nos moutons*, what was the astral attraction that incontestably bound the reminiscences of Mop to the cognominal distinction of Sir Isaac? I had prepared a very erudite and subtle treatise upon this query, enlivened by quotations from the ancient Mystics—such as Iamblicus and Proclus—as well as by a copious reference to the doctrine of the more modern Spiritualists, from Sir Kenelm Digby and Swedenbourg, to Monsieur Cahagnet and Judge Edwards: it was to be called Inquiry into the Law of Affinities, by Philomopsos: when, unluckily for my treatise, I arrived at the knowledge of a fact which, though it did not render the treatise less curious, knocked on the head the theory upon which it was based. The baptismal name of the old soldier, Mop's first proprietor and earliest preceptor, was Isaac; and his master being called in the homely household by that Christian name, the sound had entered into Mop's youngest and most endeared associations. His canine affections had done much towards ripening his scholastic education. "Where is Isaac?" "Call Isaac!" "Fetch Isaac his hat," &c. &c. Stilled was that name when the old soldier died; but when heard again, Mop's heart was moved, and in missing the old master, he felt more at home with the new. As for the title, "Sir," it was a mere expletive in his ears. Such was the fact, and such the deduction to be drawn from it. Not that it will satisfy every one. I know that philosophers who deny all that they have not witnessed, and refuse to witness what they resolve to deny, will reject the story *in toto*; and will prove, by reference to their own dogs, that a dog never recognises the name of his master—never yet could be taught arithmetic. I know also that there are Mystics who will prefer to believe that Mop was in direct spiritual communication with unseen Isaacs, or in a state of clairvoyance, or under the influence of the odic fluid. But did we ever yet find in human reason a question with only one side to it? Is not truth a polygon? Have not sages arisen in our day to deny even the principle of gravity, for which we had been so long contentedly taking the word of the great Sir Isaac? It is that blessed spirit of controversy which keeps the world going; and it is that which, perhaps, explains why Mr. Waife, when his memory was fairly put to it, could remember, out of the history of the myriads who have occupied our planet from the date of Adam to that in which I now write, so very few men whom the world will agree to call wise, and out of that very few so scant a percentage with names sufficiently known to make them more popularly significant of pre-eminent sagacity than if they had been called — Mops.

practical experience of life, in a man now so hard put to it for a livelihood. There are persons, however, who might have a good stock of talent, if they did not turn it all into small change. And you, reader, know as well as I do, that when a sovereign or a shilling is once broken into, the change scatters and dispends itself in a way quite unaccountable. Still coppers are useful in household bills; and when Waife was really at a pinch, somehow or other, by hook or by crook, he scraped together intellectual halfpence enough to pay his way.

Mrs. Saunders grew quite fond of her lodgers. Waife she regarded as a prodigy of genius; Sophy was the prettiest and best of children; Sir Isaac, she took for granted, was worthy of his owners. But the Comedian did not confide to her his dog's learning, nor the use to which he designed to put it. And in still greater precaution, when he took his leave, he extracted from Mrs. Saunders a solemn promise that she would set no one on his track, in case of impertinent inquiries.

"You see before you," said he, "a man who has enemies—such as rats are to your chickens: chickens despise rats when raised, as yours are now, above the reach of claws and teeth. Some day or other I may so raise a coop for that little one—I am too old for coops. Meanwhile, if a rat comes sneaking here after us, send it off the wrong way, with a flea in its ear."

Mrs. Saunders promised, between tears and laughter; blessed Waife, kissed Sophy, patted Sir Isaac, and stood long at her threshold watching the three, as the early sun lit their forms receding in the green narrow lane—dewdrops sparkling on the hedgerows, and the skylark springing upward from the young corn.

Then she slowly turned in-doors, and her home seemed very solitary. We can accustom ourselves to loneliness, but we should beware of infringing the custom. Once admit two or three faces seated at your hearthside, or gazing out from your windows on the laughing sun, and when they are gone, they carry off the glow from your grate and the sunbeam from your panes. Poor Mrs. Saunders! in vain she sought to rouse herself, to put the rooms to rights, to attend to the chickens, to distract her thoughts. The one-eyed cripple, the little girl, the shaggy-faced dog, still haunted her; and when at noon she dined all alone off the remnants of the last night's social supper, the very click of the renovated clock seemed to say, "Gone, gone;" and muttering, "Ah! gone," she reclined back on her chair, and indulged herself in a good womanlike cry. From this luxury she was startled by a knock at the door. "Could they have come back?" No; the door opened, and a genteel young man, in a black coat and white neckcloth, stepped in.

"I beg your pardon, ma'am—your name 's Saunders—sell poultry?"

"At your service, sir. Spring chickens?" Poor people, whatever their grief, must sell their chickens, if they have any to sell.

"Thank you, ma'am; not at this moment. The fact is, that I call to make some inquiries. Have not you lodgers here?"

Lodgers! at that word the expanding soul of Mrs. Saunders reclosed hermetically; the last warning of Waife revibrated in her ears: this white-neckclothed gentleman, was he not a rat?

"No, sir, I han't no lodgers."

"But you have had some lately, eh? a crippled elderly man and a little girl."

CHAPTER VII.

The cloud has its silver lining.

Thus turning his back on the good fortune which he had so carefully cautioned Mrs. Saunders against favouring on his behalf, the vagrant was now on his way to the ancient municipal town of Gatesboro', which, being the nearest place of fitting opulence and population, Mr. Waife had resolved to honour with the *début* of Sir Isaac as soon as he had appropriated to himself the services of that promising quadruped. He had consulted a map of the county before quitting Mr. Merle's roof, and ascertained that he could reach Gatesboro' by a short cut for foot-travellers along fields and lanes. He was always glad to avoid the high-road: doubtless for such avoidance he had good reasons. But prudential reasons were in this instance supported by vagrant inclinations. High-roads are for the prosperous. By-paths and ill-luck go together. But by-paths have their charm, and ill-luck its pleasant moments.

They passed, then, from the high-road into a long succession of green pastures, through which a straight public path conducted them into one of those charming lanes never seen out of this bowery England—a lane deep sunk amidst high banks, with overhanging oaks, and quivering ash, gnarled Wych-elm, vivid holly, and shaggy brambles, with wild convolvulus and creeping woodbine forcing sweet life through all. Sometimes the banks opened abruptly, leaving patches of greensward, and peeps through still sequestered gates, or over moss-grown pales, into the park or paddock of some rural thane.

New villas or old manor-houses on lawny uplands, knitting, as it were, together, England's feudal memories with England's freeborn hopes—the old land with its young people; for England is so old, and the English are so young! And the grey cripple and the bright-haired child often paused, and gazed upon the demesnes and homes of owners whose lots were cast in such pleasant places. But there was no grudging envy in their gaze; perhaps because their life was too remote from those grand belongings. And therefore they could enjoy and possess every banquet of the eye. For at least the beauty of what we see is ours for the moment, on the simple condition that we do not covet the thing which gives to our eyes that beauty. As the measureless sky and the unnumbered stars are equally granted to king and to beggar—and in our wildest ambition we do not sigh for a monopoly of the empyrean, or the fee-simple of the planets—so the earth too, with all its fenced gardens and embattled walls—all its landmarks of stern property and churlish ownership—is ours too by right of eye. Ours to gaze on the fair possessions with such delight as the gaze can give; grudging to the unseen owner his other, and, it may be, more troubled rights, as little as we grudge an astral proprietor his acres of light in Capricorn. Benignant is the law that saith, " *Thou shalt not covet.*"

When the sun was at the highest, our wayfarers found a shadowy nook for their rest and repast. Before

angler rose; and Waife, whose attention was attracted that way by the bark, saw him, called to Sir Isaac, and said politely, "There is no harm in my dog, sir."

The young man muttered some inaudible reply, and, lifting up his rod, as in sign of his occupation or excuse for his vicinity, came out from the intervening foliage, and stepped quietly to Waife's side. Sir Isaac followed him—sniffed again—seemed satisfied; and seated himself on his haunches, fixed his attention upon the remains of the chicken which lay defenceless on the grass. The new-comer was evidently of the rank of gentleman; his figure was slim and graceful, his face pale, meditative, refined. He would have impressed you at once with the idea of what he really was—an Oxford scholar; and you would, perhaps, have guessed him designed for the ministry of the Church, if not actually in orders.

CHAPTER VIII.

Mr. Waife excites the admiration, and benignly pities the infirmity of an Oxford scholar.

"You are sir—sir—strangers?" said the Oxonian, after a violent exertion to express himself, caused by an impediment in his speech.

WAIFE.—"Yes, sir, travellers. I trust we are not trespassing: this is not private ground, I think?"

OXONIAN.—"And if—f—f—f it were, my f—f—father would not war—n—n you off—ff—f."

"Is it your father's ground then? Sir, I beg you a thousand pardons."

The apology was made in the Comedian's grandest style—it imposed greatly on the young scholar. Waife might have been a duke in disguise; but I will do the angler the justice to say that such discovery of rank would have impressed him little more in the vagrant's favour. It had been that impromptu "grace"—that thanksgiving which the scholar felt was for something more than the carnal food—which had first commanded his respect and wakened his interest. Then that innocent careless talk, part uttered to dog and child—part soliloquised—part thrown out to the ears of the lively teeming Nature, had touched a somewhat kindred chord in the angler's soul, for he was somewhat of a poet and much of a soliloquist, and could confer with Nature, nor feel that impediment in speech which obstructed his intercourse with men. Having thus far indicated that oral defect in our new acquaintance, the reader will cheerfully excuse me for not enforcing it overmuch. Let it be among the things *subaudita*, as the sense of it gave to a gifted and aspiring nature, thwarted in the sublime career of Preacher, an exquisite mournful pain. And I no more like to raise a laugh at his infirmity behind his back, than I should before his pale, powerful, melancholy face—therefore I suppress the infirmity, in giving the reply.

OXONIAN.—"On the other side the lane where the garden slopes downward is my father's house.

CHAPTER IX.

The Nomad, entering into civilised life, adopts its arts, shaves his poodle, and puts on a black coat. Hints at the process by which a Cast-off exalts himself into a Take-in.

AT twilight they stopped at a quiet inn within eight miles of Gatesboro'. Sophy, much tired, was glad to creep to bed. Waife sate up long after her; and, in preparation for the eventful morrow, washed and shaved Sir Isaac. You would not have known the dog again; he was dazzling. Not Ulysses, rejuvinated by Pallas Athenè, could have been more changed for the better. His flanks revealed a skin most daintily mottled; his tail became leonine, with an imperial tuft; his mane fell in long curls like the beard of a Ninevite king; his boots were those of a courtier in the reign of Charles II.; his eyes looked forth in dark splendour from locks white as the driven snow. This feat performed, Waife slept the peace of the righteous, and Sir Isaac, stretched on the floor beside the bed, licked his mottled flanks and shivered—"*Il faut souffrir pour être beau.*" Much marvelling, Sophy the next morning beheld the dog; but before she was up, Waife had paid the bill and was waiting for her on the road, impatient to start. He did not heed her exclamations, half compassionate, half admiring; he was absorbed in thought. Thus they proceeded slowly on till within two miles of the town, and then Waife turned aside, entered a wood, and there, with the aid of Sophy, put the dog upon a deliberate rehearsal of the anticipated drama. The dog was not in good spirits, but he went through his part with mechanical accuracy, though slight enthusiasm.

"He is to be relied upon, in spite of his French origin," said Waife. "All national prejudice fades before the sense of a common interest. And we shall always find more genuine solidity of character in a French poodle than in an English mastiff, whenever a poodle is of use to us, and the mastiff is not. But oh, waste of care ! oh, sacrifice of time to empty names ! oh, emblem of fashionable education ! It never struck me before—does it not, child though thou art, strike thee now—by the necessities of our drama, this animal must be a French dog ?"

"Well, grandfather ?"

"And we have given him an English name ! Precious result of our own scholastic training; taught at preparatory academies precisely that which avails us nought when we are to face the world ! What is to be done ? Unlearn him his own cognomen—teach him another name; too late, too late. We cannot afford the delay."

"I don't see why he should be called any name at all. He observes your signs just as well without."

"If I had but discovered that at the beginning. Pity ! Such a fine name, too. Sir Isaac ! *Vanitas vanitatum !* What desire chiefly kindles the ambitious ? To create a name—perhaps bequeath a title—exalt into Sir Isaacs a progeny of Mops ! And after all, it is possible

Achilles is well off during his whole life, which, though distinguished, is short. On the other hand, Ulysses, who is sorely put to it, kept out of his property in Ithaca, and, in short, living on his wits, is not the less befriended by the immaculate Pallas, because his wisdom savours somewhat of stage trick and sharp practice. And as to convenient aliases and white fibs, where would have been the use of his wits, if Ulysses had disdained such arts, and been magnanimously munched up by Polyphemus? Having thus touched on the epic side of Mr. Waife's character with the clemency due to human nature, but with the caution required by the interests of society, permit him to resume a "duplex course," sanctioned by ancient precedent, but not commended to modern imitation.

Just as our travellers neared the town, the screech of a railway whistle resounded towards the right—a long train rushed from the jaws of a tunnel, and shot into the neighbouring station.

"How lucky!" exclaimed Waife; "make haste, my dear!" Was he going to take the train? Pshaw! he was at his journey's end. He was going to mix with the throng that would soon stream through those white gates into the town; he was going to purloin the respectable appearance of a passenger by the train. And so well did he act the part of a bewildered stranger just vomited forth into unfamiliar places by one of those panting steam monsters, so artfully amidst the busy competition of nudging elbows, over-bearing shoulders, and the *impedimenta* of carpet-bags, portmanteaus, babies in arms, and shin-assailing trucks, did he look round, consequentially, on the *qui vive*, turning his one eye, now on Sophy, now on Sir Isaac, and griping his bundle to his breast as if he suspected all his neighbours to be Thugs, condottieri, and swell-mob, that in an instant fly-men, omnibus-drivers, cads, and porters marked him for their own. "Gatesboro' Arms," "Spread Eagle," "Royal Hotel," "Saracen's Head—very comfortable, centre of High Street, opposite the Town Hall,"—were, shouted, bawled, whispered, or whined into his ear. "Is there an honest porter?" asked the Comedian piteously. An Irishman presented himself. "And is it meself can serve your honour?"—"Take this bundle, and walk on before me to the High Street."—"Could not I take the bundle, grandfather? The man will charge so much," said the prudent Sophy. "Hush! you indeed!" said the *Père Noble*, as if addressing an exiled *Altesse royale*—"you take a bundle—Miss—Chapman!"

They soon gained the High Street. Waife examined the fronts of the various inns which they passed by, with an eye accustomed to decipher the physiognomy of hostelries. "The Saracen's Head" pleased him, though its imposing size daunted Sophy. He arrested the steps of the porter; "Follow me close," and stepped across the open threshold into the bar. The landlady herself was there, portly and imposing, with an auburn *toupet*, a silk gown, a cameo brooch, and an ample bosom.

"You have a private sitting-room, ma'am?" said the Comedian, lifting his hat. There are so many ways of lifting a hat—for instance, the way for which Louis XIV. was so renowned. But the Comedian's way on the present occasion rather resembled that of the late Duke of D ° ° °—not quite royal, but as near to royalty as becomes a subject. He added, recovering his head—"And on the first floor?" The landlady did not curtsy, but she bowed,

please — at seven o'clock. Stay, I beg your pardon for detaining you; but where does the Mayor live?"

"His private residence is a mile out of the town; but his counting-house is just above the Town Hall — to the right, sir!"

"Name?"

"Mr. Hartopp!"

"Hartopp! Ah! to be sure! Hartopp. His political opinions, I think, are" (ventures at a guess) "enlightened?"

LANDLADY. — "Very much so, sir. Mr. Hartopp is highly respected."

WAIFE. — "The chief municipal officer of a town so thriving — fine shops and much plate glass — must march with the times. I think I have heard that Mr. Hartopp promotes the spread of intelligence and the propagation of knowledge."

LANDLADY (rather puzzled). — "I dare say, sir. The Mayor takes great interest in the Gatesboro' Athenæum and Literary Institute."

WAIFE. — "Exactly what I should have presumed from his character and station. I will detain you no longer, ma'am" (Ducal bow). The landlady descended the stairs. Was her guest a candidate for the representation of the town at the next election? March with the times! — spread of intelligence! All candidates she ever knew had that way of expressing themselves — "March" and "Spread." Not an address had parliamentary aspirant put forth to the freemen and electors of Gatesboro', but what

"March" had been introduced by the candidate, and "Spread" been suggested by the committee. Still she thought that her guest, upon the whole, looked and bowed more like a member of the Upper House. Perhaps one of the amiable though occasionally prosy peers who devote the teeth of wisdom to the cracking of those very hard nuts — "How to educate the masses," "What to do with our criminals," and suchlike problems, upon which already have been broken so many jawbones tough as that with which Samson slew the Philistines.

"Oh, grandfather," sighed Sophy, "what are you about? We shall be ruined — you, too, who are so careful not to get into debt. And what have we left to pay the people here?"

"Sir Isaac! and THIS!" returned the Comedian, touching his forehead. "Do not alarm yourself — stay here and repose — and don't let Sir Isaac out of the room on any account!"

He took off his hat, brushed the nap carefully with his sleeve, replaced it on his head — not jauntily aside — not like a *jeune premier*, but with equilateral brims, and in composed fashion, like a *père noble* — then, making a sign to Sir Isaac to rest quiet, he passed to the door; there he halted, and turning towards Sophy, and meeting her wistful eyes, his own eye moistened. "Ah!" he murmured, "heaven grant I may succeed now, for if I do, then you shall indeed be a little lady!"

He was gone.

to take in this request. Mr. C. may add that of late he has earnestly directed his attention to the best means of extracting new uses from those noble but undeveloped institutions. — *Saracen's Head, &c.*"

This epistle, duly sealed and addressed, Waife delivered to the care of Mike Callaghan — and simultaneously he astounded that functionary with no less a gratuity than half a crown. Cutting short the fervent blessings which this generous donation naturally called forth, the Comedian said, with his happiest combination of suavity and loftiness, "And should the Mayor ask you what sort of person I am—for I have not the honour to be known to him, and there are so many adventurers about, that he might reasonably expect me to be one—perhaps you can say that I don't look like a person he need be afraid to admit. You know a gentleman by sight! Bring back an answer as soon as may be; perhaps I shan't stay long in the town. You will find me in the High Street, looking at the shops."

The porter took to his legs—impatient to vent his overflowing heart upon the praises of this munificent stranger. A gentleman, indeed—Mike should think so. If Mike's good word with the Mayor was worth money, Gentleman Waife had put his half-crown out upon famous interest.

The Comedian strolled along the High Street, and stopped before a stationer's shop, at the window of which was displayed a bill, entitled—

GATESBORO' ATHENÆUM AND LITERARY INSTITUTE.

LECTURE ON CONCHOLOGY,
BY PROFESSOR LONG,
Author of "Researches into the Natural History of Limpets."

Waife entered the shop, and lifted his hat,—"Permit me, sir, to look at that hand-bill."

"Certainly, sir; but the lecture is over—you can see by the date; it came off last week. We allow the bills of previous proceedings at our Athenæum to be exposed at the window till the new bills are prepared—keeps the whole thing alive, sir."

"Conchology," said the Comedian, "is a subject which requires deep research, and on which a learned man may say much without fear of contradiction. But how far is Gatesboro' from the British Ocean?"

"I don't know exactly, sir—a long way."

"Then, as shells are not familiar to the youthful remembrances of your fellow-townsmen, possibly the lecturer may have found an audience rather select than numerous."

"It was a very attentive audience, sir—and highly respectable—Miss Grieve's young ladies (the genteelest seminary in the town) attended."

WAIFE.—"Highly creditable to the young ladies. But, pardon me, is your Athenæum a *Mechanic's* institute?"

SHOPMAN.—"It was so called at first. But, some how or other, the mere operatives fell off, and it was thought advisable to change the word 'Mechanics' into the word 'Literary.' Gatesboro' is not a manufacturing town, and the mechanics here do not realise the expectations of that taste for abstract science on which the originators of these societies founded their——"

WAIFE (insinuatingly interrupting).—"Their calculations of intellectual progress and their tables of pecuniary return. Few of these societies, I am told, are really self-supporting—I suppose Professor Long is!—and if he resides in Gates-

and honours flowed in from a brimmed horn. The surliest man in the town would have been ashamed of saying a rude thing to Jos. Hartopp. If he spoke in public, though he hummed and hawed lamentable, no one was so respectfully listened to. As for the parliamentary representation of the town, he could have returned himself for one seat and Mike Callaghan for the other, had he been so disposed. But he was too full of the milk of humanity to admit into his veins a drop from the gall of party. He suffered others to legislate for his native land, and (except on one occasion, when he had been persuaded to assist in canvassing, not indeed the electors of Gatesboro', but those of a distant town, in which he possessed some influence, on behalf of a certain eminent orator) Jos. Hartopp was only visible in politics whenever Parliament was to be petitioned in favour of some humane measure, or against a tax that would have harassed the poor.

If anything went wrong with him in his business, the whole town combined to set it right for him. Was a child born to him, Gatesboro' rejoiced as a mother. Did measles or scarlatina afflict his neighbourhood, the first anxiety of Gatesboro' was for Mr. Hartopp's nursery. No one would have said Mrs. Hartopp's nursery; and when in such a department the man's name supersedes the woman's, can more be said in proof of the tenderness he excites? In short, Jos. Hartopp was a notable instance of a truth not commonly recognised — viz., that affection is power, and that, if you do make it thoroughly and unequivocally clear that you love your neighbours, though it may not be quite so well as you love yourself,— still, cordially and disinterestedly, you will find your neighbours much better fellows than Mrs. Grundy gives them credit for,—but always provided that your talents be not such as to excite their envy, nor your opinions such as to offend their prejudices.

MR. HARTOPP.—"You take an interest, you say, in literary institutes, and have studied the subject?"

THE COMEDIAN.—"Of late, those institutes have occupied my thoughts as presenting the readiest means of collecting liberal ideas into a profitable focus."

MR. HARTOPP.—"Certainly it is a great thing to bring classes together in friendly union."

THE COMEDIAN.—"For laudable objects."

MR. HARTOPP.—"To cultivate their understandings."

THE COMEDIAN. — "To warm their hearts."

MR. HARTOPP.—"To give them useful knowledge."

THE COMEDIAN.—"And pleasurable sensations."

MR. HARTOPP.—"In a word, to instruct them."

THE COMEDIAN. — "And to amuse."

"Eh!" said the Mayor—"amuse!"

Now, every one about the person of this amiable man was on the constant guard to save him from the injurious effects of his own benevolence; and accordingly his foreman, hearing that he was closeted with a stranger, took alarm, and entered on pretence of asking instructions about an order for hides,—in reality, to glower upon the intruder, and keep his master's hands out of imprudent pockets.

Mr. Hartopp, who, though not brilliant, did not want for sense, and was a keener observer than was generally supposed, divined, the kindly intentions of his assistant. "A gentleman interested in the Gatesboro' Athenæum. My fore-

effort successful, as I feel sure it will be, I will leave it to you, gentlemen, to continue my undertaking. But I cannot stay long here. If the day after to-morrow—"

"That is our ordinary soirée night," said the Mayor. "But you said a dog, sir—dogs not admitted—Eh, Williams?"

Mr. Williams.—"A mere bye-law, which the sub-committee can suspend if necessary. But would not the introduction of a live animal be less dignified than—"

"A dead failure," put in the Comedian, gravely. The Mayor would have smiled, but he was afraid of doing so, lest it might hurt the feelings of Mr. Williams, who did not seem to take the joke.

"We are a purely intellectual body," said that latter gentleman, "and a dog—"

"A learned dog, I presume?" observed the Mayor.

Mr. Williams (nodding).—"Might form a dangerous precedent for the introduction of other quadrupeds. We might thus descend even to the level of a learned pig. We are not a menagerie, Mr.—Mr.—"

"Chapman," said the Mayor, urbanely.

"Enough," said the Comedian, rising, with his grand air: "if I considered myself at liberty, gentlemen, to say who and what I am, you would be sure that I am not trifling with what I consider a very grave and important subject. As to suggesting anything derogatory to the dignity of science, and the eminent repute of the Gatesboro' Athenæum, it would be idle to vindicate myself. These grey hairs are—"

He did not conclude that sentence, save by a slight waive of the hand. The two burgesses bowed reverentially, and the Comedian went on—

"But when you speak of precedent, Mr. Williams, allow me to refer you to precedents in point. Aristotle wrote to Alexander the Great for animals to exhibit to the Literary Institute of Athens. At the colleges in Egypt lectures were delivered on a dog called Anubis, as inferior, I boldly assert, to that dog which I have referred to, as an Egyptian College to a British Institute. The ancient Etrurians, as is shown by the erudite Schweighæuser, in that passage—you understand Greek, I presume, Mr. Williams?"

Mr. Williams could not say he did.

The Comedian.—"Then I will not quote that passage in Schweighæuser upon the Molossian dogs in general, and the dog of Alcibiades in particular. But it proves beyond a doubt, that, in every ancient literary institute, learned dogs were highly estimated; and there was even a philosophical Academy called the Cynic—that is, Doggish, or Dog-school, of which Diogenes was the most eminent professor. He, you know, went about with a lanthorn looking for an honest man, and could not find one! Why? Because the Society of Dogs had raised his standard of human honesty to an impracticable height. But I weary you; otherwise I could lecture on in this way for the hour together, if you think the Gatesboro' operatives prefer erudition to amusement."

"A great scholar," whispered Mr. Williams.—Aloud; "and I've nothing to say against your precedents, sir. I think you have made out that part of the case. But, after all, a learned dog is not so very uncommon as to be in itself the striking attraction which you appear to suppose."

"It is not the mere learning of my dog of which I boast," replied the Comedian. "Dogs may be learned, and men too; but it is the way that learning is imparted,

other; and without appearing at the time to profit much by observation, without perhaps being himself conscious that he did profit, there was something in the very *enfantillage* of his loosest prattle, by which, with a glance of the one lustrous eye, and a twist of the mobile lip, he could convey the impression of an original genius playing with this round world of ours—tossing it up, catching it again—easily as a child plays with its particoloured ball. His mere book-knowledge was not much to boast of, though early in life he must have received a fair education. He had a smattering of the ancient classics, sufficient, perhaps, to startle the unlearned. If he had not read them, he had read about them; and at various odds and ends of his life he had picked up acquaintance with the popular standard modern writers. But literature with him was the smallest stripe in the particoloured ball. Still it was astonishing how far and wide the Comedian could spread the sands of lore that the winds had drifted round the door of his playful busy intellect. Where, for instance, could he ever have studied the nature and prospects of Mechanics' Institutes? and yet how well he seemed to understand them. Here, perhaps, his experience in one kind of audience helped him to the key to all miscellaneous assemblages. In fine, the man was an Actor; and if he had thought fit to act the part of Professor Long himself, he would have done it to the life.

The two burghers had not spent so pleasant an evening for many years. As the clock struck twelve, the Mayor, whose gig had been in waiting a whole hour to take him to his villa, rose reluctantly to depart.

"And," said Williams, "the bills must be out to-morrow. What shall we advertise?"

"The simpler the better," said Waife; "only pray head the performance with the assurance that it is under the special patronage of his worship the Mayor."

The Mayor felt his breast swell as if he had received some overwhelming personal obligation.

"Suppose it run thus," continued the Comedian—

"Illustrations from Domestic Life and Natural History, with LIVE examples: PART 1ST—THE DOG!"

"It will take," said the Mayor; "dogs are such popular animals!"

"Yes," said Williams; "and though for that very reason some might think that by the 'live example of a dog' we compromised the dignity of the Institute—still the importance of Natural History—"

"And," added the Comedian, "the sanctifying influences of domestic life—"

"May," concluded Mr. Williams, "carry off whatever may seem to the higher order of minds a too familiar attraction in the—dog!"

"I do not fear the result," said Waife, "provided the audience be sufficiently numerous; for that (which is an indispensable condition to a fair experiment) I issue handbills—only where distributed by the Mayor."

"Don't be too sanguine. I distributed bills on behalf of Professor Long, and the audience was not numerous. However, I will do my best. Is there nothing more in which I can be of use to you, Mr. Chapman?"

"Yes, later." Williams took alarm, and approached the Mayor's breast-pocket protectingly. The Comedian withdrew him aside and whispered, "I intend to give the Mayor a little outline of the exhibi-

CHAPTER XII.

In which everything depends on Sir Isaac's success in discovering the Law of Attraction.

On the appointed evening, at eight o'clock, the great room of the Gatesboro' Athenæum was unusually well filled. Not only had the Mayor exerted himself to the utmost for that object, but the handbill itself promised a rare relief from the proainess of abstract enlightenment and elevated knowledge. Moreover, the stranger himself had begun to excite speculation and curiosity. He was an amateur, not a cut-and-dry professor. The Mayor and Mr. Williams had both spread the report that there was more in him than appeared on the surface; prodigiously learned, but extremely agreeable—fine manners, too!—Who could he be? Was Chapman his real name? &c. &c.

The Comedian had obtained permission to arrange the room beforehand. He had the raised portion of it for his stage, and he had been fortunate enough to find a green curtain to be drawn across it. From behind this screen he now emerged and bowed. The bow redoubled the first conventional applause. He then began a very short address — extremely well delivered, as you may suppose, but rather in the conversational than the oratorical style. He said it was his object to exhibit the intelligence of that Universal Friend of Man—the Dog, in some manner appropriate, not only to its sagacious instincts, but to its affectionate nature, and to convey thereby the moral that talents, however great, learning, however deep, were of no avail, unless rendered serviceable to Man. (Applause.) He must be pardoned then, if, in order to effect this object, he was compelled to borrow some harmless effects from the stage. In a word, his dog would represent to them the plot of a little drama. And he, though he could not say that he was altogether unaccustomed to public speaking (here a smile, modest, but august as that of some famous parliamentary orator who makes his first appearance at a vestry), still wholly new to its practice in the special part he had undertaken, would rely on their indulgence to efforts aspiring to no other merit than that of aiding the Hero of the Piece in a familiar illustration of those qualities in which Dogs might give a lesson to humanity. Again he bowed, and retired behind the curtain. A pause of three minutes; the curtain drew up. Could that be the same Mr. Chapman whom the spectators beheld before them? Could three minutes suffice to change the sleek, respectable, prosperous-looking gentleman who had just addressed them, into that image of threadbare poverty and hunger-pinched dejection? Little aid from theatrical costume: the clothes seemed the same, only to have grown wondrous aged and rusty. The face, the figure, the man —*these* had undergone a transmutation beyond the art of the mere stage wardrobe, be it ever so amply stored, to effect. But for the patch over the eye, you could not have recognised Mr. Chapman. There was, indeed, about him, still, an air of dignity; but it was the dignity of

proaches the table, raises itself on its hind-legs, surveys the table dolefully, shakes its head, whines, comes to its master, pulls him by the skirt, looks into his face inquisitively.

What does all this mean? It soon comes out, and very naturally. The dog belonged to an old fellow-soldier, who had gone to the Isle of France to claim his share in the inheritance of a brother who had settled and died there, and who, meanwhile, had confided it to the care of our veteran, who was then in comparatively easy circumstances, since ruined by the failure and fraud of a banker to whom he had intrusted his all; and his small pension, including the yearly sum to which his cross entitled him, had been forestalled and mortgaged to pay the petty debts which, relying on his dividend from the banker, he had innocently incurred. The dog's owner had been gone for months; his return might be daily expected. Meanwhile the dog was at the hearth, but the wolf at the door. Now, this sagacious animal had been taught to perform the duties of messenger and majordomo. At stated intervals he applied to his master for sous, and brought back the supplies which the sous purchased. He now, as usual, came to the table for the accustomed coin —the last sou was gone—the dog's occupation was at an end. But could not the dog be sold? Impossible— it was the property of another—a sacred deposit; one would be as bad as the fraudulent banker if one could apply to one's own necessities the property one holds in trust. These little biographical particulars came out in that sort of bitter and pathetic humour which a study of Shakespeare, or the experience of actual life, had taught the Comedian to be a natural relief to an intense sorrow. The dog meanwhile aided the narrative by his by-play. Still intent upon the sous, he thrust his nose into his master's pockets—he appealed touchingly to the child, and finally put back his head and vented his emotion in a lugubrious and elegiacal howl. Suddenly there is heard without the sound of a showman's tin trumpet! Whether the actor had got some obliging person to perform on that instrument, or whether, as more likely, it was but a trick of ventriloquism, we leave to conjecture. At that note, an idea seemed to seize the dog. He ran first to his master, who was on the threshold about to depart; pulled him back into the centre of the room; next he ran to the child, dragging her towards the same spot, though with great tenderness, and then, uttering a joyous bark, he raised himself on his hind-legs, and, with incomparable solemnity, performed a minuet step! The child catches the idea from the dog. "Was he not more worth seeing than the puppet-show in the streets? might not people give money to see him, and the old soldier still keep his cross. To-day there is a public fête in the gardens yonder; that showman must be going thither; why not go too?" What! he the old soldier —he stoop to show off a dog! he!" he! The dog looked at him deprecatingly, and stretched himself on the floor—lifeless.

Yes, that is the alternative—shall his child die too, and he be too proud to save her? Ah! and if the cross can be saved also! But pshaw! what did the dog know that people would care to see? Oh, much, much. When the child was alone and sad, it would come and play with her. See those old dominoes! She ranged them on the floor, and the dog leapt up and came to prove his skill. Artfully, then, the Comedian had planned that the dog should make some sad mistakes, al-

cheers and laughter. And the Comedian's face, unmoved by such demonstrations—so shy and sad—insinuated its pathos underneath cheer and laugh. You now learned through the child that a dance, on which the company had been supposed to be gazing was concluded, and that they would not be displeased by an interval of some other diversion. Now was the time! The dog, as if to convey a sense of the prevalent ennui, yawned audibly, patted the child on the shoulder, and looked up in her face. "A game of dominoes," whispered the little girl. The dog gleefully grinned assent. Timidly she stole forth the old dominoes, and ranged them on the ground; on which she slipped from her chair; the dog slipped from his; they began to play. The experiment was launched; the soldier saw that the curiosity of the company was excited—that the show would commence—the rows follow; and as if he at least would not openly shame his service and his Emperor, he turned aside, slid his hand to his breast, tore away his cross, and hid it. Scarce a murmured word accompanied the action —the acting mid all; and a noble thrill ran through the audience. Oh, sublime art of the mime!

The Mayor sate very near where the child and dog were at play. The Comedian had (as he before implied he would do) discreetly prepared that gentleman for direct and personal appeal. The little girl turned her blue eyes innocently towards Mr. Hartopp, and said, "The dog beats me, sir; will you try what you can do?"

A roar, and universal clapping of hands, amidst which the worthy magistrate stepped on the stage. At the command of its young mistress, the dog made the magistrate a polite bow, and straight to the game went magistrate and dog. From that time the interest became, as it were, personal to all present. "Will you come, sir?" said the child to a young gentleman, who was straining his neck to see how the dominoes were played; "and observe that it is all fair. You too, sir?" to Mr. Williams. The Comedian stood beside the dog, whose movements he directed with undetected skill, while appearing only to fix his eyes on the ground in conscious abasement. Those on the rows from behind now pressed forward; those in advance either came on the stage, or stood up intently contemplating. The Mayor was defeated, the crowd became too thick, and the caresses bestowed on the dog seemed to fatigue him. He rose and retreated to a corner haughtily. "Manners, sir," said the soldier; "It is not for the like of us to be proud; excuse him, ladies and gentlemen."—"He only wishes to please all," said the child deprecatingly. "Say how many would you have round us at a time, so that the rest may not be prevented seeing you?" She spread the multiplication figures before the dog; the dog put his paw on 10. "Astonishing!" said the Mayor.

"Will you choose them yourself, sir?"

The dog nodded, walked leisurely round, keeping one eye towards the one eye of his master, and selected ten persons, amongst whom were the Mayor, Mr. Williams, and three pretty young ladies, who had been induced to ascend the stage. The others were chosen no less judiciously.

The dog was then led artfully on from one accomplishment to another, much within the ordinary range which bounds the instruction of learned animals. He was asked to say how many ladies were on the stage; he spelt three. What were

who needs your aid is not one of that soldiery which devastated Europe. But he has fought in battles as severe, and been left by fortune to as stern a desolation. True, he is not a Frenchman: he is one of a land you will not love less than France,—it is your own. He, too, has a child whom he would save from famine. He, too, has nothing left to sell or to pawn for bread—except—oh, not this gilded badge, see, this is only foil and cardboard—except, I say, the thing itself, of which you respect even so poor a symbol—nothing left to sell or to pawn but Honour! For these I have pleaded this night as a showman; for those, less haughty than the Frenchman, I stretch my hands towards you without shame; for these I am a beggar."

He was silent. The dog quietly took up the hat and approached the Mayor again. The Mayor extracted the half-crown he had previously deposited, and dropped into the hat two golden sovereigns. Who does not guess the rest? All crowded forward—youth and age, man and woman. And most ardent of all were those whose life stands most close to vicissitude—most exposed to beggary—most sorely tried in the alternative between bread and honour. Not an Operative there but spared his mite.

CHAPTER XIII.

Omne ignotum pro Magnifico.—Humour, knowing nothing of his antecedents, exalts Gentleman Waife into Don Magnifico.

THE Comedian and his two coadjutors were followed to the Saracen's Head Inn by a large crowd, but at respectful distance. Though I know few things less pleasing than to have been decoyed and entrapped into an unexpected demand upon one's purse—when one only counted, too, upon an agreeable evening—and hold, therefore, in just abhorrence the circulating plate which sometimes follows a public oration, homily, or other eloquent appeal to British liberality; yet, I will venture to say, there was not a creature whom the Comedian had surprised into impulsive beneficence, who regretted his action, grudged its cost, or thought he had paid too dear for his entertainment. All had gone through a series of such pleasurable emotions, that all had, as it were, wished a vent for their gratitude—and when the vent was found, it became an additional pleasure. But, strange to say, no one could satisfactorily explain to himself these two questions—for what, and to whom had he given his money? It was not a general conjecture that the exhibitor wanted the money for his own uses. No, despite the evidence in favour of that idea, a person so respectable, so dignified—addressing them, too, with that noble assurance to which a man who begs for himself is not morally entitled—a person thus characterised must be some high-hearted philanthropist who condescended to display his powers at an institute purely intellectual, perhaps on behalf of an eminent but decayed author, whose name, from the respect due to letters, was deli-

but his spirits were too much exhilarated to allow him to notice the unusual flush upon her cheek, except with admiration of the increased beauty which the heightened colour gave to her soft features.

"Well," said he, "you *are* a pretty child!—a very pretty child—and you act wonderfully. You would make a fortune on the stage; but—"

SOPHY (eagerly).—"But—no, no, never!—not the stage!"

WAIFE.—"I don't wish you to go on the stage, as you know. A private exhibition—like the one to-night, for instance—has" (thrusting his hand into his pocket) "much to recommend it."

SOPHY (with a sigh).—"Thank Heaven! that is over now—and you'll not be in want of money for a long, long time! Dear Sir Isaac!"

She began caressing Sir Isaac, who received her attentions with solemn pleasure. They were now in Sophy's room; and Waife, after again pressing the child in vain to take some refreshment, bestowed on her his kiss and blessing, and whistled *Malbrook s'en va-t-en guerre* to Sir Isaac, who, considering that melody an invitation to supper, licked his lips, and stalked forth, rejoicing, but decorous.

Left alone, the child breathed long and hard, pressing her hands to her bosom, and sunk wearily on the foot of the bed. There were no shutters to the window, and the moonlight came in gently, stealing across that part of the wall and floor which the ray of the candle left in shade. The girl raised her eyes slowly towards the window—towards the glimpse of the blue sky, and the slanting lustre of the moon. There is a certain epoch in our childhood, when what is called the romance of sentiment first makes itself vaguely felt. And ever with the dawn of that sentiment, the moon and the stars take a strange and haunting fascination. Few persons in middle life—even though they be genuine poets—feel the peculiar spell in the severe stillness and mournful splendour of starry skies which impresses most of us, even though no poets at all, in that mystic age when Childhood nearly touches upon Youth, and turns an unquiet heart to those marvellous riddles within us and without, which we cease to conjecture when experience has taught us that they have no solution upon this side the grave. Lured by the light, the child rose softly, approached the window, and, resting her upturned face upon both hands, gazed long into the heavens, communing evidently with herself, for her lips moved and murmured indistinctly. Slowly she retired from the casement, and again seated herself at the foot of the bed, disconsolate. And then her thoughts ran somewhat thus, though she might not have shaped them exactly in the same words: "No! I cannot understand it. Why was I contented and happy before I knew *him*? Why did I see no harm, no shame in this way of life—not even on that stage with those people—until *he* said, 'It was what he wished I had never stooped to.' And grandfather says our paths are so different, they cannot cross each other again. There is a path of life, then, which I can never enter—there is a path on which I must always, always walk, always, always, always that path—no escape! Never to come into that other one where there is no disguise, no hiding, no false names—never, never!"—she started impatiently, and with a wild look—"It is killing me!"

Then, terrified by her own impetuosity, she threw herself on the bed, weeping low. Her heart had now gone back to her grandfather; it was smiting her for ingratitude to

ingly offended, retreated under the sofa, whence he peered forth through his deciduous ringlets, with brows knit in grave rebuke. Nor was it without deliberate caution — a whisker first, and then a paw — that he emerged from his retreat, when a plate, heaped with the remains of the feast, was placed upon the hearth-rug.

The supper over, and the attendant gone, the negus still left, Waife lighted his pipe, and, gazing on Sir Isaac, thus addressed that canine philosopher: "Illustrious member of the Quadrupedal Society of Friends to Man, and, as possessing those abilities for practical life which but few friends to man ever display in his service, promoted to high rank—Commissary-General of the Victualling Department, and Chancellor of the Exchequer—I have the honour to inform you that a vote of thanks in your favour has been proposed in this house, and carried unanimously." Sir Isaac, looking shy, gave another lick to the plate, and wagged his tail. "It is true that thou wert once (shall I say it?) in fault at 'Beauty and Worth,'—thy memory deserted thee; thy peroration was on the verge of a breakdown; but 'Nemo mortalium omnibus horis sapit,' as the Latin grammar philosophically expresseth it. Mortals the wisest, not only on two legs, but even upon four, occasionally stumble. The greatest general, statesman, sage, is not he who commits no blunder, but he who best repairs a blunder, and converts it to success. This was thy merit and distinction! It hath never been mine! I recognise thy superior genius. I place in thee unqualified confidence; and consigning thee to the arms of Morpheus, since I see that panegyric acts on thy nervous system as a salubrious soporific, I now move that this House do resolve itself into a Committee of Ways and Means for the Consideration of the Budget!"

Therewith, while Sir Isaac fell into a profound sleep, the Comedian deliberately emptied his pockets on the table; and, arranging gold and silver before him, thrice carefully counted the total, and then divided it into sundry small heaps.

"That's for the bill," quoth he—"Civil List !—a large item. That's for Sophy, the darling! She shall have a teacher, and learn Music—Education Grant — Current expenses for the next fortnight;—Miscellaneous Estimates; tobacco—we'll call that Secret-Service Money. Ah, scamp-vagrant, is not Heaven kind to thee at last! A few more such nights, and who knows but thine old age may have other roof than the workhouse? And Sophy? —Ah, what of her! Merciful Providence, spare my life till she has outgrown its uses!" A tear came to his eye; he brushed it away quickly, and recounting his money, hummed a joyous tune.

The door opened; Waife looked up in surprise, sweeping his hand over the coins, and restoring them to his pocket.

The Mayor entered.

As Mr. Hartopp walked slowly up the room, his eye fixed Waife's; and that eye was so searching, though so mild, that the Comedian felt himself change colour. His gay spirits fell—falling lower and lower, the nearer the Mayor's step came to him; and when Hartopp, without speaking, took his hand—not in compliment—not in congratulation, but pressed it as if in deep compassion, still looking him full in the face, with those pitying, penetrating eyes, the Actor experienced a sort of shock as if he were read through, despite all his histrionic disguises—read through to his heart's core; and, as

have amply repaid us. We are public servants; according as we act in public—hiss us or applaud. Are we to submit to an inquisition into our private character? Are you to ask how many mutton bones has that dog stolen! how many cats has he worried! or how many shirts has the showman in his wallet! how many debts has he left behind him! what is his rent-roll on earth, and his account with heaven!—go and put those questions to ministers, philosophers, generals, poets. When they have acknowledged your right to put them, come to me and the other dog!"

MR. HARTOPP (rising and drawing on his gloves).—"I beg your pardon! I have done, sir. And yet I conceived an interest in you. It is because I have no talents myself that I admire those who have. I felt a mournful anxiety, too, for your poor little girl—so young, so engaging. And is it necessary that you should bring up that child in a course of life certainly equivocal, and to females dangerous?"

The Comedian lifted his eyes suddenly, and stared hard at the face of his visitor, and in that face there was so much of benevolent humanity —so much sweetness contending with authoritative rebuke—that the vagabond's hardihood gave way! he struck his breast, and groaned aloud.

MR. HARTOPP (pressing on the advantage he had gained).—"And have you no alarm for her health? Do you not see how delicate she is? Do you not see that her very talent comes from her susceptibility to emotions, which must wear her away?"

WAIFE.—"No, no! stop, stop, stop! you terrify me, you break my heart. Man, man! it is all for her that I toil, and show, and beg—if you call it begging. Do you think I care what becomes of this battered bulk? Not a straw. What am I to do? What! what! You tell me to confide in you—wherefore? How can you help me? Who can help me? Would you give me employment? What am I fit for? Nothing! You could find work and bread for an Irish labourer, nor ask who or what he was; but to a man who strays towards you, seemingly from that sphere in which, if Poverty enters, she drops a curtsy, and is called 'genteel,' you cry, 'Hold, produce your passport; where are your credentials — references?' I have none. I have slipped out of the world I once moved in. I can no more appeal to those I knew in it than if I had transmigrated from one of yon stars, and said, 'See there what I was once!' Oh, but you do not think she looks ill!—do you? do you? Wretch that I am! And I thought to save her!"

The old man trembled from head to foot, and his cheek was as pale as ashes.

Again the good magistrate took his hand, but this time the clasp was encouraging. "Cheer up; where there is a will there is a way; you justify the opinion I formed in your favour, despite all circumstances to the contrary. When I asked you to confide in me, it was not from curiosity, but because I would serve you, if I can. Reflect on what I have said. True, you can know but little of me. Learn what is said of me by my neighbours before you trust me further. For the rest, to-morrow you will have many proposals to renew your performance. Excuse me if I do not actively encourage it. I will not, at least, interfere to your detriment; but—"

"But," exclaimed Waife, not much heeding this address—"but you think she looks ill? you think this is injuring her? you think I am

CHAPTER XVI.

In every civilised society there is found a race of men who retain the instincts of the aboriginal cannibal, and live upon their fellow-men as a natural food. These interesting but formidable bipeds, having caught their victim, invariably select one part of his body on which to fasten their relentless grinders. The part thus selected is peculiarly susceptible, Providence having made it alive to the least nibble; it is situated just above the hip-joint, it is protected by a tegument of exquisite fibre, vulgarly called "THE SENSIBLE POCKET." The thoroughbred Anthropophagite usually begins with his own relations and friends; and so long as he confines his voracity to the domestic circle, the Laws interfere little, if at all, with his venerable propensities. But when he has exhausted all that allows itself to be edible in the bosom of private life, the Man-eater falls loose on Society, and takes to prowling—thro' "Suave qui peut!" the Laws rouse themselves, put on their spectacles, call for their wigs and gowns, and the Anthropophagite turned prowler is not always sure of his dinner. It is when he has arrived at this stage of development that the man-eater becomes of importance, enters into the domain of History, and occupies the thoughts of Moralists."

ON the same morning in which Waife thus went forth from the "Saracen's Head" in quest of the doctor, but at a later hour, a man, who, to judge by the elaborate smartness of his attire, and the jaunty assurance of his saunter, must have wandered from the gay purlieus of Regent Street, threaded his way along the silent and desolate thoroughfares that intersect the remotest districts of Bloomsbury. He stopped at the turn into a small street still more sequestered than those which led to it, and looked up to the angle on the wall whereon the name of the street should have been inscribed. But the wall had been lately whitewashed, and the whitewash had obliterated the expected epigraph. The man muttered an impatient execration; and turning round as if to seek a passenger of whom to make inquiry, beheld on the opposite side of the way another man apparently engaged in the same research. Involuntarily each crossed over the road towards the other.

"Pray, sir," quoth the second wayfarer in that desert, "can you tell me if this is a street that is called a Place—Podden Place, Upper?"

"Sir," returned the sprucer wayfarer, "it is the question I would have asked of you."

"Strange!"

"Very strange indeed that more than one person can, in this busy age, employ himself in discovering a Podden Place! Not a soul to enquire of—not a shop that I see—not an orange-stall!"

"Ha!" cried the other, in a hoarse sepulchral voice—"Ha! there is a pot-boy! Boy—boy—boy! I say; Hold, there! hold! Is this Podden Place—Upper?"

"Yes, it be," answered the pot-boy, with a sleepy air, caught in that sleepy atmosphere; and chiming his pewter against an area rail with a dull clang, he chanted forth "Pots oho!" with a note as dirge-like as that which in the City of the Plague chanted "Out with the dead!"

Meanwhile the two wayfarers exchanged bows and parted — the sprucer wayfarer, whether from the indulgence of a reflective mood, or from an habitual indifference to

"Ha! then I yield you the precedence; I yield it, sir, but conditionally. You will not be long?"

"Not a moment longer than I can help; the land will be clear for you in an hour or less."

"Or less, so please you, let it be or less. Servant, sir."

"Sir, yours — Come, my Hebe; truck the dancers, that is, go up the stairs, and let me renew the dreams of youth in the eyes of Bella!"

The old woman, meanwhile, had been turning over the card in her withered palm, looking from the card to the visitor's face, and then to the card again, and mumbling to herself. At length she spoke:

"You, Mr. Losely — you! — Jasper Losely! how you be changed! what ha' ye done to yourself? where's your comeliness? where's the look that stole ladies' hearts? — you, Jasper Losely! you are his goblin!"

"Hold your peace, old hussey!" said the visitor, evidently annoyed at remarks so disparaging. "I am Jasper Losely, more bronzed of cheek, more iron of hand." He raised his switch with a threatening gesture, that might be in play, for the lips wore smiles, or might be in earnest, for the brows were bent; and pushing into the passage, and shutting the door, said — "Is your mistress up-stairs? show me to her room, or — ." The old crone gave him one angry glance, which sunk frightened beneath the cruel gleam of his eyes, and hastening up the stairs with a quicker stride than her age seemed to warrant, cried out — "Mistress, mistress! here is Mr. Losely! — Jasper Losely himself!" By the time the visitor had reached the landing-place of the first floor, a female form had emerged from a room above; — a female face peered over the banisters. Losely looked up, and started as he saw it. A haggard face — the face of one over whose life there has passed a blight. When last seen by him it had possessed beauty, though of a masculine rather than womanly character. Now of that beauty not a trace! the cheeks, sunk and hollow, left the nose sharp, long, beaked as a bird of prey. The hair, once glossy in its ebon hue, now grizzled, harsh, neglected, hung in tortured tangled meshes — a study for an artist who would paint a fury. But the eyes were bright — brighter than ever; bright now with a glare that lighted up the whole face bending over the man. In those burning eyes was there love? was there hate? was there welcome? was there menace? Impossible to distinguish; but at least one might perceive that there was joy.

"So," said the voice from above — "so we do meet at last, Jasper Losely; you are come!"

Drawing a loose kind of dressing-robe more closely round her, the mistress of the house now descended the stairs — rapidly, flittingly, with a step noiseless as a spectre's, and, grasping Losely firmly by the hand, led him into a chill, dank, sunless drawing-room, gazing into his face fixedly all the while.

He winced and writhed. "There, there, let us sit down, my dear Mrs. Crane."

"And once I was called Bella."

"Ages ago! *Basta!* All things have their end. Do take those eyes of yours off my face; they were always so bright! — and — really now they are perfect burning-glasses! How close it is! Peuh! I am dead tired. May I ask for a glass of water — a drop of wine in it — or — brandy will do as well?"

"Ho! you have come to brandy and morning drams — oh, Jasper?" said Mrs. Crane, with a strange dreary accent. "I too once tried if fire could burn up thought, but

A darker shade fell over Arabella Crane's face, as she said—

"The child—she is not here! I have disposed of her long ago."

"Eh!—disposed of her! what do you mean?"

"Do you ask as if you feared I had put her out of the world? No! Well, then—you come to England to see the child? You miss—you love, the child of that—of that—" She paused, checked herself, and added in an altered voice—" of that honest, high-minded gentlewoman, whose memory must be so dear to me — you love that child; very natural, Jasper."

"Love her! a child I have scarcely seen since she was born! —do talk common sense. No. But have I not told you that she ought to be money's worth to me—ay, and she shall be yet, despite that proud man's disdainful insolence."

"That proud man — what, you have ventured to address him— visit him—since your return to England?"

"Of course. That's what brought me over. I imagined the man would rejoice at what I told him—open his purse-strings — lavish blessings and bank notes. And the brute would not even believe me—all because——"

"Because you had sold the right to be believed before. I told you, when I took the child, that you would never succeed there—that I would never encourage you in the attempt. But you had sold the future as you sold your past—too cheaply, it seems, Jasper."

"Too cheaply, indeed. Who could ever have supposed that I should have been fobbed off with such a pittance?"

"Who, indeed, Jasper! You were made to spend fortunes, and call them pittances when spent, Jasper! You should have been a prince, Jasper — such princely tastes! Trinkets and dress, horses and dice, and plenty of ladies to look and die. Such princely spirit too!—bounding all return for loyal sacrifice to the honour you vouchsafed in accepting it!"

Uttering this embittered irony, which nevertheless seemed rather to please than to offend her guest, she kept moving about the room, and (whether from some drawer in the furniture, or from her own person, Losely's careless eye did not observe) she suddenly drew forth a miniature, and, placing it before him, exclaimed—" Ah, but you are altered from those days—see what you then were!"

Losely's gaze, thus abruptly invited, fixed itself on the effigies of a youth eminently handsome, and of that kind of beauty which, without being effeminate, approaches to the fineness and brilliancy of the female countenance—a beauty which renders its possessor inconveniently conspicuous, and too often, by winning that ready admiration which it costs no effort to obtain, withdraws the desire of applause from successes to be achieved by labour, and hardens egotism by the excuses it lends to self-esteem. It is true that this handsome face had not the elevation bestowed by thoughtful expression; but thoughtful expression is not the attribute a painter seeks to give to the abstract comeliness of early youth—and it is seldom to be acquired without that constitutional wear and tear which is injurious to mere physical beauty. And over the whole countenance was diffused a sunny light, the freshness of buxom health, of luxuriant vigour, so that even that arrogant vanity which an acute observer might have detected as the prevailing mental characteristic, seemed but

were never of a mercenary temper. I trust you are happy, and so forth —I wish I were; things don't prosper with me. If you could conveniently lend me a five-pound note—"

"You would borrow of me, Jasper? Ah! you come to me in your troubles. You shall have the money—five pounds—ten pounds—what you please, but you will call again for it—you need me now—you will not utterly desert me now?"

"Best of creatures!—never!" He seized her hand and kissed it. She withdrew it quickly from his clasp, and, glancing over him from head to foot, said, "But are you really in want?—you are well dressed, Jasper; that you always were."

"Not always; three days ago very much the reverse; but I have had a trifling aid, and—"

"Aid in England? from whom? where? Not from him whom, you say, you had the courage to seek?"

"From whom else? Have I no claim? A miserable alms flung to me. Curse him! I tell you that man's look and language so galled me—so galled," echoed Losely, shifting his hold from the top of his switch to the centre, and bringing the murderous weight of the lead down on the palm of his other hand, "that, if his eye had quitted mine for a moment, I think I must have brained him, and been—"

"Hanged!" said Mrs. Crane.

"Of course, hanged," returned Losely, resuming the reckless voice and manner in which there was that peculiar levity which comes from hardness of heart, as from the steel's hardness comes the blade's play. "But if a man did not sometimes forget consequences, there would be an end of the gallows. I am glad that his eye never left mine." And the leaden head of the switch fell with a dull dumb sound on the floor.

Mrs. Crane made no immediate rejoinder, but fixed on her lawless visitor a gaze in which there was no womanly fear (though Losely's aspect and gesture might have sent a thrill through the nerves of many a hardy man), but which was not without womanly compassion, her countenance gradually softening more and more, as if under the influence of recollections mournful but not hostile. At length she said in a low voice, "Poor Jasper! Is all the vain ambition that made you so false shrunk into a ferocity that finds you so powerless? Would your existence, after all, have been harder, poorer, meaner, if your faith had been kept to me?"

Evidently disliking that turn in the conversation, but checking a reply which might have been rude had no visions of five pounds—ten pounds—loomed in the distance, Mr. Losely said, "Pshaw! Bella, pshaw! I was a fool, I daresay, and a sad dog—a very sad dog; but I had always the greatest regard for you, and always shall! Hillo, what's that? A knock at the door! Oh, by the by, a queer-looking man, in a white hat, called at the same time I did, to see you on private business —gave way to me—said he should come again; may I ask who he is?"

"I cannot guess; no one ever calls here on business except the tax-gatherer."

The old woman-servant now entered. "A gentleman, ma'am—says his name is Rugge."

"Rugge—Rugge—let me think."

"I am here, Mrs. Crane," said the manager, striding in. "You don't perhaps call me to mind by name; but—oho—not gone, sir! Do I intrude prematurely?"

"No, I have done; good-day, my dear Mrs. Crane."

"Stay, Jasper. I remember you now, Mr. Rugge; take a chair."

my property, as, morally speaking, Juliet Araminta most undoubtedly is. That's why I call—leaving my company, to which I am a father, orphans for the present. But I have missed that little girl—that young lady, sir. I called her a phenomenon, ma'am—missed her much—it is natural, sir; I appeal to you. No man can be done out of a valuable property and not feel it, if he has a heart in his bosom. And if I had her back safe, I should indulge ambition. I have always had ambition. The theatre at York, sir —that is my ambition; I had it from a child, sir; dreamed of it three times, ma'am. If I had back my property in that phenomenon, I would go at the thing, slap bang, take the York, and bring out the phenomenon, with a claw!"

LOSELY (musingly).—"You say the young lady is a phenomenon, and for this phenomenon you are willing to pay something handsome —a vague expression. Put it into £. s. d."

RUGGE.—"Sir, if she can be bound to me legally for three years, I would give £100. I did offer to Waife £50—to you, sir, £100."

Losely's eyes flashed, and his hands opened restlessly. "But, confound it, where is she? have you no clue?"

RUGGE.—"No, but we can easily find one; it was not worth my while to hunt them up, before I was quite sure that, if I regained my property in that phenomenon, the law would protect it."

MRS. CRANE (moving to the door). —"Well, Jasper Losely, you will sell the young lady, I doubt not; and when you have sold her, let me know." She came back and whispered, "You will not perhaps now want money from me, but I shall see you again; for, if you would find the child, you will need my aid."

"Certainly, my dear friend, I will call again; honour bright."

Mrs. Crane here bowed to the gentlemen, and swept out of the room.

Thus left alone, Losely and Rugge looked at each other with a shy and yet cunning gaze—Rugge's hands in his trousers pockets, his head thrown back—Losely's hands involuntarily expanded, his head bewitchingly bent forward, and a little on one side.

"Sir," said Rugge at length, "what do you say to a chop and a pint of wine? Perhaps we could talk more at our ease elsewhere. I am only in town for a day—left my company thirty miles off—orphans, as I said before."

"Mr. Rugge," said Losely, "I have no desire to stay in London, or indeed in England; and the sooner we can settle this matter the better. Grant that we find the young lady, you provide for her board and lodging—teach her your honourable profession—behave, of course, kindly to her—"

"Like a father."

"And give to me the sum of £100?"

"That is, if you can legally make her over to me. But, sir, may I inquire by what authority you would act in this matter?"

"On that head it will be easy to satisfy you; meanwhile I accept your proposal of an early dinner. Let us adjourn—is it to your house?"

"I have no exact private house in London; but I know a public one—commodious."

"Be it so. After you, sir."

As they descended the stairs, the old woman-servant stood at the street door. Rugge went out first —the woman detained Losely.

"Do you find her altered?"

"Whom? Mrs. Crane?—why,

Mrs. Crane to accompany him to the village, and aid in the requisite investigations—entertaining a tacit but instinctive belief in the superiority of her acuteness. "Set a female to catch a female," quoth Mr. Rugge.

On the day and in the place thus fixed, the three hunters opened their chase. They threw off at the Cobbler's stall. They soon caught the same scent which had been followed by the lawyer's clerk. They arrived at Mrs. Saunders'—there the two men would have been at fault like their predecessor. But the female was more astute. To drop the metaphor, Mrs. Saunders could not stand the sharp cross-examination of one of her own sex. "That woman deceives us," said Mrs. Crane, on leaving the house. "They have not gone to London. What could they do there? Any man with a few stage juggling tricks can get on in country villages, but would be lost in cities. Perhaps, as it seems he has got a dog—we have found out that from Mrs. Saunders —he will make use of it for an itinerant puppet-show."

"Punch!" said Mr. Rugge— "not a doubt of it."

"In that case," observed Mrs. Crane, "they are probably not far off. Let us print handbills, offering a reward for their clue, and luring the old man himself by an assurance that the inquiry is made in order that he may learn of something to his advantage."

In the course of the evening the handbills were printed. The next day they were posted up on the walls, not only of that village, but on those of the small towns and hamlets for some miles round. The handbills ran invitingly thus: "If William Waife, who left —— on the 20th ult., will apply at the Red Lion Inn at ——, for X. X., he will learn of something greatly to his advantage. A reward of £5 will be given to any one who will furnish information where the said William Waife, and the little girl who accompanies him, may be found. The said William Waife is about sixty years of age, of middle stature, strongly built, has lost one eye, and is lame of one leg. The little girl, called Sophy, is twelve years old, but looks younger; has blue eyes and light brown hair. They had with them a white French poodle dog. This bill is printed by the friends of the missing party." The next day passed—no information; but on the day following, a young gentleman of good mien, dressed in black, rode into the town, stopped at the Red Lion Inn, and asked to see X. X. The two men were out on their researches—Mrs. Crane stayed at home to answer inquiries.

The gentleman was requested to dismount, and walk in. Mrs. Crane received him in the inn parlour, which swarmed with flies. She stood in the centre—vigilant, grim spider of the place.

"I ca-ca-call," said the gentleman, stammering fearfully, "in con-conse-quence of a b-b-bill—I—ch-ch-chanced to see in my ri-ri-ri-ride yesterday —on a wa-wa-wall:—You—you, I —sup-sup——"

"Am X. X." put in Mrs. Crane, growing impatient, "one of the friends of Mr. Waife, by whom the handbill has been circulated; it will indeed be a great relief to us to know where they are—the little girl more especially."

Mrs. Crane was respectably dressed—in silk, iron-grey; she had crisped her flaky tresses into stiff hard ringlets, that fell like long screws from under a black velvet band. Mrs. Crane never wore a cap —nor could you fancy her in a cap;

"I see, ma'am. I cannot hesitate after this. It is a good many miles off where I met the persons whom I have no doubt that you seek; and two or three days ago my father received a letter from a very worthy, excellent man, with whom he is often brought into communication upon benevolent objects — a Mr. Hartopp, the Mayor of Gatesboro', in which, among other matters, the Mayor mentioned briefly that the Literary Institute of that town had been much delighted by the performance of a very remarkable man with one eye, about whom there seemed some mystery, with a little girl and a learned dog; and I can't help thinking that the man, the girl, and the dog, must be those whom I saw, and you seek."

MRS. CRANE.—"At Gatesboro'? is that far?"

OXONIAN.—"Some way; but you can get a cross train from this village. I hope that the old man will not be separated from the little girl; they seemed very fond of each other."

MRS. CRANE.—"No doubt of it; very fond; it would be cruel to separate them. A comfortable home for both. I don't know, sir, if I dare offer to a gentleman of your evident rank the reward,—but for the poor of your parish."

OXONIAN. — "Oh, ma'am, our poor want for nothing; my father is rich. But if you would oblige me by a line after you have found these interesting persons—I am going to a distant part of the country tomorrow — to Montfort Court, in ——shire."

MRS. CRANE.—"To Lord Montfort—the head of the noble family of Vipont?"

OXONIAN.—"Yes; do you know any of the family, ma'am? If you could refer me to one of them, I should feel more satisfied as to—"

MRS. CRANE (hastily).—"Indeed, sir, every one must know that great family by name and repute. I know no more. So you are going to Lord Montfort's! The Marchioness, they say, is very beautiful?"

OXONIAN.—"And good as beautiful. I have the honour to be connected both with her and Lord Montfort; they are cousins, and my grandfather was a Vipont. I should have told you my name—Morley; George Vipont Morley."

Mrs. Crane made a profound curtsy, and, with an unmistakable smile of satisfaction, said, as if half in soliloquy—"So it is to one of that noble family—to a Vipont—that the dear child will owe her restoration to my embrace! Bless you, sir!"

"I hope I have done right," said George Vipont Morley, as he mounted his horse. "I must have done right, surely!" he said again, when he was on the high-road. "I fear I have not done right," he said a third time, as the face of Mrs. Crane began to haunt him; and when at sunset he reached his home, tired out, horse and man, with an unusually long ride, and the green water-bank on which he had overheard poor Waife's simple grace and joyous babble came in sight—"After all," he said, dolefully, "it was no business of mine. I meant well; but—" His little sister ran to the gate to greet him—"Yes! I did quite right. How should I like my sister to be roving the country, and acting at Literary Institutes with a poodle dog? Quite right; kiss me, Jane!"

of that damp theatre, sir, you might as well talk of the—"

Suddenly the door flew open, and pushing aside a clerk who designed to announce him, in burst Mr. Chapman himself.

He had evidently expected to find the Mayor alone, for at the sight of that throng he checked himself, and stood mute at the threshold. The levee for a moment was no less surprised, and no less mute. But the good folks soon recovered themselves. To many it was a pleasure to accost and congratulate the man who the night before had occasioned to them emotions so agreeable. Cordial smiles broke out — friendly hands were thrust forth. Brief but hearty compliments, mingled with entreaties to renew the performance to a larger audience, were showered round. The Comedian stood hat in hand, mechanically passing his sleeve over its nap, muttering half inaudibly, "You see before you a man"— and turning his single eye from one face to the other, as if struggling to guess what was meant, or where he was. The Mayor rose and came forward—"My dear friends," said he, mildly, "Mr. Chapman calls by appointment. Perhaps he may have something to say to me confidentially."

The three serious gentlemen, who had hitherto remained aloof, eyeing Mr. Chapman, much as three inquisitors might have eyed a Jew, shook three solemn heads, and set the example of retreat. The last to linger were the rival proprietors of the theatre and the city concert-room. Each whispered the stranger—one the left ear, one the right. Each thrust into his hand a printed paper. As the door closed on them the Comedian let fall the papers; his arm drooped to his side; his whole frame seemed to collapse. Hartopp took him by the hand, and led him gently to his own arm-chair beside the table. The Comedian dropped on the chair, still without speaking.

MR. HARTOPP.—"What is the matter? What has happened?"

WAIFE.—"She is very ill;—in a bad way; the doctor says so—Dr. Gill."

MR. HARTOPP (feelingly).—"Your little girl in a bad way! Oh, no; doctors always exaggerate in order to get more credit for the cure. Not that I would disparage Dr. Gill—fellow-townsman — first-rate man. Still 'tis the way with doctors to talk cheerfully if one is in danger, and to look solemn if there is nothing to fear."

WAIFE.—"Do you think so—you have children of your own, sir?— of her age, too?—Eh! eh!"

MR. HARTOPP.—"Yes; I know all about children—better, I think, than Mrs. H. does. What is the complaint?"

WAIFE.—"The doctor says it is low fever."

MR. HARTOPP.—"Caused by nervous excitement, perhaps."

WAIFE (looking up).—"Yes—that's what he says—nervous excitement."

MR. HARTOPP.—"Clever sensitive children, subjected precociously to emulation and emotion, are always liable to such maladies. My third girl, Anna Maria, fell into a low fever, caused by nervous excitement in trying for school prizes."

WAIFE.—"Did she die of it, sir?"

MR. HARTOPP (shuddering). — "Die — no! I removed her from school—set her to take care of the poultry—forbade all French exercises, made her take English exercise instead—and ride on a donkey. She's quite another thing now—checks as red as an apple, and as firm as a cricket-ball."

WAIFE.—"I will keep poultry; I

easy-chair. Yet, were the Mayor's sympathetic liking and respectful admiration wholly unaccountable? Runs there not between one warm human heart and another the electric chain of a secret understanding? In that maimed outcast, so stubbornly hard to himself—so tremulously sensitive for his sick child—was there not the majesty to which they who have learned that Nature has her nobles, reverently bow the head! A man, true to man's grave religion, can no more despise a life wrecked in all else, while a hallowing affection stands out sublime through the rents and chinks of fortune, than he can profane with rude mockery a temple in ruins—if still left there the altar.

CHAPTER XIX.

Very well so far as it goes.

MR. HARTOPP.—"I cannot presume to question you further, Mr. Chapman. But to one of your knowledge of the world, I need not say that your silence deprives me of the power to assist yourself. We'll talk no more of that."

WAIFE.—"Thank you gratefully, Mr. Mayor."

MR. HARTOPP.—"But for the little girl, make your mind easy—at least for the present. I will place her at my farm cottage. My bailiff's wife, a kind woman, will take care of her, while you pursue your calling elsewhere. As for this money, you will want it yourself; your poor little child shall cost you nothing. So that's settled. Let me come up and see her. I am a bit of a doctor myself. Every man blest with a large family, in whose house there is always some interesting case of small-pox, measles, hooping-cough, scarlatina, &c., has a good private practice of his own. I'm not brilliant in book-learning, Mr. Chapman. But as to children's complaints in a practical way," added Hartopp, with a glow of pride, "Mrs. H. says she'd rather trust the little ones to me than to Dr. Gill. I'll see your child, and set her up, I'll be bound. But now I think of it," continued Hartopp, softening more and more, "if exhibit you must, why not stay at Gatesboro' for a time? More may be made in this town than elsewhere."

"No, no; I could not have the heart to act here again without her. I feel at present as if I can never again act at all! Something else will turn up. Providence is so kind to me, Mr. Mayor."

Waife turned to the door—"You will come soon?" he said, anxiously.

The Mayor, who had been locking up his ledgers and papers, replied, "I will but stay to give some orders; in a quarter of an hour I shall be at your hotel."

SOPHY (passionately).—"I thought so; I thought he meant that. I tried not to believe it; go away—you? and who's to take care of you? who'll understand you? I want care! I—I! No, no, it is you—you who want care. I shall be well to-morrow—quite well, don't fear. He shall not be sent away from me; he shall not, sir. Oh, grandfather, grandfather, how could you?" She flung herself on his breast, clinging there—clinging as if infancy and age were but parts of the same whole.

"But," said the Mayor, "it is not as if you were going to school, my dear; you are going for a holiday. And your grandfather must leave you—must travel about—'tis his calling. If you fell ill and were with him, think how much you would be in his way. Do you know," he added, smiling, "I shall begin to fear that you are selfish."

"Selfish!" exclaimed Waife, angrily.

"Selfish!" echoed Sophy, with a melancholy scorn that came from a sentiment so deep that mortal eye could scarce fathom it. "Oh, no, sir! can you say it is for *his* good, not for, what he supposes, mine, that you want us to part? The pretty cottage, and all for me—and what for him?—tramp tramp along the hot dusty roads. Do you see that he is lame? Oh, sir, I know him—you don't. Selfish! he would have no merry ways that make you laugh without me; would you, Grandy, dear? Go away, you are a naughty man—go, or I shall hate you as much as that dreadful Mr. Rugge."

"Rugge—who is he?" said the Mayor, curiously, catching at any clue.

"Hush, my darling!— hush!" said Waife, fondling her on his breast. "Hush! What is to be done, sir?"

Hartopp made a sly sign to him, to say no more before Sophy, and then replied, addressing himself to her—

"What is to be done? Nothing shall be done, my dear child, that you dislike. I don't wish to part you two. Don't hate me—lie down again—that's a dear. There, I have smoothed your pillow for you; oh, here's your pretty doll again."

Sophy snatched at the doll petulantly, and made what the French call a *moue* at the good man as she suffered her grandfather to replace her on the sofa.

"She has a strong temper of her own," muttered the Mayor; "so has Anna Maria a strong temper!"

Now, if I were anyway master of my own pen, and could write as I pleased, without being hurried along helter-skelter, by the tyrannical exactions of that "young Rapid" in buskins and chiton, called "THE HISTORIC MUSE," I would break off this chapter, open my window, rest my eyes on the green lawn without, and indulge in a rhapsodical digression upon that beautifier of the moral life which is called "Good Temper." Ha—the Historic Muse is dozing. By her leave!—Softly.

as Shakespeare, to distinguish those subtle emotions which we grown folks have outlived.

"She has a strong temper," said the Mayor, when Sophy snatched the doll from his hand a second time, and pouted at him, spoiled child, looking so divinely cross, so petulantly pretty. And how on earth could the Mayor know what associations with that stupid doll made her think it profaned by the touch of a stranger? Was it to her eyes as to his—mere waxwork and frippery, or a symbol of holy remembrances, of gleams into a fairer world, of "devotion to something afar from the sphere of her sorrow?" Was not the evidence of "strong temper" the very sign of affectionate depth of heart? Poor little Sophy. Hide it again—safe out of sight—close, inscrutable, unguessed, as childhood's first treasures of sentiment ever are!

CHAPTER XXII.

The object of Civilisation being always to settle people one way or the other, the Mayor of Gatesboro' entertains a statesmanlike ambition to settle Gentleman Waife: no doubt a wise conception, and in accordance with the genius of the Nation.—Every Session of Parliament, England is employed in settling folks, whether at home or at the Antipodes, who ignorantly object to be settled in her way; in short, "I'll settle them," has become a vulgar idiom, tantamount to a threat of uttermost extermination or smash.—Therefore the Mayor of Gatesboro', harbouring that benignant idea with reference to "Gentleman Waife," all kindly readers will exclaim, "Dii Meliora! What will he do with it?"

THE doll once more safe behind the pillow, Sophy's face gradually softened; she bent forward, touched the Mayor's hand timidly, and looked at him with pleading, penitent eyes, still wet with tears—eyes that said, though the lips were silent —"I'll not hate you. I was ungrateful and peevish; may I beg pardon?"

"I forgive you with all my heart," cried the Mayor, interpreting the look aright. "And now try and compose yourself and sleep while I talk with your grandpapa below."

"I don't see how it is possible that I can leave her," said Waife, when the two men had adjourned to the sitting-room.

"I am sure," quoth the Mayor, seriously, "that it is the best thing for her; her pulse has much nervous excitability; she wants a complete rest; she ought not to move about with you on any account. But come—though I must not know, it seems, who and what you are, Mr. Chapman—I don't think you will run off with my cows, and if you like to stay at the bailiff's cottage for a week or two with your grandchild, you shall be left in peace, and asked no questions. I will own to you a weakness of mine—I value myself on being seldom or never taken in. I don't think I could forgive the man who did take me in. But taken in I certainly shall be, if, despite all your mystery, you are not as honest a fellow as ever stood upon shoe-leather! So come to the cottage."

CHAPTER XXIII.

A pretty trifle in its way, no doubt, is the love between youth and youth—Gay varieties of the bauble spread the counter of the Great Toy-Shop—But thou, courteous Dame Nature, raise thine arm to yon shelf, somewhat out of everyday reach, and bring me down that obsolete, neglected, unconsidered thing, the Love between Age and Childhood.

The next day Sophy was better—the day after, improvement was more visible—and on the third day Waife paid his bill, and conducted her to the rural abode to which, credulous at last of his promises to share it with her for a time, he enticed her fated steps. It was little more than a mile beyond the suburbs of the town, and though the walk tired her, she concealed fatigue, and would not suffer him to carry her. The cottage now smiled out before them — thatched gable roof, with fancy barge-board—half Swiss, half what is called Elizabethan—all the fences and sheds round it, as only your rich traders, condescending to turn farmers, construct and maintain—sheds and fences, trim and neat, as if models in waxwork. The breezy air came fresh from the new haystacks—from the woodbine round the porch—from the breath of the lazy kine, as they stood knee-deep in the pool, that, belted with weeds and broad-leaved water-lilies, lay calm and gleaming amidst level pastures.

Involuntarily they arrested their steps, to gaze on the cheerful landscape and inhale the balmy air. Meanwhile the Mayor came out from the cottage porch, his wife leaning on his arm, and two of his younger children bounding on before, with joyous faces, giving chase to a gaudy butterfly which they had started from the woodbine.

Mrs. Hartopp had conceived a lively curiosity to see and judge for herself of the objects of her liege lord's benevolent interest. She shared, of course, the anxiety which formed the standing excitement of all those who lived but for one godlike purpose, that of preserving Josiah Hartopp from being taken in. But whenever the Mayor specially wished to secure his wife's countenance to any pet project of his own, and convince her either that he was not taken in, or that to be discreetly taken in is in this world a very popular and sure mode of getting up, he never failed to attain his end. That man was the cunningest creature! As full of wiles and stratagems in order to get his own way—in benevolent objects — as men who set up to be clever are for selfish ones. Mrs. Hartopp was certainly a good woman, but a *made* good woman. Married to another man, I suspect that she would have been a shrew. Petruchio would never have tamed her, I'll swear. But she, poor lady, had been gradually, but completely, subdued, subjugated, absolutely cowed beneath the weight of her spouse's despotic mildness; for in Hartopp there was a weight of soft quietude, of placid oppression, wholly irresistible. It would have buried a Titaness under a Pelion of moral featherbeds. Mass upon mass of downy influence descended upon you, seemingly yielding as it fell, enveloping, overbearing, stifling you—not pre-

the back-garden, my darling," said Waife. "I see an arbour there, where I will compose myself with a pipe, a liberty I should not like to take in-doors." They stepped across the threshold, and gained the arbour, which stood at the extreme end of the small kitchen-garden, and commanded a pleasant view of pastures and cornfields, backed by the blue outline of distant hills. Afar were faintly heard the laugh of the Mayor's happy children, now and then a tinkling sheep-bell, or the tap of the wood-pecker, unrepressed by the hush of the midmost summer, which stills the more tuneful choristers amidst their coverts. Waife lighted his pipe, and smoked silently; Sophy, resting her head on his bosom, silent also. She was exquisitely sensitive to nature; the quiet beauty of all round her was soothing a spirit lately troubled, and health came stealing gently back through fame and through heart. At length she said softly — "We could be so happy here, grandfather! It cannot last, can it?"

"'Tis no use in this life, my dear," returned Waife, philosophising; "no use at all disturbing present happiness by asking 'can it last?' To-day is man's, to-morrow his Maker's. But tell me frankly, do you really dislike so much the idea of exhibiting? I don't mean as we did in Mr. Rugge's show. I know you hate that; but in a genteel private way, as the other night. You sigh! Out with it."

"I like what you like, Grandy."

"That's not true. I like to smoke; you don't. Come, you do dislike acting? Why? you do it so well—wonderfully. Generally speaking, people like what they do well."

"It is not the acting itself, Grandy dear, that I don't like. When I am in some part, I am carried away—I am not myself. I am some one else!"

"And the applause?"

"I don't feel it? I daresay I should miss it if it did not come; but it does not seem to me as if I were applauded. If I felt that, I should stop short, and get frightened. It is as if that somebody else into whom I was changed was making friends with the audience; and all my feeling is for that somebody—just as, Grandy dear, when it is over, and we two are alone together, all my feeling is for you—at least (hanging her head) it used to be; but lately, somehow, I am ashamed to think how I have been feeling for myself more than for you. Is it—is it that I am growing selfish? as Mr. Mayor said. Oh no. Now we are here—not in those noisy towns—not in the inns and on the highways;—now here, here, I do feel again for you—all for you!"

"You are my little angel, you are," said Waife, tremulously. "Selfish! you! a good joke that! Now you see, I am not what is called Demonstrative—a long word, Sophy, which means, that I don't show to you always how fond I am of you: and, indeed," he added ingenuously. "I am not always aware of it myself. I like acting—I like the applause, and the lights, and the excitement, and the illusion—the make-belief of the whole thing; it takes me out of memory and thought—it is a world that has neither past, present, nor future, an interlude in time—an escape from space. I suppose it is the same with poets when they are making verses. Yes, I like all this; and when I think of it, I forget you too much. And I never observed, Heaven forgive me! that you were pale and drooping, till it was pointed out to me. Well, take away your arms. Let us consult! As soon as you get quite, quite well—how shall we live? what shall we do? You are as wise as a little woman, and

hundred times, only I did not dare to speak first."

Waife listened very attentively. "I can make very good baskets," said he, rubbing his chin, "famous baskets (if one could hire a bit of osier ground), and, as you say, there might be other fancy articles I could turn out prettily enough, and you could work samplers, and urn-rugs, and doyleys, and pin-cushions, and so forth; and what with a rood or two of garden-ground, and poultry (the Mayor says poultry is healthy for children), upon my word, if we could find a safe place, and people would not trouble us with their gossip— and we could save a little money for you when I am—"

"Bees too—honey?" interrupted Sophy, growing more and more interested and excited.

"Yes, bees—certainly. A cottage of that kind in a village would not be above £6 a-year, and £20 spent on materials for fancy-works would set us up. Ah! but furniture— beds and tables—monstrous dear!"

"O no, very little would do at first."

"Let us count the money we have left," said Waife, throwing himself down on a piece of sward that encircled a shady mulberry-tree. Old man and child counted the money, bit by bit, gaily yet anxiously—babbling, interrupting each other— scheme upon scheme; they forgot past and present as much as in acting plays—they were absorbed in the future—innocent simple future —innocent as the future planned by two infants fresh from Robinson Crusoe or fairy tales.

"I remember—I remember; just the place for us," cried Waife, suddenly. "It is many, many, many years since I was there; I was courting my Lizzy at the time— alas—alas! But no sad thoughts now!—just the place, near a large town, but in a pretty village quite retired from it. 'Twas there I learned to make baskets. I had broken my leg—fall from a horse— nothing to do. I lodged with an old basket-maker; he had a capital trade. Rivulet at the back of his house; reeds, osiers, plentiful. I see them now, as I saw them from my little casement while my leg was setting. And Lizzy used to write to me such dear letters; my baskets were all for her. We had baskets enough to have furnished a house with baskets; could have dined in baskets, sat in baskets, slept in baskets. With a few lessons I could soon recover the knack of the work. I should like to see the place again; it would be shaking hands with my youth once more. None who could possibly recognise me could be now living. Saw no one but the surgeon, the basket-maker, and his wife; all so old, they must be long since gathered to their fathers. Perhaps no one carries on the basket trade now. I may revive it and have it all to myself; perhaps the cottage itself may be easily hired." Thus, ever disposed to be sanguine, the vagabond chattered on, Sophy listening fondly, and smiling up to his face. "And a fine large park close by; the owners, great lords, deserted it then; perhaps it is deserted still. You might wander over it as if it were your own, Sophy. Such wonderful trees—such green solitudes; and pretty shy hares running across the vistas—stately deer too! We will make friends with the lodgekeepers, and we will call the park yours, Sophy; and I shall be a genius who weaves magical baskets, and you shall be the enchanted princess concealed from all evil eyes, knitting doyleys of pearl under leaves of emerald, and catching no sound from the world of perishable life, except as the boughs whisper and the birds sing."

money; it slips out of my hands like an eel. Heaven bless you, sir; your kindness seems like a miracle vouchsafed to me for that child's dear sake. No evil can chance to her with you; and if I should fall ill and die, even then you, who would have aided the tricksome vagrant, will not grudge the saving hand to the harmless child."

The letter to Sophy ran thus,—

"Darling, forgive me; I have stolen away from you, but only for a few days, and only in order to see if we cannot gain the magic home where I am to be the Genius, and you the Princess. I go forth with such a light heart, Sophy dear. I shall be walking thirty miles a-day, and not feel an ache in the lame leg; you could not keep up with me —you know you could not. So think over the cottage and the basket-work, and practise at samplers and pin-cushions, when it is too hot to play; and be stout and strong against I come back. That, I trust, will be this day week—'tis but seven days; and then we will only act fairy dramas to nodding trees, with linnets for the orchestra; and even Sir Isaac shall not be demeaned by mercenary tricks, but shall employ his arithmetical talents in casting up the weekly bills, and he shall never stand on his hind-legs except on sunny days, when he shall carry a parasol to shade an enchanted princess. Laugh, darling—let me fancy I see you laughing; but don't fret—don't fancy I desert you. Do try and get well—quite, quite well; I ask it of you on my knees."

The letter and the bag were taken over at sunrise to Mr. Hartopp's villa. Mr. Hartopp was an early man. Sophy overslept herself; her room was to the west; the morning beams did not reach its windows; and the cottage without children woke up to labour, noiseless and still. So when at last she shook off sleep, and tossing her hair from her blue eyes, looked round and became conscious of the strange place, she still fancied the hour early. But she got up, drew the curtain from the window, saw the sun high in the heavens, and, ashamed of her laziness, turned, and lo! the letter on the chair! Her heart at once misgave her; the truth flashed upon a reason prematurely quick in the intuition which belongs to the union of sensitive affection and active thought. She drew a long breath, and turned deadly pale. It was some minutes before she could take up the letter, before she could break the seal. When she did, she read on noiselessly, her tears dropping over the page, without effort or sob. She had no egotistical sorrow, no grief in being left alone with strangers; it was the pathos of the old man's lonely wanderings, of his bereavement of his counterfeit glee, and genuine self-sacrifice—this it was that suffused her whole heart with unutterable yearnings of tenderness, gratitude, pity, veneration. But when she had wept silently for some time, she kissed the letter with devout passion, and turned to that Heaven to which the outcast had taught her first to pray.

Afterwards she stood still, musing a little while, and the sorrowful shade gradually left her face. Yes; she would obey him—she would not fret—she would try and get well and strong. He would feel, at the distance, that she was true to his wishes—that she was fitting herself to be again his companion;—seven days would soon pass. Hope, that can never long quit the heart of childhood, brightened over her meditations, as the morning sun over a landscape that just before had lain red amidst twilight and under rain.

When she came down-stairs, Mrs.

Nay, more, he could not but feel that the event would long affect his personal comfort and independence; he would be more than ever under the affectionate tyranny of Mr. Williams—more than ever be an object of universal surveillance and espionage. There would be one thought paramount throughout Gatesboro'. "The Mayor, God bless him! has been taken in—this must not occur again! or Gatesboro' is dishonoured, and Virtue indeed a name!" Mr. Hartopp felt not only mortified but subjugated—he who had hitherto been the soft subjugator of the hardest. He felt not only subjugated, but indignant at the consciousness of being so. He was too meekly convinced of Heaven's unerring justice not to feel assured that the man who had taken him in would come to a tragic end. He would not have hanged that man with his own hands—he was too mild for vengeance. But if he had seen that man hanging, he would have said piously, "Fitting retribution," and passed on his way soothed and comforted. Taken in!—taken in at last!—he, Josiah Hartopp, taken in by a fellow with one eye!

CHAPTER II.

The Mayor is so protected that he cannot help himself.

A COMMOTION without—a kind of howl—a kind of hoot. Mr. Williams—the warehousemen, the tanners, Mike Callaghan, share between them the howl and the hoot. The Mayor started—is it possible! His door is burst open, and, scattering all who sought to hold him back—scattering them to the right and left from his massive torso, in rushed the man who had taken in the Mayor—the fellow with one eye, and with that fellow, shaggy and travel-soiled, the other dog!

"What have you done with the charge I intrusted to you? My child—my child—where is she?"

Waife's face was wild with the agony of his emotions, and his voice was so sharply terrible that it went like a knife into the heart of the man, who, thrust aside for the moment, now followed him, fearful, into the room.

"Mr.—Mr. Chapman, sir," faltered the Mayor, striving hard to recover dignity and self-possession, "I am astonished at your—your—"

"Audacity!" interposed Mr. Williams.

"My child—my Sophy—my child! answer me, man!"

"Sir," said the Mayor, drawing himself up, "have you not got the note which I left at my bailiff's cottage in case you called there?"

"Your note—this thing!" said Waife, striking a crumpled paper with his hand, and running his eye over its contents. "You have rendered up, you say, the child to her lawful protector? Gracious heavens! did I trust her to you, or not?"

"Leave the room all of you," said the Mayor, with a sudden return of his usual calm vigour.

"You go—you, sirs; what the deuce do you do here?" growled Williams to the meaner throng. "Out!—I stay; never fear, man, I'll take care of him!"

alone with the vagrant, and to have said the soothing things he did not dare to say before Williams, who sate there mute and grim, guarding him from being once more "taken in." "If you had confided in me at first, Mr. Chapman," he said, pathetically, "or even if now, I could aid you in an honest way of life!"

"Aid him—now!" said Williams, with a snort. "At it again! you're not a man, you're an angel!"

"But if he is penitent, Williams."

"So! so! so!" murmured Waife. "Thank Heaven it was not he who spoke against me—it was but a strange woman. Oh!" he suddenly broke off with a groan. "Oh—but that strange woman—who, what can she be? and Sophy with her and him. Distraction! Yes, yes, I take the money. I shall want it all. Sir Isaac, pick up that bag. Gentlemen, good-day to you!" He bowed; such a failure that bow! Nothing ducal in it! bowed and turned towards the door; then, when he gained the threshold, as if some meeker, holier thought restored to him dignity of bearing, his form rose, though his face softened, and stretching his right hand towards the Mayor, he said:—"You did but as all perhaps would have done on the evidence before you. You meant to be kind to her. If you knew all, how you would repent! I do not blame—I forgive you."

He was gone: the Mayor stood transfixed. Even Williams felt a cold comfortless thrill. "He does not look like it," said the foreman. "Cheer up, sir, no wonder you were taken in — who would not have been?"

"Hark! that hoot again. Go, Williams, don't let the men insult him. Go, do—I shall be grateful."

But before Williams got to the door, the cripple and his dog had vanished; vanished down a dark narrow alley on the opposite side of the street. The rude workmen had followed him to the mouth of the alley, mocking him. Of the exact charge against the Comedian's good name they were not informed; that knowledge was confined to the Mayor and Mr. Williams. But the latter had dropped such harsh expressions, that bad as the charge might really be, all in Mr. Hartopp's employment probably deemed it worse, if possible, than it really was. And wretch indeed must be the man by whom the Mayor had been confessedly taken in, and whom the Mayor had indignantly given up to the reproaches of his own conscience. But the cripple was now out of sight, lost amidst those labyrinths of squalid homes which, in great towns, are thrust beyond view, branching off abruptly behind High Streets and Market Places, so that strangers passing only along the broad thoroughfares, with glittering shops and gas-lit causeways, —exclaim, "Where do the Poor live?"

abroad—was already out of the country. But the woman with Losely, he had not heard her described; his guesses did not turn towards Mrs. Crane; the woman was evidently hostile to him—it was the woman who had spoken against him—not Losely; the woman whose tongue had poisoned Hartopp's mind, and turned into scorn all that admiring respect which had before greeted the great Comedian. Why was that woman his enemy? Who could she be? What had she to do with Sophy? He was half beside himself with terror. It was to save her less even from Losely than from such direful women as Losely made his confidants and associates, that Waife had taken Sophy to himself. As for Mrs. Crane, she had never seemed a foe to *him*—she had ceded the child to him willingly—he had no reason to believe, from the way in which she had spoken of Losely when he last saw her, that she could henceforth aid the interests, or share the schemes, of the man whose perfidies she then denounced; and as to Rugge, he had not appeared at Gatesboro'. Mrs. Crane had prudently suggested that his presence would not be propitiatory or discreet, and that all reference to him, or to the contract with him, should be suppressed. Thus Waife was wholly without one guiding evidence—one groundwork for conjecture—that might enable him to track the lost; all he knew was, that she had been given up to a man whose whereabouts it was difficult to discover—a vagrant, of life darker and more hidden than his own.

But how had the hunters discovered the place where he had treasured up his Sophy—how dogged that retreat? Perhaps from the village in which we first saw him. Ay, doubtless, learned from Mrs. Saunders of the dog he had purchased, and the dog would have served to direct them on his path. At that thought he pushed away Sir Isaac, who had been resting his head on the old man's knee—pushed him away angrily; the poor dog slunk off in sorrowful surprise, and whined.

"Ungrateful wretch that I am!" cried Waife, and he opened his arms to the brute, who bounded forgivingly to his breast.

"Come, come, we will go back to the village in Surrey. Tramp, tramp!" said the cripple, rousing himself. And at that moment, just as he gained his feet, a friendly hand was laid on his shoulder, and a friendly voice said—

"I have found you! the crystal said so! Marbellous!"

"Merle," faltered out the vagrant—"Merle, you here! Oh, perhaps you come to tell me good news; you have seen Sophy—you know where she is!"

The Cobbler shook his head. "Can't see her just at present. Crystal says nout about her. But I know she was taken from you—and—and—you shake tremenjous! Lean on me, Mr. Waife, and call off that big animal. He's a suspicating my calves and circumtittyvating them. Thank ye, sir. You see I was born with sinister aspects in my Twelfth House, which appertains to big animals and enemies;—and dogs of that size about one's calves are—malefics!"

As Merle now slowly led the cripple, and Sir Isaac, relinquishing his first suspicions, walked droopingly beside them, the Cobbler began a long story, much encumbered by astrological illustrations and moralising comments. The substance of his narrative is thus epitomised: Rugge, in pursuing Waife's track, had naturally called on Merle in company with Losely and Mrs.

how or other became acquainted with Rugge, and sold Sophy to the manager. Where Rugge was, there would Sophy be. It could not be very difficult to find out the place in which Rugge was now exhibiting; and then—ah then! Waife whistled to Sir Isaac, tapped his forehead, and smiled triumphantly. Meanwhile the Cobbler had led him back into the suburb, with the kind intention of offering him food and bed for the night at his sister's house. But Waife had already formed his plan; in London, and in London alone, could he be sure to learn where Rugge was now exhibiting; in London there were places at which that information could be gleaned at once. The last train to the metropolis was not gone. He would slink round the town to the station: he and Sir Isaac at that hour might secure places unnoticed.

When Merle found it was in vain to press him to stay over the night, the good-hearted Cobbler accompanied him to the train, and, while Waife shrunk into a dark corner, bought the tickets for dog and master. As he was paying for these, he overheard two citizens talking of Mr. Chapman. It was indeed Mr. Williams explaining to a fellow-burgess just returned to Gatesboro', after a week's absence, how and by what manner of man Mr. Hartopp had been taken in. At what Williams said, the Cobbler's cheek paled. When he joined the Comedian, his manner was greatly altered; he gave the tickets without speaking, but looked hard into Waife's face, as the latter repaid him the fares. "No," said the Cobbler suddenly, "I don't believe it."

"Believe what?" asked Waife, startled.

"That you are——"

The Cobbler paused, bent forward, and whispered the rest of the sentence close in the vagrant's ear. Waife's head fell on his bosom, but he made no answer.

"Speak," cried Merle; "say 'tis a lie." The poor cripple's lip writhed, but he still spoke not.

Merle looked aghast at that obstinate silence. At length, but very slowly, as the warning bell summoned him and Sir Isaac to their several places in the train, Waife found voice. "So you too, you too desert and despise me! God's will be done!" He moved away—spiritless, limping, hiding his face as well as he could. The porter took the dog from him, to thrust it into one of the boxes reserved for such four-footed passengers.

Waife thus parted from his last friend—I mean the dog—looked after Sir Isaac wistfully, and crept into a third-class carriage, in which luckily there was no one else. Suddenly Merle jumped in, snatched his hand, and pressed it tightly. "I don't despise, I don't turn my back on you; whenever you and the little one want a home and a friend, come to Kit Merle as before, and I'll bite my tongue out if I ask any more questions of you; I'll ask the stars instead."

The Cobbler had but just time to splutter out these comforting words, and redescend the carriage, when the train put itself into movement, and the life-like iron miracle, fuming, hissing, and screeching, bore off to London its motley convoy of human beings, each passenger's heart a mystery to the other, all bound the same road, all wedged close within the same whirling mechanism; what a separate and distinct world in each! Such is Civilization! How like we are one to the other in the mass! how strangely dissimilar in the abstract.

is necessarily a distortion of the reasoning faculty; and man, accustomed from the cradle rather to reason than to feel, has that faculty more firm against abrupt twists and lesions than it is in woman; where virtue may have left him, logic may still linger; and he may decline to push evil to a point at which it is clear to his understanding that profit vanishes and punishment rests; while woman, once abandoned to ill, finds sufficient charm in its mere excitement; and, regardless of consequences, where the man asks, "Can I?" raves out, "I will!" Thus man may be criminal through cupidity, vanity, love, jealousy, fear, ambition; rarely in civilised, that is, reasoning life, through hate and revenge; for hate is a profitless investment, and revenge a ruinous speculation. But when women are thoroughly depraved and hardened, nine times out of ten it is hatred or revenge that makes them so. Arabella Crane had not, however, attained to that last state of wickedness, which, consistent in evil, is callous to remorse; she was not yet unsexed. In her nature was still that essence, "varying and mutable," which distinguishes woman while womanhood is left to her. And now, as she sate gazing on the throng below, her haggard mind recoiled perhaps from the conscious shadow of the Evil Principle which, invoked as an ally, remains as a destroyer. Her dark front relaxed; she moved in her seat uneasily. "Must it be always thus!" she muttered—"always this hell here! Even now, if in one large pardon I could include the undoer, the earth, myself, and again be human—human, even as those slight triflers or coarse brawlers that pass yonder! Oh for something in common with common life!"

Her lips closed, and her eyes again fell upon the crowded street. At that moment three or four heavy vans or waggons filled with operatives or labourers and their wives, coming back from the race-course, obstructed the way; two outriders with satin jackets were expostulating, cracking their whips, and seeking to clear space for an open carriage with four thoroughbred impatient horses. Towards that carriage every gazer from the windows was directing eager eyes; each foot-passenger on the pavement lifted his hat—evidently in that carriage some great person! Like all who are at war with the world as it is, Arabella Crane abhorred the great, and despised the small for worshipping the great. But still her own fierce dark eyes mechanically followed those of the vulgar. The carriage bore a marquess's coronet on its panels, and was filled with ladies; two other carriages bearing a similar coronet, and evidently belonging to the same party, were in the rear. Mrs. Crane started. In that first carriage, as it now slowly moved under her very window, and paused a minute or more till the obstructing vehicles in front were marshalled into order—there flashed upon her eyes a face radiant with female beauty in its most glorious prime. Amongst the crowd at that moment was a blind man, adding to the various discords of the street by a miserable hurdy-gurdy. In the movement of the throng to get nearer to a sight of the ladies in the carriage, this poor creature was thrown forward; the dog that led him, an ugly brute, on his own account or his master's, took fright, broke from the string, and ran under the horses' hoofs, snarling. The horses became restive; the blind man made a plunge after his dog, and was all but run over. The lady in the first carriage, alarmed

in that miserable affair of which you told me?"

"Not a miserable affair for her—but certainly I never got any good from it. Trouble for nothing! Barta. No use looking back."

"No use; but who can help it!" said Arabella Crane, sighing heavily; then, as if eager to change the subject, she added abruptly, "Mr. Rugge has been here twice this morning, highly excited—the child will not act. He says you are bound to make her do so!"

"Nonsense. That is his look-out. I see after children, indeed!"

MRS. CRANE (with a visible effort).—"Listen to me, Jasper Losely. I have no reason to love that child, as you may suppose. But now that you so desert her, I think I feel compassion for her; and when, this morning, I raised my hand to strike her for her stubborn spirit, and saw her eyes unflinching, and her pale, pale, but fearless face, my arm fell to my side powerless. She will not take to this life without the old man. She will waste away and die."

LOSELY.—"How you bother me! Are you serious? What am I to do?"

MRS. CRANE.—"You have won money, you say; revoke the contract; pay Rugge back his £100. He is disappointed in his bargain; he will take the money."

LOSELY.—"I daresay he will, indeed. No—I have won to-day, it is true, but I may lose to-morrow, and, besides, I am in want of so many things; when one gets a little money, one has an immediate necessity for more—ha! ha! Still I would not have the child die; and she may grow up to be of use. I tell you what I will do; if, when the races are over, I find I have gained enough to afford it, I will see about buying her off. But £100 is too much! Rugge ought to take half the money, or a quarter, because, if she don't act, I suppose she does eat."

Odious as the man's words were, he said them with a laugh that seemed to render them less revolting —the laugh of a very handsome mouth, showing teeth still brilliantly white. More comely than usual that day, for he was in great good-humour, it was difficult to conceive that a man with so healthful and fair an exterior was really quite rotten at heart.

"Your own young laugh," said Arabella Crane, almost tenderly. "I know not how it is, but this day I feel as if I were less old—altered though I be in face and mind. I have allowed myself to pity that child; while I speak, I can pity you. Yes! pity—when I think of what you were. Must you go on thus? To what? Jasper Losely," she continued, sharply, eagerly, clasping her hands—"hear me—I have an income, not large, it is true, but assured; you have nothing but what, as you say, you may lose to-morrow; share my income! Fulfil your solemn promises — marry me. I will forget whose daughter that girl is—I will be a mother to her. And for yourself, give me the right to feel for you again as I once did, and I may find a way to raise you yet—higher than you can raise yourself. I have some wit, Jasper, as you know. At the worst you shall have the pastime, I the toil. In your illness I will nurse you; in your joys I will intrude no share. Whom else can you marry? to whom else could you confide? who else could—"

She stopped short as if an adder had stung her, uttering a shriek of rage, of pain; for Jasper Losely, who had hitherto listened to her, stupefied, astounded, here burst into a fit of merriment, in which there

CHAPTER V.

The most submissive where they love may be the most stubborn where they do not love—Sophy is stubborn to Mr. Rugge—That injured man summons to his side Mrs. Crane, imitating the policy of those potentates who would retrieve the failures of force by the successes of diplomacy.

Mr. Rugge has obtained his object. But now comes the question, "What will he do with it?" Question with as many heads as the Hydra; and no sooner does an Author dispose of one head than up springs another.

Sophy has been bought and paid for—she is now, legally, Mr. Rugge's property. But there was a wise peer who once bought Punch—Punch became his property, and was brought in triumph to his lordship's house. To my lord's great dismay, Punch would not talk. To Rugge's great dismay, Sophy would not act.

Rendered up to Jasper Losely and Mrs. Crane, they had not lost an hour in removing her from Gatesboro' and its neighbourhood. They did not, however, go back to the village in which they had left Rugge, but returned straight to London, and wrote to the manager to join them there.

Sophy, once captured, seemed stupefied; she evinced no noisy passion—she made no violent resistance. When she was told to love and obey a father in Jasper Losely, she lifted her eyes to his face—then turned them away, and shook her head, mute and incredulous. That man her father! she did not believe it. Indeed, Jasper took no pains to convince her of the relationship, or win her attachment. He was not unkindly rough—he seemed wholly indifferent—probably he was so. For the ruling vice of the man was in his egotism. It was not so much that he had bad principles and bad feelings, as that he had no principles and no feelings at all, except as they began, continued, and ended in that system of centralisation, which not more paralyses healthful action in a state, than it does in the individual man. Self-indulgence with him was absolute. He was not without power of keen calculation, not without much cunning. He could conceive a project for some gain far off in the future, and concoct, for its realisation, schemes subtly woven, astutely guarded. But he could not secure their success by any long-sustained sacrifices of the caprice of one hour or the indolence of the next. If it had been a great object to him for life to win Sophy's filial affection, he would not have bored himself for five minutes each day to gain that object. Besides, he had just enough of shame to render him uneasy at the sight of the child he had deliberately sold. So, after chucking her under the chin, and telling her to be a good girl and be grateful for all that Mrs. Crane had done for her, and meant still to do, he consigned her almost solely to that lady's care.

When Rugge arrived, and Sophy was informed of her intended destination, she broke silence—her colour went and came quickly—she declared, folding her arms upon her breast, that she would never act if separated from her grandfather. Mrs.

calico-flowers into the child's tresses, stood the senior matron of the establishment—not a bad sort of woman—who kept the dresses, nursed the sick, revered Rugge, told fortunes on a pack of cards which she always kept in her pocket, and acted occasionally in parts where age was no drawback and ugliness desirable— such as a witch, or duenna, or whatever in the dialogue was poetically called "Hag." Indeed, Hag was the name she usually took from Rugge—that which she bore from her defunct husband was Gormerick. This lady, as she braided the garland, was also bent on the soothing system, saying, with great sweetness, considering that her mouth was full of pins, "Now, deary—now, dovey —look at oneself in the glass; we could beat oo, and pinch oo, and stick pins into oo, dovey, but we won't. Dovey will be good, I know;" and a great patch of rouge came on the child's pale cheeks. The clown therewith, squatting before her with his hands on his knees, grinned lustily, and shrieked out— "My eyes, what a beauty!"

Rugge, meanwhile, one hand thrust in his bosom, contemplated the diplomatic efforts of his ministers, and saw, by Sophy's compressed lips and unwinking eyes, that their cajoleries were unsuccessful. He approached and hissed into her ear—"Don't madden me! don't —you will act, eh!"

"No," said Sophy, suddenly rising; and, tearing the wreath from her hair, she set her small foot on it with force. "No! not if you kill me!"

"Gods!" faltered Rugge. "And the sum I have paid! I am diddled! Who has gone for Mrs. Crane?"

"Tom," said the clown.

The word was scarcely out of the clown's mouth ere Mrs. Crane herself emerged from a side scene, and, putting off her bonnet, laid both hands on the child's shoulders, and looked her in the face without speaking. The child as firmly returned the gaze. Give that child a martyr's cause, and in that frail body there would have been a martyr's soul. Arabella Crane, not inexperienced in children, recognised a power of will stronger than the power of brute force, in that tranquillity of eye— the spark of calm light in its tender blue—blue, pure as the sky; light, steadfast as the star.

"Leave her to me, all of you," said Mrs. Crane. "I will take her to your private room, Mr. Rugge;" and she led the child away to a sort of recess, room it could not be rightly called, fenced round with boxes and crates, and containing the manager's desk and two stools.

"Sophy," then said Mrs. Crane, "you say you will not act unless your grandfather be with you. Now, hear me. You know that I have been always stern and hard with you. I never professed to love you —nor do I. But you have not found me untruthful. When I say a thing seriously, as I am speaking now, you may believe me. Act to-night, and I will promise you faithfully that I will either bring your grandfather here, or I will order it so that you shall be restored to him. If you refuse, I make no threat, but I shall leave this place; and my belief is that you will be your grandfather's death."

"His death—his death—I!"

"By first dying yourself. Oh, you smile; you think it would be happiness to die. What matter that the old man you profess to care for is broken-hearted! Brat, leave selfishness to boys — you are a girl!— Suffer!"

"Selfish!" murmured Sophy, "selfish! that was said of me before. Selfish!—ah, I understand. No, I

"Oh you are blind, are you? but we are not deaf. There's a penny not to play. What black thing have you got there by a string?"

"My dog, sir!"

"Deuced ugly one—not like a dog—more like a boar, with horns!"

"I say, master," cries the clown, "here's a blind man come to see the Phenomenon!"

The crowd laugh; they make way for the blind man's black dog. They suspect, from the clown's address, that the blind man has something to do with the company.

You never saw two uglier specimens of their several species than the blind man and his black dog. He had rough red hair and a red beard, his face had a sort of twist that made every feature seem crooked. His eyes were not bandaged, but the lids were closed, and he lifted them up piteously as if seeking for light. He did not seem, however, like a common beggar: had rather the appearance of a reduced sailor. Yes, you would have bet ten to one he had been a sailor, not that his dress belonged to that noble calling, but his build, the roll of his walk, the tie of his cravat, a blue anchor tattoed on that great brown hand—certainly a sailor—a British tar! poor man.

The dog was hideous enough to have been exhibited as a *lusus naturæ*,—evidently very aged—for its face and ears were grey, the rest of it a rusty reddish black; it had immensely long ears, pricked up like horns; it was a dog that must have been brought from foreign parts; it might have come from Acheron, sire by Cerberus, so portentous, and (if not irreverent the epithet) so infernal was its aspect, with that grey face, those antlered ears, and its ineffably weird demeanour altogether. A big dog, too, and evidently a strong one. All prudent folks would have made way for a man led by that dog. Whine creaked the hurdy-gurdy, and bow-wow all of a sudden barked the dog. Sophy stifled a cry, pressed her hand to her breast, and such a ray of joy flashed over her face, that it would have warmed your heart for a month to have seen it.

But do you mean to say, Mr. Author, that that British Tar (gallant, no doubt, but hideous) is Gentleman Waife, or that Stygian animal the snowy-curled Sir Isaac? Upon my word, when I look at them myself, I, the Historian, am puzzled. If it had not been for that bow-wow, I am sure Sophy would not have suspected. Tara-tarantara. Walk in, ladies and gentlemen, walk in; the performance is about to commence! Sophy lingers last.

"Yes, sir," said the blind man, who had been talking to the apprentice—"Yes, sir," said he, loud and emphatically, as if his word had been questioned. "The child was snowed up, but luckily the window of the hut was left open: Exactly at two o'clock in the morning, that dog came to the window, set up a howl, and—"

Sophy could hear no more—led away behind the curtain by the King's Lieutenant. But she had heard enough to stir her heart with an emotion that set all the dimples round her lip into undulating play.

CHAPTER VIII

Corollaries from the problem suggested in Chapters VI. and VII.

BROAD daylight, nearly nine o'clock indeed, and Jasper Losely is walking back to his inn from the place at which he had dined the evening before. He has spent the night drinking, gambling, and though he looks heated, there is no sign of fatigue. Nature, in wasting on this man many of her most glorious elements of happiness, had not forgotten a herculean constitution—always restless and never tired, always drinking and never drunk. Certainly it is some consolation to delicate invalids, that it seldom happens that the sickly are very wicked. Criminals are generally athletic—constitution and conscience equally tough; large backs to their heads—strong suspensorial muscles—digestions that save them from the overfine nerves of the virtuous. The native animal must be vigorous in the human being, when the moral safeguards are daringly overleapt. Jasper was not alone, but with an acquaintance he had made at the dinner, and whom he invited to his inn to breakfast; they were walking familiarly arm-in-arm. Very unlike the brilliant Losely—a young man under thirty, who seemed to have washed out all the colours of youth in dirty water. His eyes dull, their whites yellow; his complexion sodden. His form was thickset and heavy; his features pug, with a cross of the bulldog. In dress, a specimen of the flash style of sporting man, as exhibited on the Turf, or more often, perhaps, in the Ring; Belcher neckcloth, with an immense pin representing a jockey at full gallop; cut-away coat, corduroy breeches, and boots with tops of a chalky white. Yet, withal, not the air and walk of a genuine born and bred sporting man, even of the vulgar order. Something about him which reveals the pretender. A would-be hawk with a pigeon's liver—a would-be sportsman with a Cockney's nurture.

Samuel Adolphus Poole is an orphan of respectable connections. His future expectations chiefly rest on an uncle from whom, as godfather, he takes the loathed name of Samuel. He prefers to sign himself Adolphus; he is popularly styled Dolly. For his present existence he relies ostensibly on his salary as an assistant in the house of a London tradesman in a fashionable way of business, Mr. Latham, his employer, has made a considerable fortune, less by his shop than by discounting the bills of his customers, or of other borrowers whom the loan draws into the net of the custom. Mr. Latham connives at the sporting tastes of Dolly Poole. Dolly has often thus been enabled to pick up useful pieces of information as to the names and repute of such denizens of the sporting world as might apply to Mr. Latham for temporary accommodation. Dolly Poole has many sporting friends; he has also many debts. He has been a dupe, he is now a rogue; but he wants decision of character to put into practice many valuable ideas that his experience of dupe and his development into rogue suggest to his ambition. Still, however, now and

hungry?—No!—I am! Hillo—who's that?"

His arm was seized by Mr. Rugge. "She's gone—fled," gasped the manager, breathless. "Out of the lattice—fifteen feet high—not dashed to pieces—vanished."

"Go on and order breakfast," said Losely to Mr. Poole, who was listening too inquisitively. He drew the manager away. "Can't you keep your tongue in your head before strangers? the girl is gone?"

"Out of the lattice, and fifteen feet high!"

"Any sheets left hanging out of the lattice?"

"Sheets! No."

"Then she did not go without help—somebody must have thrown up to her a rope-ladder—nothing so easy—done it myself scores of times for the descent of 'maids who love the moon,' Mr. Rugge. But at her age there is not a moon—at least there is not a man in the moon; one must dismiss, then, the idea of a rope-ladder—too precocious. But are you quite sure she is gone? not hiding in some cupboard? *Sacre!* —very odd. Have you seen Mrs. Crane about it?"

"Yes, just come from her; she thinks that villain Waife must have stolen her. But I want you, sir, to come with me to a magistrate."

"Magistrate! I—why?—nonsense—set the police to work."

"Your deposition that she is your lawful child, lawfully made over to me, is necessary for the Inquisition —I mean Police."

"Hang it, what a bother! I hate magistrates, and all belonging to them. Well, I must breakfast! I'll see to it afterwards. Oblige me by not calling Mr. Waife a villain— good old fellow in his way."

"Good! Powers above!"

"But if he took her off, how did he get at her? It must have been preconcerted."

"Ha! true. But she has not been suffered to speak to a soul not in the company—Mrs. Crane excepted."

"Perhaps at the performance last night some signal was given?"

"But if Waife had been there I should have seen him; my troop would have known him; such a remarkable face—one eye, too."

"Well, well, do what you think best. I'll call on you after breakfast; let me go now. *Basta! Basta!*"

Losely wrenched himself from the manager, and strode off to the inn ; then, ere joining Poole, he sought Mrs. Crane.

"This going before a magistrate," said Losely, "to depose that I have made over my child to that blackguard showman—in this town too— after such luck as I have had, and where bright prospects are opening on me, is most disagreeable. And supposing, when we have traced Sophy, she should be really with the old man—awkward! In short, my dear friend, my dear Bella"—(Losely could be very coaxing when it was worth his while)—"you just manage this for me. I have a fellow in the next room waiting to breakfast; as soon as breakfast is over I shall be off to the race-ground, and so shirk that ranting old bore ; you'll call on him instead, and settle it somehow." He was out of the room before she could answer.

Mrs. Crane found it no easy matter to soothe the infuriate manager when he heard Losely was gone to amuse himself at the race-course. Nor did she give herself much trouble to pacify Mr. Rugge's anger, or assist his investigations. Her interest in the whole affair seemed over. Left thus to his own devices, Rugge, however, began to institute a sharp, and what pro-

Genius, till he has paid his penny to Charon, and his passport to immortality has been duly examined by the custom-house officers of Styx! When one half the world drag forth that same next-door neighbour, place him on a pedestal, and have him cried, "O yes! O yes! Found a Man of Genius! Public property —open to inspection!" does not the other half the world put on its spectacles, turn up its nose, and cry, "That a Man of Genius, indeed! Pelt him!—pelt him!" Then of course there is a clatter, what the vulgar call "a shindy," round the pedestal. Squeezed by his believers, shied at by his scoffers, the poor man gets horribly mauled about, and drops from the perch in the midst of the row. Then they shovel him over, clap a great stone on his relics, wipe their foreheads, shake hands, compromise the dispute, the one half the world admitting that though he was a genius he was still an ordinary man; the other half allowing, that though he was an ordinary man, he was still a genius. And so on to the next pedestal with its "Hic stet," and the next great stone with its "Hic jacet."

The manager of the Grand Theatrical Exhibition gazed on the blind sailor, and did not know him from Adam!

CHAPTER IX.

The aboriginal Man-eater, or Pocket-Cannibal, is susceptible of the refining influence of Civilisation. He decorates his lair with the skins of his victims; he adorns his person with the spoils of those whom he devours. Mr. Losely introduced to Mr. Poole's friends—dressed for dinner; and, combining elegance with appetite, eats them up.

ELATED with the success which had rewarded his talents for pecuniary speculation, and dismissing from his mind all thoughts of the fugitive Sophy and the spoliated Ruggs, Jasper Losely returned to London in company with his new friend, Mr. Poole. He left Arabella Crane to perform the same journey, unattended; but that grim lady, carefully concealing any resentment at such want of gallantry, felt assured that she should not be long in London without being honoured by his visits.

In renewing their old acquaintance, Mrs. Crane had contrived to establish over Jasper that kind of influence which a vain man, full of schemes that are not to be told to all the world, but which it is convenient to discuss with some confidential friend who admires himself too highly not to respect his secrets, mechanically yields to a woman whose wits are superior to his own.

It is true that Jasper, on his return to the metropolis, was not magnetically attracted towards Podden Place; nay, days and even weeks elapsed, and Mrs. Crane was not gladdened by his presence. But she knew that her influence was only suspended—not extinct. The body attracted was for the moment kept from the body attracting, by the abnormal weights that had dropped into its pockets. Restore the body thus temporarily counterpoised to its former lightness, and it

side, lounged into the saloons of theatres, accompanied by a cohort of juvenile admirers, their hats on one side also, and returned to the pleasantest little suppers in his own apartment. There "the goblet" flowed—and after the goblet, cigars for some, and a rubber for all.

So puissant Losely's vitality, and so blest by the stars his luck, that his form seemed to wax stronger and his purse fuller by this "life." No wonder he was all for a life of that kind; but the slight beings who tried to keep up with him grew thinner and thinner, and poorer and poorer; a few weeks made their cheeks spectral and their pockets a dismal void. Then as some dropped off from sheer inanition, others whom they had decoyed by their praises of "Life" and its hero, came into the magic circle to fade and vanish in their turn.

In a space of time incredibly brief, not a whist-player was left upon the field; the victorious Losely had trumped out the last; some few whom Nature had endowed more liberally than Fortune, still retained strength enough to sup—if asked;

"But none who came to sup remained to play."

"Plague on it," said Losely to Poole, as one afternoon they were dividing the final spoils, "your friends are mightily soon cleaned out; could not even get up double dummy last night; and we must hit on some new plan for replenishing the coffers! You have rich relations; can't I help you to make them more useful?"

Said Dolly Poole, who was looking exceedingly bilious, and had become a martyr to chronic headache,

"My relations are prigs! Some of them give me the cold shoulder, others—a great deal of jaw. But as for tin, I might as well scrape a flint for it. My uncle Sam is more anxious about my sins than the other codgers, because he is my godfather, and responsible for my sins, I suppose; and he says he will put me in the way of being respectable. My head's splitting—"

"Wood does split till it is seasoned," answered Losely. "Good fellow, uncle Sam! He'll put you in the way of tin; nothing else makes a man respectable."

"Yes—so he says; a girl with money—"

"A wife—tin canister! Introduce me to her, and she shall be tied to you."

Samuel Dolly did not appear to relish the idea of such an introduction. "I have not been introduced to her myself," said he. "But if you advise me to be spliced, why don't you get spliced yourself? a handsome fellow like you can be at no loss for an heiress."

"Heiresses are the most horrid cheats in the world," said Losely: "there is always some father, or uncle, or fusty Lord Chancellor whose consent is essential, and not to be had. Heiresses in scores have been over head and ears in love with me. Before I left Paris, I sold their locks of hair to a wig-maker—three great trunksful. Honour bright. But there were only two whom I could have safely allowed to run away with me; and they were so closely watched, poor things, that I was forced to leave them to their fate—early graves! Don't talk to me of heiresses, Dolly, I have been the victim of heiresses. But a rich widow is an estimable creature. Against widows,if rich, I have not a word to say; and to tell you the truth, there is a widow whom I suspect I have fascinated, and whose connection I have a particular private reason for deeming desirable! She has a whelp of a son, who is a

ones) in the house opposite, discover, by the help of a telescope, that the drawing-rooms have been new papered, canary-coloured ground—festoon borders, and that the mouldings of the shutters have been gilt. Gilt shutters! that looks ominous of an ostentatious and party-giving tenant.

Then carts full of furniture have stopped at the door—carpets, tables, chairs, beds, wardrobes — all seemingly new, and in no inelegant taste, have been disgorged into the hall. It has been noticed, too, that every day a lady of slight figure and genteel habiliments has come, seemingly to inspect progress—evidently the new tenant. Sometimes she comes alone; sometimes with a dark-eyed handsome lad, probably her son. Who can she be? what is she? what is her name? her history? has she a right to settle in Gloucester Place, Portman Square? The detective police of London is not peculiarly vigilant; but its defects are supplied by the voluntary efforts of unmarried ladies. The new-comer was a widow; her husband had been in the army; of good family; but a mauvais sujet; she had been left in straitened circumstances with an only son. It was supposed that she had unexpectedly come into a fortune—on the strength of which she had removed from Pimlico into Gloucester Place. At length—the preparations completed —one Monday afternoon the widow, accompanied by her son, come to settle. The next day a footman in genteel livery (brown and orange) appeared at the door. Then, for the rest of the week, the baker and butcher called regularly. On the following Sunday, the lady and her son appeared at church.

No reader will be at a loss to discover in the new tenant of No.— Gloucester Place, the widowed mother of Lionel Haughton. The letter for that lady which Darrell had intrusted to his young cousin, had, in complimentary and cordial language, claimed the right to provide for her comfortable and honourable subsistence; and announced that, henceforth, £800 a-year would be placed quarterly to her account at Mr. Darrell's banker, and that an additional sum of £1,200 was already there deposited in her name, in order to enable her to furnish any residence to which she might be inclined to remove. Mrs. Haughton, therewith, had removed to Gloucester Place.

She is seated by the window in her front drawing-room—surveying with proud though grateful heart the elegancies by which she is surrounded. A very winning countenance—lively eyes, that in themselves may be over-quick and petulant; but their expression is chastened by a gentle kindly mouth. And over the whole face, the attitude, the air, even the dress itself, is diffused the unmistakable simplicity of a sincere natural character. No doubt Mrs. Haughton has her tempers and her vanities, and her little harmless feminine weaknesses; but you could not help feeling in her presence that you were with an affectionate, warmhearted, honest, good woman. She might not have the refinements of tone and manner which stamp the high-bred gentlewoman of convention; she might evince the deficiencies of an imperfect third-rate education; but she was saved from vulgarity by a certain undefinable grace of person and music of voice—even when she said or did things that well-bred people do not say or do; and there was an engaging intelligence in those quick hazel eyes that made you sure that she was sensible, even when she uttered what was silly.

again into Gloucester Place, on foot. On that occasion Mrs. Haughton was with her son, and the gentleman would not seem to perceive her. The next day he returned; she was then alone, and just as she gained her door, he advanced—"I beg you ten thousand pardons, madam; but if I am rightly informed, I have the honour to address Mrs. Charles Haughton!"

The lady bowed in surprise.

"Ah, madam, your lamented husband was one of my most particular friends."

"You don't say so!" cried Mrs. Haughton: And looking more attentively at the stranger, there was in his dress and appearance something that she thought very stylish; a particular friend of Charles Haughton's was sure to be stylish—to be a man of the first water. And she loved the poor Captain's memory, her heart warmed to any "particular friend of his."

"Yes," resumed the gentleman, noting the advantage he had gained, "though I was considerably his junior, we were great cronies—excuse that familiar expression—in the Hussars together—"

"The Captain was not in the Hussars, sir; he was in the Guards."

"Of course he was; but I was saying—In the Hussars, together with the Guards, there were some very fine fellows—very fine—he was one of them. I could not resist paying my respects to the widowed lady of so fine a fellow. I know it is a liberty, ma'am, but 'tis my way. People who know me well—and I have a large acquaintance—are kind enough to excuse my way. And to think that villanous horse, which I had just bought out of Lord Bolton's stud — (200 guineas, ma'am, and cheap)—should have nearly taken the life of Charles Haughton's lovely relict. If anybody else had been driving that brute, I shudder to think what might have been the consequences; but I have a wrist of iron. Strength is a vulgar qualification—very vulgar—but when it saves a lady from perishing, how can one be ashamed of it? But I am detaining you. Your own house, Mrs. Haughton?"

"Yes, sir, I have just taken it, but the workmen have not finished. I am not yet settled here."

"Charming situation! My friend left a son, I believe? In the army already?"

"No, sir, but he wishes it very much."

"Mr. Darrell, I think, could gratify that wish."

"What! you know Mr. Darrell, that most excellent generous man. All we have we owe to him."

The gentleman abruptly turned aside—wisely—for his expression of face at that praise might have startled Mrs. Haughton.

"Yes, I knew him once. He has had many a fee out of my family. Goodish lawyer—cleverish man—and rich as a Jew. I should like to see my old friend's son, ma'am. He must be monstrous handsome with such parents!"

"Oh, sir, very like his father. I shall be proud to present him to you."

"Ma'am, I thank you. I will have the honour to call—"

And thus is explained how Jasper Losely has knocked at Mrs. Haughton's door—has walked up her stairs—has seated himself in her drawing-room, and is now edging his chair somewhat nearer to her, and throwing into his voice and looks a degree of admiration, which has been sincerely kindled by the aspect of her elegant apartments.

Jessica Haughton was not one of those women, if such there be, who do not know when a gentleman is

already taken up the sentence which he was accustomed to delight
Lionel left uncompleted, and says, and ensnare the young friends of
as he bows over Mrs. Haughton's Mr. Poole, and hurried on: "But in
hand, "come on purpose to claim an innocent way, ma'am, such as
acquaintance with an old friend's mothers would approve. We'll fix
widow, a young friend's mother." an evening for it when I have the
Mrs. HAUGHTON.—"I am sure, honour to call again. Good morning,
Colonel Morley, I am very much Mrs. Haughton. Your hand again,
flattered. And you, too, knew the sir (to Lionel).—Ah, we shall be
poor dear Captain; 'tis so pleasant great friends, I guess! You must
to think that his old friends come let me take you out in my cab—
round us now. This gentleman, teach you to handle the ribbons,
also, was a particular friend of dear eh? 'Gad, my old friend Charles
Charles's." was a whip. Ha! ha! Good-day,

The Colonel had somewhat small good-day!"
eyes, which moved with habitual Not a muscle had moved in the
slowness. He lifted those eyes, let Colonel's face during Mr. Losely's
them drop upon Jasper (who still jovial monologue. But when Jasper
stood in the middle of the room, had bowed himself out, Mrs. Haugh-
with one hand still half-extended ton, curtseying, and ringing the bell
towards Lionel), and letting the for the footman to open the street-
eyes rest there while he spoke, re- door, the man of the world (and, as
peated, man of the world, Colonel Morley
"Particular friend of Charles was consummate) again raised those
Haughton's—the only one of his small slow eyes—this time towards
particular friends whom I never had her face—and dropped the words,—
the honour to see before." "My old friend's particular friend

Jasper, who, whatever his de- is—not bad looking, Mrs. Haugh-
ficiency in other virtues, certainly ton!"
did not lack courage, made a strong "And so lively and pleasant,"
effort at self-possession, and without returned Mrs. Haughton, with a
replying to the Colonel, whose slight rise of colour, but no other
remark had not been directly ad- sign of embarrassment. "It may
dressed to himself, said in his most be a nice acquaintance for Lionel."
rollicking tone—"Yes, Mrs. Haugh- "Mother!" cried that ungrateful
ton, Charles was my particular boy, "you are not speaking seriously.
friend, but"—lifting his eye-glass— I think the man is odious. If he
"but this gentleman was," dropping were not my father's friend, I should
the eye-glass negligently, "not in say he was—"
our set, I suppose." Then advancing "What, Lionel?" asked the
to Lionel, and seizing his hand, "I Colonel, blandly—"was what?"
must introduce myself—the image "Snobbish, sir."
of your father, I declare! I was "Lionel, how dare you!" ex-
saying to Mrs. Haughton how much claimed Mrs. Haughton. "What
I should like to see you—proposing vulgar words boys do pick up at
to her, just as you came in, that we school, Colonel Morley."
should go to the play together. Oh, "We must be careful that they
ma'am, you may trust him to me do not pick up worse than words
safely. Young men should see when they leave school, my dear
LIFE." Here Jasper tipped Lionel madam. You will forgive me, but
one of those knowing winks with Mr. Darrell has so expressly—of

CHAPTER XI.

A man of the world, having accepted a troublesome charge, considers "what he will do with it;" and, having promptly decided, is sure, first, that he could not have done better; and, secondly, that much may be said to prove that he could not have done worse.

RESERVING to a later occasion any more detailed description of Colonel Morley, it suffices for the present to say that he was a man of a very fine understanding, as applied to the special world in which he lived. Though no one had a more numerous circle of friends, and though with many of those friends he was on that footing of familiar intimacy which Darrell's active career once, and his rigid seclusion of late, could not have established with any idle denizen of that brilliant society in which Colonel Morley moved and had his being, yet to Alban Morley's heart (a heart not easily reached) no friend was so dear as Guy Darrell. They had entered Eton on the same day—left it the same day—lodged while there in the same house; and though of very different characters, formed one of those strong, imperishable brotherly affections which the Fates weave into the very woof of existence.

Darrell's recommendation would have secured to any young *protégé* Colonel Morley's gracious welcome and invaluable advice. But, both as Darrell's acknowledged kinsman, and as Charles Haughton's son, Lionel called forth his kindliest sentiments, and obtained his most sagacious deliberations. He had already seen the boy several times, before waiting on Mrs. Haughton, deeming it would please her to defer his visit until she could receive him in all the glories of Gloucester Place; and he had taken Lionel into high favour, and deemed him worthy of a conspicuous place in the world. Though Darrell in his letter to Colonel Morley had emphatically distinguished the position of Lionel, as a favoured kinsman, from that of a presumptive or even a probable heir, yet the rich man had also added: "But I wish him to take rank as the representative to the Haughtons; and whatever I may do with the bulk of my fortune, I shall insure to him a liberal independence. The completion of his education, the adequate allowance to him, the choice of a profession, are matters in which I entreat you to act for yourself, as if you were his guardian. I am leaving England—I may be abroad for years." Colonel Morley, in accepting the responsibilities thus pressed on him, brought to bear upon his charge subtle discrimination, as well as conscientious anxiety.

He saw that Lionel's heart was set upon the military profession, and that his power of application seemed lukewarm and desultory when not cheered and concentred by enthusiasm, and would, therefore, fail him if directed to studies which had no immediate reference to the objects of his ambition. The Colonel, accordingly, dismissed the idea of sending him for three years to an University. Alban Morley summed up his theories on the collegiate ordeal in these succinct aphorisms: "Nothing so good as an University education, nor worse

Continent, just when she was so respectably settled! What was the good of money if she was to be parted from her boy! Mr. Darrell might take the money back if he pleased— she would write and tell him so. Colonel Morley had no feeling; and she was shocked to think Lionel was in such unnatural hands. She saw very plainly that he no longer cared for her—a serpent's tooth, &c. &c. But as soon as the burst was over, the sky cleared, and Mrs. Haughton became penitent and sensible. Then her grief for Lionel's loss was diverted by preparations for his departure. There was his wardrobe to see to—a patent portmanteau to purchase and to fill. And, all done, the last evening mother and son spent together, though painful at the moment, it would be happiness for both hereafter to recall! Their hands clasped in each other—her head leaning on his young shoulder—her tears kissed so soothingly away. And soft words of kindly motherly counsel, sweet promises of filial performance. Happy, thrice happy, as an after remembrance, be the final parting between hopeful son and fearful parent, at the foot of that mystic bridge, which starts from the threshold of home—lost in the dimness of the far-opposing shore!—bridge over which goes the boy who will never return but as the man.

CHAPTER XII.

The Pocket-Cannibal baits his woman's trap with love-letters—And a Widow allured steals timidly towards it from under the weeds.

JASPER LOSELY is beginning to be hard up! The infallible calculation at *rouge-et-noir* has carried off all that capital which had accumulated from the savings of the young gentlemen whom Dolly Poole had contributed to his exchequer. Poole himself is beset by duns, and pathetically observes "that he has lost three stone in weight, and that he believes the calves to his legs are gone to enlarge his liver."

Jasper is compelled to put down his cabriolet—to discharge his groom —to retire from his fashionable lodgings; and just when the prospect even of a dinner becomes dim, he bethinks himself of Arabella Crane, and remembers that she promised him £5, nay £10, which are still due from her. He calls—he is received like the prodigal son. Nay, to his own surprise, he finds Mrs. Crane has made her house much more inviting —the drawing-rooms are cleaned up; the addition of a few easy articles of furniture gives them quite a comfortable air. She herself has improved in costume—though her favourite colour still remains iron-grey. She informs Jasper that she fully expected him—that these preparations are in his honour—that she has engaged a very good cook— that she hopes he will dine with her when not better engaged—in short, lets him feel himself at home in Podden Place.

Jasper at first suspected a sinister design, under civilities that his conscience told him were unmerited—a design to entrap him into that matrimonial alliance which he had so ungallantly scouted, and from which

important and attractive, was alien to the levity and fickleness of his temper. But in this instance he had other motives than those on the surface for unusual perseverance.

A man like Jasper Losely never reposes implicit confidence in any one. He is garrulous, indiscreet—lets out much that Machiavel would have advised him not to disclose; but he invariably has nooks and corners in his mind which he keeps to himself. Jasper did not confide to his adopted mother his designs upon his intended bride. But she knew them through Poole, to whom he was more frank; and when she saw him looking over her select and severe library—taking therefrom the *Polite Letter-Writer* and the *Elegant Extracts*, Mrs. Crane divined at once that Jasper Losely was meditating the effect of epistolary seduction upon the widow of Gloucester Place.

Jasper did not write a bad love-letter in the florid style. He had at his command, in especial, certain poetical quotations, the effect of which repeated experience had assured him to be as potent upon the female breast as the incantations or *Carmina* of the ancient sorcery. The following in particular:

"Had I a heart for falsehood framed,
I ne'er could injure you."

Another—generally to be applied when confessing that his career had been interestingly wild, and would, if pity were denied him, be pathetically short:

"When he who adores thee has left but the name
Of his faults and his follies behind."

Armed with these quotations—many a sentence from the *Polite Letter-Writer* or the *Elegant Extracts*—and a quire of rose-edged paper, Losely sat down to Ovidian composition. But as he approached the close of Epistle the First, it occurred to him that a signature and address were necessary. The address not difficult. He could give Poole's (hence his confidence to that gentleman)—Poole had a lodging in Bury Street, St. James', a fashionable locality for single men. But the name required more consideration. There were insuperable objections against signing his own, to any person who might be in communication with Mr. Darrell—a pity, for there was a good old family of the name of Losely. A name of aristocratic sound might indeed be readily borrowed from any lordly proprietor thereof without asking a formal consent. But this loan was exposed to danger. Mrs. Haughton might very naturally mention such name, as borne by her husband's friend, to Colonel Morley, and Colonel Morley would most probably know enough of the connections and relations of any peer so honoured, to say "there is no such Greville, Cavendish, or Talbot." But Jasper Losely was not without fertility of invention and readiness of resource. A grand idea, worthy of a master, and proving that, if the man had not been a rogue in grain, he could have been reared into a very clever politician, flashed across him. He would sign himself "SMITH." Nobody could say there is no such Smith; nobody could say that a Smith might not be a most respectable, fashionable, highly-connected man. There are Smiths who are millionaires—Smiths who are large-acred squires—substantial baronets—peers of England, and pillars of the State. You can no more question a man's right to be a Smith than his right to be a Briton; and wide as the diversity of rank, lineage, virtue, and genius in Britons, is the

Haughton's answer to Dolly Poole, and began seriously to speculate on the probable amount of the widow's income, and the value of her movables in Gloucester Place. Thence he repaired to Mrs. Crane; and, emboldened by the hope, for ever, to escape from her maternal tutelage, braved her scoldings, and asked for a couple of sovereigns. He was sure that he should be in luck that night. She gave to him the sum, and spared the scoldings. But, as soon as he was gone, conjecturing from the bravado of his manner what had really occurred, Mrs. Crane put on her bonnet and went out.

CHAPTER XIII.

Unhappy is the man who puts his trust in—a woman.

LATE that evening a lady, in a black veil, knocked at No. ** Gloucester Place, and asked to see Mrs. Haughton on urgent business. She was admitted. She remained but five minutes.

The next day, when, "gay as a bridegroom prancing to his bride," Jasper Losely presented himself at the widow's door, the servant placed in his hand a packet, and informed him bluffly that Mrs. Haughton had gone out of town. Jasper with difficulty suppressed his rage, opened the packet—his own letters returned, with these words,—"Sir, your name is not Courtenay Smith. If you trouble me again, I shall apply to the police." Never from female hand had Jasper Losely's pride received such a slap on its face. He was literally stunned. Mechanically he hastened to Arabella Crane; and having no longer any object in concealment, but, on the contrary, a most urgent craving for sympathy, he poured forth his indignation and wrongs. No mother could be more consolatory than Mrs. Crane. She soothed, she flattered, she gave him an excellent dinner; after which, she made him so comfortable—what with an easy chair and complimentary converse, that, when Jasper rose late to return to his lodging, he said: "After all, if I had been ugly and stupid, and of a weakly constitution, I should have been of a very domestic turn of mind."

her had often proved himself—though no man could less deserve one kindly sentiment in a female heart—though she knew that he cared nothing for her, still it was pleasing to know that he cared for nobody else—that he was sitting in the same room—and Arabella Crane felt, that if that existence could continue, she could forget the past, and look contented towards the future. Again I say, strange creature is woman—and in this instance, creature more strange, because so grim! But as her eyes soften, and her fingers work, and her mind revolves schemes for making that lawless wild beast an innocuous tame animal, who can help feeling for and with grim Arabella Crane?

Poor woman! And will not the experiment succeed? Three evenings does Jasper Losely devote to this sinless life and its peaceful occupation. He completes his task—he receives the ten guineas. (How much of that fee came out of Mrs. Crane's privy purse?) He detects three mistakes, which justify suspicion of the book-keeper's integrity. Set a thief to catch a thief! He is praised for acuteness, and promised a still lighter employment, to be still better paid. He departs, declaring that he will come the next day, earlier than usual—he volunteers an eulogium upon work in general—he vows that evenings so happy he has not spent for years; he leaves Mrs. Crane so much impressed by the hope of his improvement, that if a good clergyman had found her just at that moment, she might almost have been induced to pray. But—

"Heu quoties Adam
Mutatosque deos flebit!"

Jasper Losely returns not, neither to Podden Place nor to his lodging in the neighbourhood. Days elapse; still he comes not; even Poole does not know where he has gone; even Poole has not seen him! But that latter worthy is now laid up with a serious rheumatic fever—confined to his room and water gruel. And Jasper Losely is not the man to intrude himself on the privacy of a sick-chamber. Mrs. Crane, more benevolent, visits Poole—cheers him up—gets him a nurse—writes to Uncle Sam. Poole blesses her. He hopes that Uncle Sam, moved by the spectacle of his sick-bed, will say, "Don't let your debts fret you —I will pay them!" Whatever her disappointment or resentment at Jasper's thankless and mysterious evasion, Arabella Crane is calmly confident of his return. To her servant, Bridgett Greggs, who was perhaps the sole person in the world who entertained affection for the lone gaunt woman, and who held Jasper Losely in profound detestation, she said, with tranquil sternness, "That man has crossed my life, and darkened it. He passed away, and left Night behind him. He has dared to return. He shall never escape me again, till the grave yawn for one of us."

"But, Lor love you, Miss, you would not put yourself in the power of such a black-hearted villing?"

"In *his* power! No, Bridgett; fear not, he must be in mine—sooner or later in mine—hand and foot. Patience!"

As she was thus speaking — a knock at the door—"It is he—I told you so—quick!"

But it was not Jasper Losely. It was Mr. Rugge.

Rugge. "However, I have set a minister of justice—that is, ma'am, a detective police—at work; and what I now ask of you is simply this: should it be necessary for Mr. Losely to appear with me before the senate—that is to say, ma'am, a metropolitan police-court—in order to prove my legal property in my own bought and paid-for Phenomenon, will you induce that bold bad man not again to return the poisoned chalice to my lips?"

"I do not even know where Mr. Losely is—perhaps not in London."

"Ma'am, I saw him last night at the theatre—Princess's. I was in the shilling gallery. He who owes me £100, ma'am—he in a private box!"

"Ah! you are sure; by himself?"

"With a lady, ma'am—a lady in a shawl from Ingee. I 'know them shawls. My father taught me to know them in early childhood, for he was an ornament to British commerce—a broker, ma'am—pawn! And," continued Rugge, with a withering smile, "that man in a private box, which at the Princess's costs two pounds two, and with the spoils of Ingee by his side, lifted his eye-glass and beheld me—me in the shilling gallery!—and his conscience did not say 'should we not change places if I paid that gentleman £100?' Can such things be, and overcome us, ma'am, like a summer cloud, without our special—I put it to you, ma'am—wonder?"

"Oh, with a lady, was he?" exclaimed Arabella Crane—her wrath, which, while the manager spoke, gathered fast and full, bursting now into words: "His ladies shall know the man who sells his own child for a show; only find out where the girl is, then come here again before you stir further. Oh, with a lady! Go to your detective policeman, or rather, send him to me; we will first discover Mr. Losely's address. I will pay all the expenses. Rely on my zeal, Mr. Rugge."

Much comforted, the manager went his way. He had not been long gone before Jasper himself appeared. The traitor entered with a more than customary bravado of manner, as if he apprehended a scolding, and was prepared to face it; but Mrs. Crane neither reproached him for his prolonged absence, nor expressed surprise at his return. With true feminine duplicity, she received him as if nothing had happened. Jasper, thus relieved, became of his own accord apologetic and explanatory; evidently he wanted something of Mrs. Crane. "The fact is, my dear friend," said he, sinking into a chair, "that the day after I last saw you, I happened to go to the General Post-Office to see if there were any letters for me. You smile—you don't believe me. Honour bright, — here they are," and Jasper took from the side pocket of his coat a pocket-book—a new pocket-book—a brilliant pocket-book — fragrant Russian leather—delicately embossed—golden clasps — silken linings — jewelled pencil-case—malachite penknife — an arsenal of nicknacks stored in neat recesses; such a pocket-book as no man ever gives to himself. Sardanapalus would not have given that pocket-book to himself! Such a pocket-book never comes to you, oh enviable Lotharios, save as tributary keepsakes from the charmers who adore you! Grimly the Adopted Mother eyed that pocket-book. Never had she seen it before. Grimly she pinched her lips. Out of this dainty volume—which would have been of cumbrous size to a slim thread-paper exquisite, but scarcely bulged into ripple the Atlantic expanse of Jasper Losely's

"I? No; I should have had to wait for hours. A man like me, loitering about London Bridge!—I should have been too conspicuous—he would have soon caught sight of me, though I kept on his blind side. I employed a ragged boy to watch and follow him, and here is the address. Now, will you get Sophy back for me without any trouble to me, without my appearing? I would rather charge a regiment of horse-guards than bully that old man."

"Yet you would rob him of the child—his sole comfort?"

"Bother!" cried Losely, impatiently: "the child can be only a burthen to him; well out of his way; 'tis for the sake of that child he is selling matches! It would be the greatest charity we could do him to set him free from that child sponging on him, dragging him down; without her he'd find a way to shift for himself. Why, he's even cleverer than I am! And there—there—give him this money, but don't say it came from me."

He thrust, without counting, several sovereigns—at least twelve or fourteen—into Mrs. Crane's palm; and so powerful a charm has goodness the very least, even in natures the most evil, that that unusual, eccentric, inconsistent gleam of human pity in Jasper Losely's benighted soul, shed its relenting influence over the angry, wrathful, and vindictive feelings with which Mrs. Crane the moment before regarded the perfidious miscreant: and she gazed at him with a sort of melancholy wonder. What! though so little sympathising with affection, that he could not comprehend that he was about to rob the old man of a comfort which no gold could repay—what! though so contemptuously callous to his own child—yet there in her hand lay the unmistakable token that a something of humanity, compunction, compassion, still lingered in the breast of the greedy cynic; and at that thought all that was softest in her own human nature moved towards him—indulgent—gentle. But in the rapid changes of the heart feminine, the very sentiment that touched upon love brought back the jealousy that bordered upon hate. How came he by so much money? more than, days ago, he, the insatiate spendthrift, had received for his task-work? And that POCKET-BOOK!

"You have suddenly grown rich, Jasper?"

For a moment he looked confused, but replied as he re-helped himself to the brandy, "Yes, *rouge-et-noir*—luck. Now, do go and see after this affair, that's a dear good woman. Get the child to-day if you can; I will call here in the evening."

"Should you take her, then, abroad at once to this worthy lady who will adopt her? If so, we shall meet, I suppose, no more; and I am assisting you to forget that I live still."

"Abroad—that crotchet of yours again. You are quite mistaken—in fact, the lady is in London. It was for her effects that I went to the station. Oh, don't be jealous—quite elderly."

"Jealous, my dear Jasper; you forget. I am as your mother. One of your letters, then, announced this lady's intended arrival; you were in correspondence with this—elderly lady?"

"Why, not exactly in correspondence. But when I left Paris I gave the General Post-Office as my address to a few friends in France. And this lady, who took an interest in my affairs (ladies, whether old or young, who have once known me, always do), was aware that I had

And, in fact, when he rose, dinner now on the table, he picked up the pocket-book without suspicion. But it was lucky that Bridgett had not waited for the opportunity suggested by her mistress. For when Jasper put on the dressing-gown, he observed that his coat wanted brushing; and, in giving it to the servant for that purpose, he used the precaution of taking out the pocketbook, and placing it in some other receptacle of his dress.

Mrs. Crane returned in less than two hours—returned with a disappointed look, which at once prepared Jasper for the intelligence that the birds to be entrapped had flown.

"They went away this afternoon," said Mrs. Crane, tossing Jasper's sovereigns on the table as if they burned her fingers. "But leave the fugitives to me. I will find them."

Jasper relieved his angry mind by a series of guilty but meaningless expletives; and then, seeing no farther use to which Mrs. Crane's wits could be applied at present, finished the remainder of her brandy, and wished her good-night, with a promise to call again, but without any intimation of his own address. As soon as he was gone, Mrs. Crane once more summoned Bridgett.

"You told me last week that your brother-in-law, Simpson, wished to go to America, that he had the offer of employment there, but that he could not afford the fare of the voyage. I promised I would help him if it was a service to you."

"You are a hangel, Miss!" exclaimed Bridgett, dropping a low curtsy—so low that it seemed as if she was going on her knees. "And may you have your deserts in the next blessed world, where there are no black-hearted villings."

"Enough, enough," said Mrs. Crane, recoiling perhaps from that grateful benediction. "You have been faithful to me, as none else have ever been; but this time I do not serve you in return so much as I meant to do. The service is reciprocal, if your brother-in-law will do me a favour. He takes with him his daughter, a mere child. Bridgett, let them enter their names on the steam-vessel as William and Sophy Waife; they can, of course, resume their own name when the voyage is over. There is the fare for them, and something more. Pooh, no thanks. I can spare the money. See your brother-in-law the first thing in the morning; and remember they go by the next vessel, which sails from Liverpool on Thursday."

CHAPTER XVI.

Those poor Pocket-Cannibals, how Society does persecute them! Even a menial servant would give warning if disturbed at his meals. But your Man-eater is the meekest of creatures; he will never give warning, and—not often take it.

WHATEVER the source that had supplied Jasper Losely with the money, from which he had so generously extracted the sovereigns intended to console Waife for the loss of Sophy, that source either dried up, or became wholly inadequate to his wants. For elasticity was the felicitous pecu-

names if we know their handwritings."

Dolly started, and turned white. Knave he was—cheat at cards, blackleg on the turf—but forgery! that crime was new to him. The very notion of it brought on a return of fever. And while Jasper was increasing his malady by arguing with his apprehensions, luckily for Poole, Uncle Sam came in. Uncle Sam, a sagacious old tradesman, no sooner clapped eyes on the brilliant Losely than he conceived for him a distrustful repugnance, similar to that with which an experienced gander may regard a fox in colloquy with its gosling. He had already learned enough of his godson's ways, and chosen society, to be assured that Samuel Dolly had indulged in very anti-commercial tastes, and been sadly contaminated by very anti-commercial friends. He felt persuaded that Dolly's sole chance of redemption was in working on his mind while his body was still suffering, so that Poole might, on recovery, break with all former associations. On seeing Jasper in the dress of an exquisite, with the thews of a prize-fighter, Uncle Sam saw the stalwart incarnation of all the sins which a godfather had vowed that a godson should renounce. Accordingly, he made himself so disagreeable, that Losely, in great disgust, took a hasty departure. And Uncle Sam, as he helped the nurse to plunge Dolly into his bed, had the brutality to tell his nephew, in very plain terms, that if ever he found that Drummagem gent in Poole's rooms again, Poole would never again see the colour of Uncle Sam's money. Dolly beginning to blubber, the good man relenting, patted him on the back, and said: "But as soon as you are well, I'll carry you with me to my country box, and keep you out of harm's way till I find you a wife, who will comb your head for you," —at which cheering prospect Poole blubbered more dolefully than before. On retiring to his own lodging in the Gloucester Coffee-house, Uncle Sam, to make all sure, gave positive orders to Poole's landlady, who respected in Uncle Sam the man who might pay what Poole owed to her, on no account to let in any of Dolly's profligate friends, but especially the chap he had found there: adding, "'Tis as much as my nephew's life is worth; and, what is more to the purpose, as much as your bill is." Accordingly, when Jasper presented himself at Poole's door again that very evening, the landlady apprised him of her orders; and proof to his insinuating remonstrances, closed the door in his face. But a French chronicler has recorded, that when Henry IV. was besieging Paris, though not a loaf of bread could enter the walls, love-letters passed between city and camp as easily as if there had been no siege at all. And does not Mercury preside over money as well as Love? Jasper, spurred on by Madame Caumartin, who was exceedingly anxious to exchange London for St. Petersburg as soon as possible, maintained a close and frequent correspondence with Poole by the agency of the nurse, who luckily was not above being bribed by shillings. Poole continued to reject the villany proposed by Jasper; but, in course of the correspondence, he threw out rather incoherently — for his mind began somewhat to wander — a scheme equally flagitious, which Jasper, aided perhaps by Madame Caumartin's yet keener wit, caught up, and quickly reduced to deliberate method. Old Mr. Latham, amongst the bills he discounted, kept those of such more bashful customers as stipulated that their resort to temporary accommodation should be

bella's dark doubts. But still if Sophy had been regained, and the object, on regaining her, foiled (as it probably would have been), what *then* might have become of her;—lost, perhaps, for ever, to Waife—in a foreign land—and under such guardianship? Grave question, which Jasper Losely, who exercised so little foresight in the paramount question—viz. what some day or other would become of himself?—was not likely to rack his brains by conjecturing!

Meanwhile Mrs. Crane was vigilant. The detective police-officer sent to her by Mr. Bugge could not give her the information which Bugge desired, and which she did not longer need. She gave the detective some information respecting Madame Caumartin. One day towards the evening she was surprised by a visit from Uncle Sam. He called ostensibly to thank her for her kindness to his godson and nephew; and to beg her not to be offended if he had been rude to Mr. Losely, who, he understood from Dolly, was a particular friend of hers. "You see, ma'am, Samuel Dolly is a weak young man, and easily led astray; but, luckily for himself, he has no money and no stomach. So he may repent in time; and if I could find a wife to manage him, he has not a bad head for the main chance, and may become a practical man. Repeatedly I have told him he should go to prison, but that was only to frighten him,—fact is, I want to get him safe down into the country, and he don't take to that. So I am forced to say, 'My boy, home-brewed and south-down, Samuel Dolly, or a Lunnon jail, and debtors' allowance.' Must give a young man his choice, my dear lady."

Mrs. Crane, observing that what he said was extremely sensible, Uncle Sam warmed in his confidence.

"And I thought I had him, till I found Mr. Losely in his sick-room; but ever since that day, I don't know how it is, the lad has had something on his mind, which I don't half like—cracky, I think, my dear lady—cracky. I suspect that old nurse passes letters. I taxed her with it, and she immediately wanted to take her Bible-oath, and smelt of gin—two things which, taken together, look guilty."

"But," said Mrs. Crane, growing much interested, "if Mr. Losely and Mr. Poole do correspond, what then?"

"That's what I want to know, ma'am. Excuse me; I don't wish to disparage Mr. Losely—a dashing gent, and nothing worse, I dare say. But certain sure I am that he has put into Samuel Dolly's head something which has cracked it! There is the lad now up and dressed, when he ought to be in bed, and swearing he'll go to old Latham's to-morrow, and that long arrears of work are on his conscience! Never heard him talk of conscience before—that looks guilty! And it does not frighten him any longer when I say he shall go to prison for his debts; and he's very anxious to get me out of Lunnon; and when I threw in a word about Mr. Losely (slyly, my good lady—just to see its effect), he grew as white as that paper; and then he began strutting and swelling, and saying that Mr. Losely would be a great man, and that he should be a great man, and that he did not care for my money—he could get as much money as he liked. That looks guilty, my dear lady. And oh," cried Uncle Sam, clasping his hands, "I do fear that he's thinking of something worse than he has ever done before, and his brain can't stand it. And, ma'am, he has a great respect for you; and you've a friendship for Mr. Losely. Now,

then, where the watcher stood, she could just catch the glimpse of a passing form behind the muslin draperies, or hear the sound of some louder laugh. In her dark-grey dress, and still darker mantle, Arabella Crane stood motionless, her eyes fixed on those windows. The rare foot-passenger who brushed by her turned involuntarily to glance at the countenance of one so still, and then as involuntarily to survey the house to which that countenance was lifted. No such observer so incurious as not to hazard conjecture what evil to that house was boded by the dark lurid eyes that watched it with so fixed a menace. Thus she remained, sometimes, indeed, moving from her post, as a sentry moves from his, slowly pacing a few steps to and fro, returning to the same place, and again motionless; thus she remained for hours. Evening deepened into night—night grew near to dawn; she was still there in that street, and still her eyes were on that house. At length the door opened noiselessly—a tall man tripped forth with a gay light step, and humming the tune of a gay French chanson. As he came straight towards the spot where Arabella Crane was at watch, from her dark mantle stretched forth her long arm and lean hand, and seized him. He started, and recognized her.

"You here!" he exclaimed—"you!—at such an hour!—you!"

"I, Jasper Losely, here to warn you. To-morrow the officers of justice will be in that accursed house. To-morrow that woman—not for her worst crimes, they elude the law, but for her least, by which the law hunts her down—will be a prisoner——No—you shall not return to warn her as I warn you" (for Jasper here broke away, and retreated some steps towards the house); "or, if you do, share her fate. I cast you off."

"What do you mean?" said Jasper, halting, till with slow steps she regained his side. "Speak more plainly: if poor Madame Caumartin has got into a scrape, which I don't think likely, what have I to do with it?"

"The woman you call Caumartin fled from Paris to escape its tribunals. She has been tracked; the French government have claimed her—Ho!—you smile. This does not touch you?"

"Certainly not."

"But there are charges against her from English tradesmen; and if it be proved that you knew her in her proper name—the infamous Gabrielle Desmarets—if it be proved that you have passed off the French billets de banque that she stole—if you were her accomplice in obtaining goods under her false name—if you, enriched by her robberies, were aiding and abetting her as a swindler here, though you may be safe from the French law, will you be safe from the English? You may be innocent, Jasper Losely; if so, fear nothing. You may be guilty: if so, hide, or follow me!"

Jasper paused. His first impulse was to trust implicitly to Mrs. Crane, and lose not a moment in profiting by such counsels of concealment or flight as an intelligence so superior to his own could suggest. But suddenly remembering that Poole had undertaken to get the bill for £1,000 by the next day—that if flight were necessary, there was yet a chance of flight with booty—his constitutional hardihood, and the grasping cupidity by which it was accompanied, made him resolve at least to hazard the delay of a few hours. And after all, might not Mrs. Crane exaggerate? Was not this the counsel of a jealous woman?

through this solicitor pay back his £100, he rushed incontinent to Mr. Gotobed's office, and was at once admitted into the presence of that stately practitioner.

"I beg your pardon, sir," said Mr. Gotobed with formal politeness, "but I heard a day or two ago accidentally from my head-clerk, who had learned it also accidentally from a sporting friend, that you were exhibiting at Humberstone, during the race-week, a young actress, named on the play-bills (here is one) 'Juliet Araminta,' and whom, as I am informed, you had previously exhibited in Surrey and elsewhere; but she was supposed to have relinquished that earlier engagement, and left your stage with her grandfather, William Waife. I am instructed by a distinguished client, who is wealthy, and who, from motives of mere benevolence, interests himself in the said William and Sophy Waife, to discover their residence. Please, therefore, to render up the child to my charge, apprising me also of the address of her grandfather, if he be not with you; and without waiting for further instructions from my client, who is abroad, I will venture to say that any sacrifice in the loss of your juvenile actress will be most liberally compensated."

"Sir," cried the miserable and imprudent Rugge, "I paid £100 for that fiendish child—a three years' engagement—and I have been robbed. Restore me the £100, and I will tell you where she is, and her vile grandfather also."

At hearing so bad a character lavished upon objects recommended to his client's disinterested charity, the wary solicitor drew in his pecuniary horns.

"Mr. Rugge," said he, "I understand from your words that you cannot place the child Sophy, alias Juliet Araminta, in my hands. You ask £100 to inform me where she is. Have you a lawful claim on her?"

"Certainly, sir; she is my property."

"Then it is quite clear that though you may know where she is, you cannot get at her yourself, and cannot, therefore, place her in my hands. Perhaps she is—in heaven!"

"Confound her, sir! no—in America! or on the seas to it."

"Are you sure?"

"I have just come from the steam-packet office, and seen the names in their book. William and Sophy Waife sailed from Liverpool last Thursday week."

"And they formed an engagement with you — received your money; broke the one, absconded with the other. Bad characters indeed!"

"Bad! you may well say that—a set of swindling scoundrels, the whole kit and kin. And the ingratitude!" continued Rugge: "I was more than a father to that child" (he began to whimper): "I had a babe of my own once—died of convulsions in teething. I thought that child would have supplied its place, and I dreamed of the York Theatre; but"—here his voice was lost in the folds of a marvellously dirty red pocket-handkerchief.

Mr. Gotobed having now, however, learned all that he cared to learn, and not being a soft-hearted man (first-rate solicitors rarely are), here pulled out his watch, and said—

"Sir, you have been very ill-treated, I perceive. I must wish you good-day; I have an engagement in the City. I cannot help you back to your £100, but accept this trifle (a £5 note) for your loss of time in calling" (ringing the bell violently). "Door—show out this gentleman."

That evening Mr. Gotobed wrote at length to Guy Darrell, informing

lady, and allow me to add, that I put you on my free list for life."

Bugge gone; Arabella Crane summoned Bridgett to her presence.

"Lor, mim," cried Bridgett, impulsively, "who'd think you'd been up all night raking! I have not seen you look so well this many a year."

"Ah," said Arabella Crane, "I will tell you why. I have done what for many a year I never thought I should do again—a good action. That child—that Sophy—you remember how cruelly I used her?"

"Oh, miss, don't go for to blame yourself; you fed her, you clothed her, when her own father, the villing, went her away from himself to you—you of all people—you. How could you be caressing and fawning on his child—their child?"

Mrs. Crane bung her head gloomily. "What is past is past. I have lived to save that child, and a curse seems lifted from my soul. Now listen. I shall leave London—England, probably this evening. You will keep this house; it will be ready for me any moment I return. The agent who collects my house-rents will give you money as you want it. Stint not yourself, Bridgett. I have been saving, and saving, and saving, for dreary years—nothing else to interest me—and I am richer than I seem."

"But where are you going, miss?" said Bridgett, slowly recovering from the stupefaction occasioned by her mistress's announcement.

"I don't know—I don't care."

"Oh, gracious stars! Is it with that dreadful Jasper Losely?—it is, it is. You are crazed, you are bewitched, miss!"

"Possibly I am crazed—possibly bewitched; but I take that man's life to mine as a penance for all the evil mine has ever known; and a day or two since I should have said, with rage and shame, 'I cannot help it; I loathe myself that I can care what becomes of him.' Now, without rage, without shame, I say, 'The man whom I once so loved shall not die on a gibbet if I can help it; and, please Heaven, help it I will.'"

The grim woman folded her arms on her breast, and raising her head to its full height, there was in her face and air a stern gloomy grandeur, which could not have been seen without a mixed sensation of compassion and awe.

"Go, now, Bridgett; I have said all. He will be here soon; he will come—he must come—he has no choice; and then—and then—" she closed her eyes, bowed her head, and shivered.

Arabella Crane was, as usual, right in her predictions. Before noon Jasper came—came, not with his jocund swagger, but with that sidelong sinister look—look of the man whom the world cuts—triumphantly restored to its former place in his visage. Madame Caumartin had been arrested; Poole had gone into the country with Uncle Sam; Jasper had seen a police-officer at the door of his own lodgings. He slunk away from the fashionable thoroughfare—slunk to the recesses of Podden Place—slunk into Arabella Crane's prim drawing-room, and said, sullenly, "All is up; here I am!"

Three days afterwards, in a quiet street in a quiet town of Belgium—wherein a sharper, striving to live by his profession, would soon become a skeleton—in a commodious airy apartment, looking upon a magnificent street, the reverse of noisy, Jasper Losely sat secure, innocuous, and profoundly miserable. In another house, the windows of which—facing those of Jasper's sitting-room, from an upper story—commanded so good a view therein that

house; for some alcove, all honey-suckle and ivy! But the dahlias are splendid! Very true; only, dahlias, at the best, are such uninteresting prosy things. What poet ever wrote upon a dahlia! Surely Lady Montfort might have introduced a little more taste here — shown a little more fancy! Lady Montfort! I should like to see my lord's face, if Lady Montfort took any such liberty. But there is Lady Montfort walking slowly along that broad, broad, broad gravel-walk — those splendid dahlias, on either side, in their set parterres. There she walks, in full evidence from all those sixty remorseless windows on the garden front, each window exactly like the other. There she walks, looking wistfully to the far end—('tis a long way off)—where, happily, there is a wicket that carries a persevering pedestrian out of sight of the sixty windows, into shady walks, towards the banks of that immense piece of water, two miles from the house. My lord has not returned from his moor in Scotland—my lady is alone. No company in the house—it is like saying, "No acquaintance in a city." But the retinue in full. Though she dined alone, she might, had she pleased, have had almost as many servants to gaze upon her as there were windows now staring at her lonely walk, with their glassy spectral eyes.

Just as Lady Montfort gains the wicket she is overtaken by a visitor, walking fast from the gravel sweep by the front door, where he has dismounted — where he has caught sight of her; any one so dismounting might have caught sight of her — could not help it. Gardens so fine, were made on purpose for fine persons walking in them to be seen.

"Ah, Lady Montfort," said the visitor, stammering painfully, "I am so glad to find you at home."

"At home, George!" said the lady, extending her hand; "where else is it likely that I should be found? But how pale you are. What has happened?"

She seated herself on a bench, under a cedar-tree, just without the wicket, and George Morley, our old friend the Oxonian, seated himself by her side familiarly, but with a certain reverence. Lady Montfort was a few years older than himself —his cousin—he had known her from his childhood.

"What has happened!" he repeated; "nothing new. I have just come from visiting the good bishop."

"He does not hesitate to ordain you?"

"No—but I shall never ask him to do so."

"My dear cousin, are you not over-scrupulous? You would be an ornament to the Church, sufficient in all else to justify your compulsory omission of one duty, which a curate could perform for you."

Morley shook his head sadly. "One duty omitted!" said he. "But is it not that duty which distinguishes the priest from the layman? and how far extends that duty? Wherever there needs a voice to speak the Word—not in the pulpit only, but at the hearth, by the sick-bed—*there* should be the Pastor! No—I cannot, I ought not, I dare not! Incompetent as the labourer, how can I be worthy of the hire?" It took him long to bring out these words: his emotion increased his infirmity. Lady Montfort listened with an exquisite respect, visible in her compassion, and paused long before she answered.

George Morley was the younger son of a country gentleman, with a

Montfort than the House of Hapsburg. Now the House of Montfort made it a rule that all admitted to be members of the family should help each other; that the head of the House should never, if it could be avoided, suffer any of its branches to decay and wither into poverty. The House of Montfort also held it a duty to foster and make the most of every species of talent that could swell the influence or adorn the annals of the family. Having rank, having wealth, it sought also to secure intellect, and to knit together into solid union, throughout all ramifications of kinship and cousinhood, each variety of repute and power that could root the ancient tree more firmly in the land. Agreeably to this traditional policy, Mr. Carr Vipont not only desired that a Vipont Morley should not lose a very good thing, but that a very good thing should not lose a Vipont Morley of high academical distinction—a Vipont Morley who might be a bishop! He therefore drew up an admirable letter, which the Marquess signed—that the Marquess should take the trouble of copying it was out of the question —wherein Lord Montfort was made to express great admiration of the disinterested delicacy of sentiment, which proved George Vipont Morley to be still more fitted to the cure of souls; and, placing rooms at Montfort Court at his service (the Marquess not being himself there at the moment), suggested that George should talk the matter over with the present incumbent of Humberston (that town was not many miles distant from Montfort Court), who, though he had no impediment in his speech, still never himself preached nor read prayers, owing to an affection of the trachea, and who was, nevertheless, a most efficient clergyman. George Morley, therefore, had gone down to Montfort Court some months ago, just after his interview with Mrs. Crane. He had then accepted an invitation to spend a week or two with the Rev. Mr. Allsop, the Rector of Humberston—a clergyman of the old school, a fair scholar, a perfect gentleman, a man of the highest honour, goodnatured, charitable, but who took pastoral duties much more easily than good clergymen of the new school—be they high or low—are disposed to do. Mr. Allsop, who was then in his eightieth year, a bachelor with a very good fortune of his own, was perfectly willing to fulfil the engagement on which he held his living, and render it up to George; but he was touched by the earnestness with which George assured him that at all events he would not consent to displace the venerable incumbent from a tenure he had so long and honourably held—and would wait till the living was vacated in the ordinary course of nature. Mr. Allsop conceived a warm affection for the young scholar. He had a grandniece staying with him on a visit, who less openly, but not less warmly, shared that affection; and with her George Morley fell shyly and timorously in love. With that living he would be rich enough to marry— without it, no. Without it he had nothing but a fellowship, which matrimony would forfeit, and the scanty portion of a country squire's younger son. The young lady herself was dowerless, for Allsop's fortune was so settled that no share of it would come to his grand-niece. Another reason for conscience to gulp down that unhappy impediment of speech! Certainly, during this visit, Morley's scruples relaxed; but when he returned home they came back with greater force than ever— with greater force, because he felt

what a soother! If Montfort were but less prosperous or more ambitious, what a treasure, either to console or to sustain, in a mind like yours!"

As those words were said, you might have seen at once why Lady Montfort was called haughty and reserved. Her lip seemed suddenly to snatch back its sweet smile—her dark eye, before so purely, softly friend-like, became coldly distant—the tones of her voice were not the same as she answered—

"Lord Montfort values me, as it is, far beyond my merits: far," she added, with a different intonation, gravely mournful.

"Forgive me; I have displeased you. I did not mean it. Heaven forbid that I should presume either to disparage Lord Montfort—or—or to—" he stopped short, saving the hiatus by a convenient stammer. "Only," he continued, after a pause, "only forgive me this once. Recollect I was a little boy when you were a young lady, and I have pelted you with snowballs, and called you 'Caroline.'" Lady Montfort suppressed a sigh, and gave the young scholar back her gracious smile, but not a smile that would have permitted him to call her "Caroline" again. She remained, indeed, a little more distant than usual during the rest of their interview, which was not much prolonged; for Morley felt annoyed with himself that he had so indiscreetly offended her, and seized an excuse to escape. "By the by," said he, "I have a letter from Mr. Carr Vipont, asking me to give him a sketch for a Gothic bridge to the water yonder. I will, with your leave, walk down and look at the proposed site. Only do say that you forgive me."

"Forgive you, cousin George, oh yes. One word only—it is true you were a child still when I fancied I was a woman, and you have a right to talk to me upon all things, except those that relate to me and Lord Montfort; unless, indeed," she added with a bewitching half laugh, "unless you ever see cause to scold me, there. Good-by, my cousin, and in turn forgive me, if I was so petulant. The Caroline you pelted with snowballs was always a wayward, impulsive creature, quick to take offence, to misunderstand, and —to repent."

Back into the broad, broad gravel-walk, walked, more slowly than before, Lady Montfort. Again the sixty ghastly windows stared at her with all their eyes—back from the gravel-walk, through a side-door into the pompous solitude of the stately house—across long chambers, where the mirrors reflected her form, and the huge chairs, in their flaunting damask and flaring gold, stood stiff on desolate floors—into her own private room — neither large nor splendid that; plain chintzes, quiet book shelves. She need not have been the Marchioness of Montfort to inhabit a room as pleasant and as luxurious. And the rooms that she could only have owned as Marchioness, what were those worth to her happiness? I know not. "Nothing," fine ladies will perhaps answer. Yet those same fine ladies will contrive to dispose their daughters to answer, "All." In her own room Lady Montfort sunk on her chair; wearily—wearily she looked at the clock—wearily at the books on the shelves—at the harp near the window. Then she leant her face on her hand, and that face was so sad, and so humbly sad, that you would have wondered how any one could call Lady Montfort proud.

"Treasure! I — I! worthless, fickle, credulous fool!—I—I!"

The groom of the chambers entered with the letters by the after-

democratic audience. To represent a peaceful congregation that still sheet of water would do as well. Pebbles there were in plenty just by that gravelly cove, near which a young pike lay sunning his green back. Half in jest, half in earnest, the scholar picked up a handful of pebbles, wiped them from sand and mould, inserted them between his teeth cautiously, and, looking round to assure himself that none were by, began an extempore discourse. So interested did he become in that classical experiment, that he might have tortured the air and astonished the magpies (three of whom from a neighbouring thicket listened perfectly spell-bound) for more than half an hour, when, seized with shame at the ludicrous impotence of his exertions—with despair that so wretched a barrier should stand between his mind and its expression —he flung away the pebbles, and sinking on the ground, he fairly wept—wept like a baffled child.

The fact was, that Morley had really the temperament of an orator; he had the orator's gifts in warmth of passion, rush of thought, logical arrangement; there was in him the genius of a great preacher. He felt it—he knew it; and in that despair which only Genius knows, when some pitiful cause obstructs its energies and strikes down its powers—making a confidant of Solitude—he wept loud and freely.

"Do not despond, sir, I undertake to cure you," said a voice behind.

George started up in confusion; a man, elderly, but fresh and vigorous, stood beside him, in a light fustian jacket, a blue apron, and with rushes in his hands, which he continued to plait together nimbly and deftly as he bowed to the startled scholar.

"I was in the shade of the thicket yonder, sir; pardon me, I could not help hearing you."

The Oxonian rubbed his eyes, and stared at the man with a vague impression that he had seen him before—When? Where?

"You can cure me," he stuttered out; "what of?—the folly of trying to speak in public. Thank you, I am cured."

"Nay, sir, you see before you a man who can make you a very good speaker. Your voice is naturally fine. I repeat, I can cure a defect which is not in the organ, but in the management!"

"You can! you—who and what are you?"

"A basket-maker, sir; I hope for your custom."

"Surely this is not the first time I have seen you?"

"True, you once kindly suffered me to borrow a resting-place on your father's land. One good turn deserves another."

At that moment Sir Isaac peered through the brambles, and restored to his original whiteness, and relieved from his false, horned ears, marched gravely towards the water, sniffed at the scholar, slightly wagged his tail, and buried himself amongst the reeds in search of a water-rat he had therein disturbed a week before, and always expected to find again.

The sight of the dog immediately cleared up the cloud in the scholar's memory; but with recognition came back a keen curiosity and a sharp pang of remorse.

"And your little girl?" he asked, looking down abashed.

"Better than she was when we last met. Providence is so kind to us."

Poor Waife, he never guessed that to the person he thus revealed himself he owed the grief for Sophy's abduction. He divined no reason

CHAPTER III.

Could we know by what strange circumstances a man's genius became prepared for practical success, we should discover that the most serviceable items in his education were never entered in the bills which his father paid for it.

AT the end of the very first lesson, George Morley saw that all the elocution-masters to whose skill he had been consigned were blunderers in comparison to the basket-maker. Waife did not puzzle him with scientific theories. All that the great comedian required of him was to observe and to imitate. Observation, imitation, lo! the groundwork of all art! the primal elements of all genius! Not there, indeed, to halt, but there ever to commence. What remains to carry on the intellect to mastery?—Two steps—to reflect, to reproduce. Observation, imitation, reflection, reproduction. In these stands a mind complete and consummate, fit to cope with all labour, achieve all success.

At the end of the first lesson George Morley felt that his cure was possible. Making an appointment for the next day at the same place, he came thither stealthily, and so on day by day. At the end of a week he felt that the cure was nearly certain; at the end of a month the cure was self-evident. He should live to preach the Word. True, that he practised incessantly in private. Not a moment in his waking hours that the one thought, one object, were absent from his mind; true, that with all his patience, all his toil, the obstacle was yet serious, might never be entirely overcome. Nervous hurry — rapidity of action — vehemence of feeling brought back, might, at unguarded moments, always bring back the gasping breath—the emptied lungs —the struggling utterance. But the relapse — rarer and rarer now with each trial, would be at last scarce a drawback. "Nay," quoth Waife, "instead of a drawback, become but an orator, and you will convert a defect into a beauty."

Thus justly sanguine of the accomplishment of his life's chosen object, the scholar's gratitude to Waife was unspeakable. And seeing the man daily at last in his own cottage—Sophy's health restored to her cheeks, smiles to her lip, and cheered at her light fancy-work beside her grandsire's elbow-chair, with fairy legends instilling perhaps golden truths—seeing Waife thus, the scholar mingled with gratitude a strange tenderness of respect. He knew nought of the vagrant's past— his reason might admit that in a position of life so at variance with the gifts natural and acquired of the singular basket-maker, there was something mysterious and suspicious. But he blushed to think that he had ever ascribed to a flawed or wandering intellect, the eccentricities of glorious Humour— abetted an attempt to separate an old age so innocent and genial from a childhood so fostered and so fostering. And sure I am that if the whole world had risen up to point the finger of scorn at the one-eyed cripple, George Morley, the well-born gentleman—the refined scholar —the spotless churchman—would have given him his arm to lean upon, and walked by his side unashamed.

Hartopp. He had not, however returned for some months. The cottage, having been meanwhile wanted for the temporary occupation of an under gamekeeper, while his own was under repair, fortunately remained unlet. Waife, on returning, accompanied by his little girl, had referred the bailiff to a respectable house-agent and collector of street rents in Bloomsbury, who wrote word that a lady, then abroad, had authorised him, as the agent employed in the management of a house property from which much of her income was derived, not only to state that Waife was a very intelligent man, likely to do well whatever he undertook, but also to guarantee, if required, the punctual payment of the rent for any holding of which he became the occupier. On this the agreement was concluded—the basket-maker installed. In the immediate neighbourhood there was no custom for basket-work, but Waife's performances were so neat, and some so elegant and fanciful, that he had no difficulty in contracting with a large tradesman (not at Humberston, but a more distant and yet more thriving town about twenty miles off) for as much of such work as he could supply. Each week the carrier took his goods and brought back the payments; the profits amply sufficed for Waife's and Sophy's daily bread, with even more than the surplus set aside for the rent. For the rest, the basket-maker's cottage being at the farthest outskirts of the straggling village inhabited but by a labouring peasantry, his way of life was not much known, nor much inquired into. He seemed a harmless hard-working man—never seen at the beerhouse, always seen with his neatly-dressed little grandchild in his quiet corner at church on Sundays—a civil, well-behaved man too, who touched his hat to the bailiff, and took it off to the vicar.

An idea prevailed that the basket-maker had spent much of his life in foreign countries, favoured partly by a sobriety of habits which is not altogether national, partly by something in his appearance, which, without being above his lowly calling, did not seem quite in keeping with it—outlandish in short,—but principally by the fact that he had received since his arrival two letters with a foreign postmark. The idea befriended the old man; allowing it to be inferred that he had probably outlived the friends he had formerly left behind him in England, and on his return, been sufficiently fatigued with his rambles to drop contented in any corner of his native soil, wherein he could find a quiet home, and earn by light toil a decent livelihood.

George, though naturally curious to know what had been the result of his communication to Mrs. Crane —whether it had led to Waife's discovery, or caused him annoyance— had hitherto, however, shrunk from touching upon a topic which subjected himself to an awkward confession of officious intermeddling, and to which any indirect allusion might appear an indelicate attempt to pry into painful family affairs. But one day he received a letter from his father which disturbed him greatly, and induced him to break ground and speak to his preceptor frankly. In this letter, the elder Mr. Morley mentioned incidentally amongst other scraps of local news, that he had seen Mr. Hartopp, who was rather out of sorts, his good heart not having recovered the shock of having been abominably "taken in" by an impostor for whom he had conceived a great fancy, and to whose discovery George himself had providentially

matic relations with them; and our despatches and newspapers would instruct us to a T in the characters and propensities of their leading personages. But, where man has no pecuniary nor ambitious interests at stake in his commerce with any class of his fellow-creatures, his information about them is extremely confused and superficial. The best naturalists are mere generalisers, and think they have done a vast deal when they classify a species. What should we know about mankind if we had only a naturalist's definition of man? We only know mankind by knocking classification on the head, and studying each man as a class in himself. Compare Buffon with Shakespeare! Alas, sir—can we never have a Shakespeare for house-flies and minnows?"

GEORGE MORLEY.—"With all respect for minnows and house-flies, if we found another Shakespeare, he might be better employed, like his predecessor, in selecting individualities from the classifications of man."

WAIFE.—"Being yourself a man, you think so—a house-fly might be of a different opinion. But permit me, at least, to doubt whether such an investigator would be better employed in reference to his own happiness, though I grant that he would be so in reference to your intellectual amusement and social interests. Poor Shakespeare! How much he must have suffered!"

GEORGE MORLEY.—"You mean that he must have been racked by the passions he describes—bruised by collision with the hearts he dissects. That is not necessary to genius. The judge on his bench, summing up evidence, and charging the jury, has no need to have shared the temptations, or been privy to the acts, of the prisoner at the bar.

Yet how consummate may be his analysis!"

"No," cried Waife, roughly. "No. Your illustration destroys your argument. The judge knows nothing of the prisoner! There are the circumstances—there is the law. By these he generalises—by these he judges—right or wrong. But of the individual at the bar—of the world,—the tremendous world within that individual heart — I repeat — he knows nothing. Did he know, law and circumstance might vanish—human justice would be paralysed. Ho, there! place that swart-visaged, ill-looking foreigner in the dock, and let counsel open the case—hear the witnesses depose! O, horrible wretch!—a murderer — unmanly murderer!—a defenceless woman smothered by caitiff hands! Hang him up—hang him up! 'Softly,' whispers the POET, and lifts the veil from the assassin's heart. 'Lo! it is Othello the Moor!' What jury now dare find that criminal guilty?—what judge now will put on the black cap?—who now says, 'Hang him up—hang him up?'"

With such lifelike force did the Comedian vent this passionate outburst, that he thrilled his listener with an awe akin to that which the convicted Moor gathers round himself at the close of the sublime drama. Even Sir Isaac was startled; and, leaving his hopeless pursuit of the water-rat, uttered a low bark, came to his master, and looked into his face with solemn curiosity.

WAIFE (relapsing into colloquial accents).—"Why do we sympathize with those above us more than with those below? why with the sorrows of a king rather than those of a beggar? why does Sir Isaac sympathize with me more than (let that water-rat vex him ever so much) I can possibly sympathize with him?—Whatever be the cause,

Heaven ever gave to Priest, he rested his folded hands upon Waife's shoulder, and looking him full and close in the face, said thus, slowly, deliberately—not a stammer—

"You do not guess what you have done for me; you have secured to me a home and a career—the wife of whom I must otherwise have despaired—the Divine Vocation on which all my earthly hopes were set, and which I was on the eve of renouncing—do not think these are obligations which can be lightly shaken off. If there are circumstances which forbid me to disabuse others of impressions which wrong you, imagine not that their false notions will affect my own gratitude—my own respect for you!"

"Nay, sir! they ought—they must. Perhaps not your exaggerated gratitude for a service which you should not, however, measure by its effects on yourself, but by the slightness of the trouble it gave to me; not perhaps your gratitude—but your respect, yes."

"I tell you no! Do you fancy that I cannot judge of a man's nature without calling on him to trust me with all the secrets—all the errors, if you will, of his past life? Will not the calling to which I may now hold myself destined give me power and commandment to absolve all those who truly repent and unfeignedly believe? Oh, Mr. Waife! if in earlier days you have sinned, do you not repent? and how often, in many a lovely gentle sentence dropped unawares from your lips, have I had cause to know that you unfeignedly believe! Were I now clothed with sacred authority, could I not absolve you as a priest? Think you that, in the meanwhile, I dare judge you as a man? I—Life's new recruit, guarded hitherto from temptation by careful parents and favouring fortune—I presume to judge and judge harshly, the grey-haired veteran, wearied by the march, wounded in the battle!"

"You are a noble-hearted human being," said Waife, greatly affected. "And—mark my words—a mantle of charity so large you will live to wear as a robe of honour. But hear me, sir! Mr. Hartopp also is a man infinitely charitable, benevolent, kindly, and, through all his simplicity, acutely shrewd; Mr. Hartopp, on hearing what was said against me, deemed me unfit to retain my grandchild, resigned the trust I had confided to him, and would have given me alms, no doubt, had I asked them, but not his hand. Take your hands, sir, from my shoulder, lest the touch sully you."

George did take his hands from the vagrant's shoulder, but it was to grasp the hand that waived them off, and struggled to escape the pressure. "You are innocent, you are innocent! forgive me that I spoke to you of repentance as if you had been guilty. I feel you are innocent—feel it by my own heart. You turn away, I defy you to say that you are guilty of what has been laid to your charge, of what has darkened your good name, of what Mr. Hartopp believed to your prejudice. Look me in the face and say, 'I am not innocent, I have not been belied.'"

Waife remained voiceless—motionless.

The young man, in whose nature lay yet unproved all those grand qualities of heart, without which never was there a grand orator, a grand preacher—qualities which grasp the results of argument, and arrive at the end of elaborate reasoning by sudden impulse—here released Waife's hand, rose to his feet, and, facing Waife, as the old man sate with face averted, eyes

covered there, though I fancied myself an adept in disguise, and the child and the dog were never seen out of the four garret walls in which I hid them;—if you ask me, I say, to explain how that very woman was suddenly converted from a remorseless foe into a saving guardian, I can only answer by no wit, no device, no persuasive art of mine. Providence softened her heart, and made it kind, just at a moment when no other agency on earth could have rescued us from— from—"

"Say no more—I guess! the paper this woman showed me was a legal form authorising your poor little Sophy to be given up to the care of a father. I guess! of that father you would not speak ill to me; yet from that father you would save your grandchild. Say no more. And you quiet home—your humble employment, really content you!"

"Oh, if such a life can but last! Sophy is so well, so cheerful, so happy. Did not you hear her singing the other day? She never used to sing! But we had not been here a week when song broke out from her, untaught as from a bird. But if any ill report of me travel hither from Gatesboro', or elsewhere, we should be sent away, and the bird would be mute in my thorn tree— Sophy would sing no more."

"Do not fear that slander shall drive you hence. Lady Montfort, you know, is my cousin, but you know not—few do—how thoroughly generous and gentle-hearted she is. I will speak of you to her—Oh, do not look alarmed. She will take my word when I tell her, 'that is a good man;' and if she ask more, it will be enough to say, 'those who have known better days are loth to speak to strangers of the past.'"

"I thank you earnestly, sincerely," said Waife, brightening up. "One favour more—if you saw in the formal document shown to you, or retain on your memory, the name of —of the person authorised to claim Sophy as his child, you will not mention it to Lady Montfort. I am not sure if ever she heard that name, but she may have done so— and—and—" He paused a moment, and seemed to muse; then went on, not concluding his sentence. "You are so good to me, Mr. Morley, that I wish to confide in you as far as I can. Now, you see I am already an old man, and my chief object is to raise up a friend for Sophy when I am gone—a friend in her own sex, sir. Oh, you cannot guess how I long—how I yearn to view that child under the holy fostering eyes of woman. Perhaps if Lady Montfort saw my pretty Sophy, she might take a fancy to her. Oh, if she did —if she did! And Sophy," added Waife, proudly, "has a right to respect. She is not like me—any hovel is good enough for me: But for her!—Do you know that I conceived that hope—that the hope helped to lead me back here—when, months ago, I was at Humberston, intent upon rescuing Sophy; and saw, though," observed Waife, with a sly twitch of the muscles round his mouth, "I had no right at that precise moment to be seeing anything — Lady Montfort's humane fear for a blind old impostor, who was trying to save his dog—a black dog, sir, who had dyed his hair,— from her carriage wheels. And the hope became stronger still, when, the first Sunday I attended your village church, I again saw that fair —wondrously fair—face at the far end — fair as moonlight and as melancholy. Strange it is, sir, that I, naturally a boisterous mirthful man, and now a shy, skulking fugitive—feel more attracted, more allured towards a countenance, in

at it—was reduced from great wealth to great poverty. While I was laid up, my landlady read a newspaper to me, and in that newspaper was an account of his reverse and destitution. But I was accountable to him for the balance of an old debt, and that, with the doctor's bills, quite covered my £120. I hope he does not think quite so ill of me now. But the money brought good luck to him, rather than to me. Well, sir, if you were now to give me money, I should be on the lookout for some mournful calamity. Gold is not natural to me. Some day, however, by-and-by, when you are inducted into your living, and have become a renowned preacher, and have plenty to spare, with an idea that you would feel more comfortable in your mind if you had done something royal for the basket-maker, I will ask you to help me to make up a sum, which I am trying by degrees to save—an enormous sum—almost as much as I paid away from my railway compensation—I owe it to the lady who lent it to release Sophy from an engagement which I—certainly without any remorse of conscience—made the child break."

"Oh yes! What is the amount? Let me at least repay that debt."

"Not yet. The lady can wait—and she would be pleased to wait, because she deserves to wait — it would be unkind to her to pay it off at once. But, in the meanwhile, if you could send me a few good books for Sophy;—instructive; yet not very, very dry. And a French dictionary—I can teach her French when the winter days close in. You see I am not above being paid, sir. But, Mr. Morley, there is a great favour you can do me."

"What is it? Speak."

"Cautiously refrain from doing me a great dis-service! You are going back to your friends and relations. Never speak of me to them. Never describe me and my odd ways. Name not the lady, nor—nor—nor — the man who claimed Sophy. Your friends might not hurt me, others might. Talk travels. The Hare is not long in its form when it has a friend in a Hound that gives tongue. Promise what I ask. Promise it as 'man and gentleman.'"

"Certainly. Yet I have one relation to whom I should like, with your permission, to speak of you, with whom I could wish you acquainted. He is so thorough a man, of the world that he might suggest some method to clear your good name, which you yourself would approve. My uncle, Colonel Morley—"

"On no account!" cried Waife, almost fiercely, and he evinced so much anger and uneasiness, that it was long before George could pacify him by the most earnest assurances that his secret should be inviolably kept, and his injunctions faithfully obeyed. No men of the world consulted how to force him back to the world of men that he fled from! No colonels to scan him with martinet eyes, and hint how to pipeclay a tarnish! Waife's apprehensions gradually allayed, and his confidence restored, one fine morning George took leave of his eccentric benefactor.

Waife and Sophy stood gazing after him from their garden-gate. The cripple leaning lightly on the child's arm. She looked with anxious fondness into the old man's thoughtful face, and clung to him more closely as she looked.

"Will you not be dull, poor grandy?—will you not miss him?"

"A little at first," said Waife, rousing himself. "Education is a great thing. An educated mind,

Henry II.—one of the thousand fighting men who sailed from Milford Haven with the stout Earl of Pembroke, on that strange expedition which ended in the conquest of Ireland. This gallant man obtained large grants of land in that fertile island—some Mac or some O' vanished, and the House of Vipont rose.

During the reign of Richard I., the House of Vipont, though recalled to England (leaving its Irish acquisitions in charge of a fierce cadet, who served as middleman), excused itself from the Crusade, and, by marriage with a rich goldsmith's daughter, was enabled to lend monies to those who indulged in that exciting but costly pilgrimage. In the reign of John, the House of Vipont foreclosed its mortgages on lands thus pledged, and became possessed of a very fair property in England, as well as its fiefs in the sister isle.

The House of Vipont took no part in the troublesome politics of that day. Discreetly obscure, it attended to its own fortunes, and felt small interest in *Magna Charta*. During the reigns of the Plantagenet Edwards, who were great encouragers of mercantile adventure, the House of Vipont, shunning Creci, Bannockburn, and such profitless brawls, intermarried with London traders, and got many a good thing out of the Genoese. In the reign of Henry IV. the House of Vipont reaped the benefit of its past forbearance and modesty. Now, for the first time, the Viponts appear as belted knights—they have armorial bearings—they are Lancasterian to the backbone—they are exceedingly indignant against heretics—they burn the Lollards—they have places in the household of Queen Joan, who was called a witch, but a witch is a very good friend when she wields a sceptre instead of a broomstick. And, in proof of its growing importance, the House of Vipont marries a daughter of the then mighty House of Darrell. In the reign of Henry V., during the invasion of France, the House of Vipont—being afraid of the dysentery which carried off more brave fellows than the field of Agincourt—contrived to be a minor. The Wars of the Roses puzzled the House of Vipont sadly. But it went through that perilous ordeal with singular tact and success. The manner in which it changed sides, each change safe, and most changes lucrative, is beyond all praise.

On the whole, it preferred the Yorkists; it was impossible to be actively Lancasterian, with Henry VI. of Lancaster always in prison. And thus, at the death of Edward IV., the House of Vipont was Baron Vipont of Vipont, with twenty manors. Richard III. counted on the House of Vipont, when he left London to meet Richmond at Bosworth—he counted without his host. The House of Vipont became again intensely Lancasterian, and was amongst the first to crowd round the litter in which Henry VII. entered the metropolis. In that reign it married a relation of Empson's—did the great House of Vipont! and as nobles of elder date had become scarce and poor, Henry VII. was pleased to make the House of Vipont an earl—the Earl of Montfort. In the reign of Henry VIII., instead of burning Lollards, the House of Vipont was all for the Reformation—it obtained the lands of two priories and one abbey. Gorged with that spoil, the House of Vipont, like an anaconda in the process of digestion, slept long. But no, it slept not. Though it kept itself still as a mouse during the reign of Bloody Queen Mary (only

of Vipont had gone on prospering and progressive. It was to the aristocracy what the *Times* newspaper is to the press. The same quick sympathy with public feeling—the same unity of tone and purpose—the same adaptability—and something of the same lofty tone of superiority to the petty interests of party. It may be conceded that the House of Vipont was less brilliant than the *Times* newspaper, but eloquence and wit, necessary to the duration of a newspaper, were not necessary to that of the House of Vipont. Had they been so, it would have had them!

The head of the House of Vipont rarely condescended to take office. With a rent-roll loosely estimated at about £170,000 a-year, it is beneath a man to take from the public a paltry five or six thousand a-year, and undergo all the undignified abuse of popular assemblies, and "a ribald press." But it was a matter of course that the House of Vipont should be represented in any cabinet that a constitutional monarch could be advised to form. Since the time of Walpole, a Vipont was always in the service of his country, except in those rare instances when the country was infamously misgoverned. The cadets of the House, or the senior member of the great commoner's branch of it, sacrificed their ease to fulfil that duty. The Montfort marquesses in general were contented with situations of honour in the household, as of Lord Steward, Lord Chamberlain, or Master of the Horse, &c.— not onerous dignities; and even these they only deigned to accept on those especial occasions when danger threatened the Star of Brunswick, and the sense of its exalted station forbade the House of Vipont to leave its country in the dark.

Great Houses like that of Vipont assist the work of civilisation by the law of their existence. They are sure to have a spirited and wealthy tenantry, to whom, if but for the sake of that popular character which doubles political influence, they are liberal and kindly landlords. Under their sway, fens and sands become fertile — agricultural experiments are tested on a large scale—cattle and sheep improve in breed — national capital augments, and, springing beneath the ploughshare, circulates indirectly to speed the ship and animate the loom. Had there been no Woburn, no Holkham, no Montfort Court, England would be the poorer by many a million. Our great Houses tend also to the refinement of national taste; they have their show places, their picture-galleries, their beautiful grounds. The humblest drawing-rooms owe an elegance or comfort—the smallest garden a flower or esculent—to the importations which luxury borrowed from abroad, or the inventions it stimulated at home, for the original benefit of great Houses. Having a fair share of such merits, in common with other great Houses, the House of Vipont was not without good qualities peculiar to itself. Precisely because it was the most egotistical of Houses, filled with the sense of its own identity, and guided by the instincts of its own conservation, it was a very civil, good-natured House—courteous, generous, hospitable; a House (I mean the Head of it, not of course all its subordinate members, including even the august Lady Selina) that could bow graciously and shake hands with you. Even if you had no vote yourself, you might have a cousin who had a vote. And once admitted into the family, the House adopted you; you had only to marry one of its remotest relations, and the House sent you a wedding present; and at

'Lady Montfort influences my lord." Accordingly, not only the management of his estates fell to Carr Vipont, but even of his gardens, his household, his domestic arrangements. It was Carr Vipont or Lady Selina who said to Lady Montfort, "Give a ball"—"You should ask so and so to dinner "— "Montfort was much hurt to see the old lawn at the Twickenham Villa broken up by those new bouquets. True, it is settled on you as a jointure-house, but for that very reason Montfort is sensitive," &c, &c. In fact, they were virtually as separated, my lord and my lady, as if legally disunited, and as if Carr Vipont and Lady Selina were trustees or intermediaries in any polite approach to each other. But, on the other hand, it is fair to say that where Lady Montfort's sphere of action did not interfere with her husband's plans, habits, likings, dislikings, jealous apprehensions that she should be supposed to have any ascendancy over what exclusively belonged to himself as *Roi fainéant* of the Viponts, she was left free as air. No attempt at masculine control or conjugal advice. At her disposal was wealth without stint— every luxury the soft could desire— every gewgaw the vain could covet. Had her pin-money, which in itself was the revenue of an ordinary peeress, failed to satisfy her wants —had she grown tired of wearing the family diamonds, and coveted new gems from Golconda—a single word to Carr Vipont or Lady Selina would have been answered by a *carte blanche* on the Bank of England. But Lady Montfort had the misfortune not to be extravagant in her tastes. Strange to say, in the world Lord Montfort's marriage was called a love match: he had married a portionless girl, daughter to one of his poorest and obscurest cousins, against the uniform policy of the House of Vipont, which did all it could for poor cousins except marrying them to its chief. But Lady Montfort's conduct in these trying circumstances was admirable and rare. Few affronts can humiliate us unless we resent them—and in vain. Lady Montfort had that exquisite dignity which gives to submission the grace of cheerful acquiescence. That in the gay world flatterers should gather round a young wife so eminently beautiful, and so wholly left by her husband to her own guidance, was inevitable. But at the very first insinuated compliment or pathetic condolence, Lady Montfort, so meek in her household, was haughty enough to have daunted Lovelace. She was thus very early felt to be beyond temptation, and the boldest passed on, nor presumed to tempt. She was unpopular; called "proud and freezing;" she did not extend the influence of "The House;" she did not confirm its fashion—fashion which necessitates social ease, and which no rank, no wealth, no virtue can of themselves suffice to give. And this failure on her part was a great offence in the eyes of the House of Vipont. "She does absolutely nothing for us," said Lady Selina; but Lady Selina in her heart was well pleased that to her in reality thus fell, almost without a rival, the female representation, in the great world, of the Vipont honours. Lady Selina was fashion itself.

Lady Montfort's social peculiarity was in the eagerness with which she sought the society of persons who enjoyed a reputation for superior intellect, whether statesmen, lawyers, authors, philosophers, artists. Intellectual intercourse seemed as if it was her native atmosphere, from which she was ha-

hereditary policy of the House of Vipont. On this occasion the muster of the clan was more significant than usual; there was a "CRISIS" in the constitutional history of the British empire. A new Government had been suddenly formed within the last six weeks, which certainly portended some direful blow on our ancient institutions, for the House of Vipont had not been consulted in its arrangements, and was wholly unrepresented in the Ministry, even by a lordship of the Treasury. Carr Vipont had therefore summoned the patriotic and resentful kindred.

It is an hour or so after the conclusion of dinner. The gentlemen have joined the ladies in the state suite, a suite which the last Marquess had rearranged and redecorated in his old age—during the long illness that finally conducted him to his ancestors. During his earlier years that princely Marquess had deserted Montfort Court for a seat nearer to London, and therefore much more easily filled with that brilliant society of which he had been long the ornament and centre; railways not then existing for the annihilation of time and space, and a journey to a northern county four days with post-horses, making the invitations even of a Marquess of Montfort unalluring to languid beauties and gouty ministers. But nearing the end of his worldly career, this long neglect of the dwelling identified with his hereditary titles, smote the conscience of the illustrious sinner. And other occupations beginning to pall, his lordship, accompanied and cheered by a chaplain, who had a fine taste in the decorative arts, came resolutely to Montfort Court; and there, surrounded with architects, and gilders, and upholsterers, redeemed his errors; and, soothed by the reflection of the palace provided for his successor, added to his vaults—a coffin.

The suite expands before the eye. You are in the grand drawing-room, copied from that of Versailles. That is the picture, full length, of the late Marquess in his robes; its pendent is the late Marchioness, his wife. That table of malachite is a present from the Russian Emperor Alexander; that vase of Sèvres which rests on it was made for Marie Antoinette—see her portrait enamelled in its centre. Through the open door at the far end your eye loses itself in a vista of other pompous chambers—the music-room, the statue hall, the orangery; other rooms there are appertaining to the suite —a ball-room fit for Babylon, a library that might have adorned Alexandria, but they are not lighted, nor required, on this occasion; it is strictly a family party, sixty guests and no more.

In the drawing-room three whist-tables carry off the more elderly and grave. The piano, in the music-room, attracts younger group. Lady Selina Vipont's eldest daughter Honoria, a young lady not yet brought out, but about to be brought out the next season, is threading a wonderfully intricate German piece,—

"Link'd music, long drawn out,"

with variations. Her science is consummate. No pains have been spared on her education; elaborately accomplished, she is formed to be the sympathising spouse of a wealthy statesman. Lady Montfort is seated by an elderly duchess, who is goodnatured, and a great talker; near her are seated two middle-aged gentlemen, who had been conversing with her till the duchess, having cut in, turned dialogue into monologue.

The elder of these two gentlemen is Mr. Carr Vipont, bald, with clipped

it can be called: he believed that the House of Vipont was not merely the Corinthian capital, but the embattled keep — not merely the *dulce decus*, but the *præsidium columenque rerum* of the British monarchy. He did not boast of his connection with the House; he did not provoke your spleen by enlarging on its manifold virtues; he would often have his harmless jest against its members, or even against its pretensions, but such seeming evidences of forbearance or candour were cunning devices to mitigate envy. His devotion to the House was not obtrusive, it was profound. He loved the House of Vipont for the sake of England, he loved England for the sake of the House of Vipont. Had it been possible, by some tremendous reversal of the ordinary laws of nature, to dissociate the cause of England from the cause of the House of Vipont, the Colonel would have said, "Save at least the Ark of the Constitution! and rally round the old House!"

The Colonel had none of Guy Darrell's infirmity of family pride; he cared not a rush for mere pedigrees — much too liberal and enlightened for such obsolete prejudices. No! He knew the world too well not to be quite aware that old family and long pedigrees are of no use to a man if he has not some money or some merit. But it was of use to a man to be a cousin of the House of Vipont, though without any money, without any merit at all. It was of use to be part and parcel of a British Institution; it was of use to have a legitimate indefeasible right to share in the administration and patronage of an empire, on which (to use a novel illustration) "the sun never sets." You might want nothing for yourself — the Colonel and the Marquess equally wanted nothing for themselves; but man is not to be a selfish egotist! Man has cousins — his cousins may want something. Demosthenes denounces, in words that inflame every manly breast, the ancient Greek who does not love his POLIS or State, even though he take nothing from it but barren honour, and contribute towards it — a great many disagreeable taxes. As the POLIS to the Greek, was the House of Vipont to Alban Vipont Morley. It was the most beautiful, touching affection imaginable! Whenever the House was in difficulties — whenever it was threatened by a CRISIS — the Colonel was by its side, sparing no pains, neglecting no means, to get the Ark of the Constitution back into smooth water. That duty done, he retired again into private life, and scorned all other reward than the still whisper of applauding conscience.

"Yes," said Alban Morley, whose voice, though low and subdued in tone, was extremely distinct, with a perfect enunciation, "Yes, it is quite true, my nephew has taken orders — his defect in speech, if not quite removed, has ceased to be any obstacle, even to eloquence; an occasional stammer may be effective — it increases interest, and when the right word comes, there is the charm of surprise in it. I do not doubt that George will be a very distinguished clergyman."

MR. CARR VIPONT. — "We want one — the House wants a very distinguished clergyman; we have none at this moment — not a bishop — not even a dean; all mere parish parsons, and among them not one we could push. Very odd, with more than forty livings too. But the Viponts seldom take to the Church kindly — George must be pushed. The more I think of it, the more we want a bishop: a bishop would be useful in the present CRISIS." (Looking round the rooms proudly, and softening his voice) — "A numerous gathering, Morley! This de-

"I don't choose Guy Darrell to be invited to my house." Carr Vipont was literally stunned by a reply so contumacious. Lord Montfort demur at what Carr Vipont suggested? He could not believe his senses.

"Not choose, my dear Montfort! you are joking. A monstrous clever fellow, Guy Darrell, and at this Crisis—"

"I hate clever fellows—no such bores!" said Lord Montfort, breaking from the caressing clasp of Carr Vipont, and stalking away.

"Spare your regrets, my dear Carr," said Colonel Morley. "Darrell is not in England—I rather believe he is in Verona." Therewith the Colonel sauntered towards the group gathered round the piano. A little time afterwards Lady Montfort escaped from the Duchess, and, mingling courteously with her livelier guests, found herself close to Colonel Morley. "Will you give me my revenge at chess?" she asked, with her rare smile. The Colonel was charmed. As they sat down and ranged their men, Lady Montfort remarked carelessly—

"I overheard you say you had lately received a letter from Mr. Darrell. Does he write as if well—cheerful? You remember that I was much with his daughter, much in his house, when I was a child. He was ever most kind to me." Lady Montfort's voice here faltered.

"He writes with no reference to himself, his health or his spirits. But his young kinsman described him to me as in good health—wonderfully young-looking for his years. But cheerful—no! Darrell and I entered the world together; we were friends as much as a man so busy and so eminent as he could be friends with a man like myself, indolent by habit, and obscure out of Mayfair. I know his nature; we both know something of his family sorrows. He cannot be happy! Impossible!—alone—childless—secluded. Poor Darrell, abroad now; in Verona, too!—the dullest place! in mourning still for Romeo and Juliet!—'Tis your turn to move. In his letter Darrell talked of going on to Greece, Asia—penetrating into the depths of Africa—the wildest schemes! Dear County Guy, as we called him at Eton!—what a career his might have been! Don't let us talk of him, it makes me mournful. Like Goethe, I avoid painful subjects upon principle."

LADY MONTFORT.—"No—we will not talk of him. No—I take the Queen's pawn. No, we will not talk of him!—no!"

The game proceeded; the Colonel was within three moves of checkmating his adversary. Forgetting the resolution come to, he said, as she paused, and seemed despondently meditating a hopeless defence—

"Pray, my fair cousin, what makes Montfort dislike my old friend Darrell?"

"Dislike! Does he! I don't know. Vanquished again, Colonel Morley!" She rose; and, as he restored the chessmen to their box, she leant thoughtfully over the table. "This young kinsman, will he not be a comfort to Mr. Darrell?"

"He would be a comfort and a pride to a father; but to Darrell, so distant a kinsman—comfort!—why and how? Darrell will provide for him, that is all. A very gentlemanlike young man—gone to Paris by my advice—wants polish and knowledge of life. When he comes back he must enter society; I have put his name up at White's; may I introduce him to you?"

Lady Montfort hesitated, and after a pause, said, almost rudely, "No."

much instruction and well-balanced minds. Less authoritative with the last, because boys being not under her immediate control, her sense of responsibility allowed her to display more fondness and less dignity in her intercourse with them than with young ladies who must learn from her example, as well as her precepts, the patrician decorum which becomes the smooth result of impulse restrained and emotion checked. Boys might make a noise in the world, girls should make none. Lady Selina, then, was working the slippers for her absent son, her heart being full of him at that moment. She was describing his character, and expatiating on his promise to two or three attentive listeners, all interested, as being themselves of the Vipont blood, in the probable destiny of the heir to the Carr Viponts.

"In short," said Lady Selina, winding up, "as soon as Reginald is of age we shall get him into Parliament. Carr has always lamented that he himself was not broken into office early; Reginald must be. Nothing so requisite for public men as early training—makes them practical, and not too sensitive to what those horrid newspaper men say. That was Pitt's great advantage. Reginald has ambition; he should have occupation to keep him out of mischief. It is an anxious thing for a mother, when a son is good-looking—such danger of his being spoiled by the women.—Yes, my dear, it is a small foot, very small—his father's foot."

"If Lord Montfort should have no family," said a somewhat distant and subaltern Vipont, whisperingly and hesitating, "does not the title—"

"No, my dear," interrupted Lady Selina; "no, the title does not come to us. It is a melancholy thought, but the marquessate, in that case, is extinct. No other heir-male from Gilbert, the first Marquess. Carr says there is even likely to be some dispute about the earldom. The Barony, of course, is safe; goes with the Irish estates, and most of the English; and goes (don't you know?)—to Sir James Vipont, the last person who ought to have it; the quietest, stupidest creature; not brought up to the sort of thing—a mere gentleman farmer on a small estate in Devonshire."

"He is not here?"

"No. Lord Montfort does not like him. Very natural. Nobody does like his heir, if not his own child, and some people don't even like their own eldest sons! shocking; but so it is. Montfort is the kindest, most tractable being that ever was, except where he takes a dislike. He dislikes two or three people very much."

"True; how he did dislike poor Mrs. Lyndsay!" said one of the listeners, smiling.

"Mrs. Lyndsay, yes—dear Lady Montfort's mother. I can't say I pitied her, though I was sorry for Lady Montfort. How Mrs. Lyndsay ever took in Montfort for Caroline I can't conceive! How she had the face to think of it! He, a mere youth at the time! Kept secret from all his family—even from his grandmother—the darkest transaction. I don't wonder that he never forgave it."

FIRST LISTENER.—"Caroline has beauty enough to—"

LADY SELINA (interrupting).—"Beauty, of course—no one can deny *that*. But not at all suited to such a position, not brought up to the sort of thing. Poor Montfort! he should have married a different kind of woman altogether—a woman like his grandmother, the last Lady Montfort. Caroline does nothing

long, however, a servant entered, to say that Lady Montfort would be very happy to see Mr. Morley. George followed the servant into that unpretending sitting-room, with its simple chintzes and quiet bookshelves—room that would not have been too fine for a cottage.

CHAPTER X.

In every life, go it fast, go it slow, there are critical pausing-places. When the journey is renewed the face of the country is changed.

How well she suited that simple room—herself so simply dressed—her marvellous beauty so exquisitely subdued. She looked at home there, as if all of home that the house could give were there collected.

She had finished and sealed the momentous letters, and had come, with a sense of relief, from the table at the farther end of the room, on which those letters, ceremonious and conventional, had been written — come to the window, which, though mid-winter, was open, and the redbreast, with whom she had made friends, hopped boldly almost within reach, looking at her with bright eyes, and head curiously aslant. By the window a single chair, and a small reading-desk, with the book lying open. The short day was not far from its close, but there was ample light still in the skies, and a serene if chilly stillness in the air without.

Though expecting the relation she had just summoned to her presence, I fear she had half forgotten him. She was standing by the window deep in reverie as he entered, so deep that she started when his voice struck her ear and he stood before her. She recovered herself quickly, however, and said with even more than her ordinary kindliness of tone and manner towards the scholar—"I am so glad to see and congratulate you."

"And I so glad to receive your congratulations," answered the scholar, in smooth, slow voice, without a stutter.

"But, George, how is this?" asked Lady Montfort. "Bring that chair, sit down here, and tell me all about it. You wrote me word you were cured, at least sufficiently to remove your noble scruples. You did not say how. Your uncle tells me, by patient will, and resolute practice."

"Under good guidance. But I am going to confide to you a secret, if you will promise to keep it."

"Oh, you may trust me; I have no female friends."

The clergyman smiled, and spoke at once of the lessons he had received from the basket-maker.

"I have his permission," he said in conclusion, "to confide the service he rendered me, the intimacy that has sprung up between us, but to you alone—not a word to your guests. When you have once seen him, you will understand why an eccentric man, who has known better days, would shrink from the impertinent curiosity of idle customers. Contented with his humble livelihood, he asks but liberty and repose."

"That I already comprehend,"

so lively in its mirth, and yet so softly gay. Sir Isaac, who had hitherto lain *perdu*, watching the movements of a thrush amidst a holly-bush, now started up with a bark. Waife rose—Sophy turned half in flight. The visitors approached.

Here slowly, lingeringly, let fall the curtain. In the frank license of narrative, years will have rolled away ere the curtain rise again. Events that may influence a life often date from moments the most serene, from things that appear as trivial and unnoticeable as the great lady's visit to the basket-maker's cottage. Which of those lives will that visit influence hereafter—the woman's, the child's, the vagrant's? Whose? Probably little that passes now would aid conjecture, or be a visible link in the chain of destiny. A few desultory questions—a few guarded answers—a look or so, a musical syllable or two exchanged between the lady and the child—a basket bought, or a promise to call again. Nothing worth the telling. Be it then untold. View only the scene itself as the curtain drops reluctantly. The rustic cottage, its garden-door open, and open its old-fashioned lattice casements. You can see how neat and cleanly, how eloquent of healthful poverty, how remote from squalid penury, the whitewashed walls, the homely furniture within. Creepers lately trained around the doorway. Christmas holly, with berries red against the window-panes; the bee-hive yonder; a starling, too, outside the threshold, in its wicker cage. In the background (all the rest of the neighbouring hamlet out of sight), the church spire tapering away into the clear blue wintry sky. All has an air of repose—of safety. Close beside you is the Presence of HOME —that ineffable, sheltering, loving Presence—which, amidst solitude, murmurs "not solitary;" a Presence unvouchsafed to the great lady in the palace she has left. And the lady herself? She is resting on the rude gnarled root-stump from which the vagrant had risen; she has drawn Sophy towards her; she has taken the child's hand; she is speaking now—now listening; and on her face kindness looks like happiness. Perhaps she is happy at that moment. And Waife? he is turning aside his weatherbeaten, mobile countenance, with his hand anxiously trembling upon the young scholar's arm. The scholar whispers, "Are you satisfied with me?" and Waife answers in a voice as low, but more broken, "God reward you! Oh, joy!—if my pretty one has found at last a woman friend!" Poor vagabond, he has now a calm asylum—a fixed humble livelihood —more than that, he has just achieved an object fondly cherished. His past life—alas! what has be done with it? His actual life— broken fragment though it be—is at rest now. But still the everlasting question — mocking, terrible question—with its phrasing of farce and its enigmas of tragical sense— "WHAT WILL HE DO WITH IT?" Do with what? The all that remains to him—the all he holds:— the all which man himself, betwixt Free-will and Pre-decree, is permitted to do. Ask not the vagrant alone—ask each of the four then assembled on that flying bridge called the Moment. Time before thee— what wilt *thou* do with it? Ask thyself!—ask the wisest! Out of effort to answer that question, what dream-schools have risen, never wholly to perish! The science of seers on the Chaldee's Pur-Tor, or in the rock-caves of Delphi, grasped after and grasped at by horn-handed mechanics to-day in their lanes and

BOOK VI.—CHAPTER I.

Etchings of Hyde Park in the month of June, which, if this History escape those villains the trunk-makers, may be of inestimable value to unborn antiquarians.—Characters, long absent, reappear and give some account of themselves.

FIVE years have passed away since this history opened. It is the month of June, once more—June, which clothes our London in all its glory; fills its languid ball-rooms with living flowers, and its stony causeways with human butterflies. It is about the hour of 6 P.M. The lounge in Hyde Park is crowded; along the road that skirts the Serpentine crawl the carriages one after the other; congregate by the rails the lazy lookers-on—lazy in attitude, but with active eyes, and tongues sharpened on the whetstone of scandal; the Scaligers of Club-windows airing their vocabulary in the Park. Slowly saunter on, foot-idlers of all degrees in the hierarchy of London *idlesse*; dandies of established fame —youthful tyros in their first season. Yonder in the Ride, forms less inanimate seem condemned to active exercise; young ladies doing penance in a canter; old beaux at hard labour in a trot. Sometimes, by a more thoughtful brow, a still brisker pace, you recognise a busy member of the Imperial Parliament, who, advised by physicians to be as much on horseback as possible, snatches an hour or so in the interval between the close of his Committee and the interest of the Debate, and shirks the opening speech of a well-known bore. Among such truant law-givers (grief it is to say it) may be seen that once model member, Sir Gregory Stollhead. Grim dyspepsia seizing on him at last, "relaxation from his duties" becomes the adequate punishment for all his sins. Solitary he rides, and, communing with himself, yawns at every second. Upon chairs, beneficiently located under the trees towards the north side of the walk, are interspersed small knots and coteries in repose. There, you might see the Ladies Prymme, still the Ladies Prymme —Janet and Wilhelmina; Janet has grown fat, Wilhelmina thin. But thin or fat, they are no less Prymmes. They do not lack male attendants; they are girls of high fashion, with whom young men think it a distinction to be seen talking; of high principle, too, and high pretensions (unhappily for themselves, they are co-heiresses), by whom young men under the rank of earls need not fear to be artfully entrapped into "honourable intentions." They coquet majestically, but they never flirt; they exact devotion, but they do not ask in each victim a sacrifice on the horns of the altar; they will never

"Don't scold, Vance. I am late, I know; but I did not make allowance for interceptions."

"Body o' me, interceptions! For an absentee just arrived in London, you seem to have no lack of friends."

"Friends made in Paris, and found again here at every corner, like pleasant surprises. But no friend so welcome, and dear, as Frank Vance."

"Sensible of the honour, O Lionello the magnificent. Verily you are bon Prince! The Houses of Valois and of Medici were always kind to artists. But whither would you lead me? Back into that treadmill? Thank you, humbly; no. A crowd in fine clothes is of all mobs the dullest. I can look undismayed on the many-headed monster, wild and rampant; but when the many-headed monster buys its hats in Bond Street, and has an eye-glass at each of its inquisitive eyes, I confess I take fright. Besides, it is near seven o'clock; Putney not visible, and the flounders not fried!"

"My cab is waiting yonder; we must walk to it—we can keep on the turf, and avoid the throng. But tell me honestly, Vance, do you really dislike to mix in crowds—you, with your fame, dislike the eyes that turn back to look again, and the lips that respectfully murmur, 'Vance the Painter?' Ah, I always said you would be a great painter. And in five short years you have soared high."

"Pooh!" answered Vance, indifferently. "Nothing is pure and unadulterated in London use; not cream, nor cayenne pepper—least of all Fame;—mixed up with the most deleterious ingredients. Fame! did you read the Times' critique on my pictures in the present Exhibition? Fame indeed! Change the subject.

Nothing so good as flounders. Ho! is that your cab? Superb! Car fit for the 'Grecian youth of talents rare,' in Mr. Enfield's Speaker;—horse that seems conjured out of the Elgin Marbles. Is he quiet?"

"Not very; but trust to my driving. You may well admire the horse—present from Darrell, chosen by Colonel Morley."

When the young men had settled themselves in the vehicle, Lionel dismissed his groom, and, touching his horse, the animal trotted out briskly.

"Frank," said Lionel, shaking his dark curls with a petulant gravity, "Your cynical definitions are unworthy that masculine beard. You despise fame! what sheer affectation!

'Pulverem Olympicum
Collegisse juvat ; metaque fervidis
Evitata rotis ———.'"

"Take care," cried Vance; we shall be over." For Lionel, growing excited, teased the horse with his whip; and the horse bolting, took the cab within an inch of a watercart.

"Fame, fame!" cried Lionel, unheeding the interruption. "What would I not give to have and to hold it for an hour?"

"Hold an eel, less slippery; a scorpion, less stinging! But—added Vance, observing his companion's heightened colour.—"But," he added, seriously, and with an honest compunction, "I forgot, you are a soldier, you follow the career of arms! Never heed what is said on the subject by a querulous painter! The desire of fame may be folly in civilians, in soldiers it is wisdom. Twin-born with the martial sense of honour, it cheers the march, it warms the bivouac; it gives music to the whirr of the bullet, the roar of the ball; it plants

plexed me as a boy, when we parted. Darrell is one of those men who require a home. Between the great world and solitude, he needs the intermediate filling-up which the life domestic alone supplies: a wife to realise the sweet word helpmate—children, with whose future he could knit his own toils and his ancestral remembrances. That intermediate space annihilated, the great world and the solitude are left, each frowning on the other."

"My dear Lionel, you must have lived with very clever people; you are talking far above your years."

"Am I? True, I have lived, if not with very clever people, with people far above my years. That is a secret I learned from Colonel Morley, to whom I must present you—the subtlest intellect under the quietest manner. Once he said to me, 'Would you throughout life be up to the height of your century—always in the prime of man's reason—without crudeness and without decline — live habitually, while young, with persons older, and, when old, with persons younger, than yourself.'"

"Shrewdly said indeed. I felicitate you on the evident result of the maxim. And so Darrell has no home—no wife, and no children?"

"He has long been a widower; he lost his only son in boyhood, and his daughter—did you never hear?"

"No—what—?"—

"Married so ill—a runaway match—and died many years since, without issue."

"Poor man! It was these afflictions, then, that soured his life, and made him the hermit or the wanderer?"

"There," said Lionel, "I am puzzled; for I find that even after his son's death, and his daughter's unhappy marriage and estrangement from him, he was still in Parliament, and in full activity of career. But certainly he did not long keep it up. It might have been an effort to which, strong as he is, he felt himself unequal; or, might he have known some fresh disappointment, some new sorrow, which the world never guesses? what I have said as to his family afflictions, the world knows. But I think he will marry again. That idea seemed strong in his own mind when we parted; he brought it out bluntly, roughly. Colonel Morley is convinced that he will marry, if but for the sake of an heir."

VANCE.—"And if so, my poor Lionel, you are ousted of—"

LIONEL (quickly interrupting).—"Hush! Do not say, my dear Vance, do not you say—you!—one of those low mean things which, if said to me even by men for whom I have no esteem, make my ears tingle and my cheek blush. When I think of what Darrell has already done for me—me who have no claim on him—it seems to me as if I must hate the man who insinuates, 'Fear lest your benefactor find a smile at his own hearth, a child of his own blood—for you may be richer at his death in proportion as his life is desolate.'"

VANCE.—"You are a fine young fellow, and I beg your pardon. Take care of that milestone—thank you. But I suspect that at least two-thirds of those friendly hands that detained you on the way to me, were stretched out less to Lionel Haughton — a subaltern in the Guards—than to Mr. Darrell's heir-presumptive."

LIONEL.—"That thought sometimes galls me, but it does me good; for it goads on my desire to make myself some one whom the most worldly would not disdain to know for his own sake. Oh for active

portrait you took—you have never heard of her since?"

VANCE.—"Never! How should I! Have you?"

LIONEL.—"Only what Darrell repeated to me. His lawyer had ascertained that she and her grandfather had gone to America. Darrell gently implied, that from what he learned of them, they scarcely merited the interest I felt in their fate. But we were not deceived—were we, Vance?"

VANCE.—"No; the little girl—what was her name? Sukey? Sally?—Sophy—true, Sophy—had something about her extremely prepossessing, besides her pretty face; and, in spite of that horrid cotton print, I shall never forget it."

LIONEL.—"Her face! Nor I. I see it still before me!"

VANCE.—"Her cotton print! I see it still before me! But I must not be ungrateful. Would you believe it, that little portrait, which cost me three pounds, has made, I don't say my fortune, but my fashion?"

LIONEL.—"How! You had the heart to sell it?"

VANCE.—"No; I kept it as a study for young female heads—'with variations,' as they say in music. It was by my female heads that I became the fashion; every order I have contains the condition —'But be sure, one of your sweet female heads, Mr. Vance.' My female heads are as necessary to my canvas as a white horse to Wouvermans'. Well, that child, who cost me three pounds, is the original of them all. Commencing as a Titania, she has been in turns a 'Psyche,' a 'Beatrice Cenci,' a 'Minna,' 'A Portrait of a Nobleman's Daughter,' 'Burns's Mary in Heaven,' 'The Young Gleaner,' and 'Sabrina Fair,' in Milton's Comus.

I have led that child through all history, sacred and profane. I have painted her in all costumes (her own cotton print excepted). My female heads are my glory—even the *Times'* critic allows *that!* 'Mr. Vance, *there*, is inimitable! a type of childlike grace peculiarly his own,' &c., &c. I'll lend you the article."

LIONEL.—"And shall we never again see the original darling Sophy? You will laugh, Vance, but I have been heart-proof against all young ladies. If ever I marry, my wife must have Sophy's eyes! In America!"

VANCE.—Let us hope by this time happily married to a Yankee! Yankees marry girls in their teens, and don't ask for dowries. Married to a Yankee! not a doubt of it! a Yankee who chaws, whittles, and keeps a 'store!'"

LIONEL.—"Monster! Hold your tongue. Apropos of marriage, why are you still single?"

VANCE.—"Because I have no wish to be doubled up! Moreover, man is like a napkin, the more neatly the housewife doubles him, the more carefully she lays him on the shelf. Neither can a man once doubled know how often he may be doubled. Not only his wife folds him in two, but every child quarters him into a new double, till what was a wide and handsome substance, large enough for anything in reason, dwindles into a pitiful square that will not cover one platter — all puckers and creases—smaller and smaller with every double — with every double a new crease. Then, my friend, comes the washing-bill! and, besides all the hurts one receives in the mangle, consider the hourly wear and tear of the linen-press! In short, Shakespeare vindicates the single life, and depicts the double in the famous line—

"You knew real poverty in childhood, Frank?"

"Real poverty, covered over with sham affluence. My father was Genteel Poverty, and my mother was Poor Gentility. The sham affluence went when my father died. The real poverty then came out in all its ugliness. I was taken from a genteel school, at which, long afterwards, I genteelly paid the bills; and I had to support my mother somehow or other—somehow or other I succeeded. Alas, I fear not genteelly! But before I lost her, which I did in a few years, she had some comforts which were not appearances; and she kindly allowed, dear soul, that gentility and shams do not go well together. O! beware of debt, Lionello mio; and never call that economy meanness which is but the safeguard from mean degradation."

"I understand you at last, Vance; shake hands—I know why you are saving."

"Habit now," answered Vance, repressing praise of himself, as usual. "But I remember so well when twopence was a sum to be respected, that to this day I would rather put it by than spend it. All our ideas — like orange-plants—spread out in proportion to the size of the box which imprisons the roots. Then I had a sister." Vance paused a moment, as if in pain, but went on with seeming carelessness, leaning over the window-sill, and turning his face from his friend. "I had a sister older than myself, handsome, gentle. I was so proud of her! Foolish girl! my love was not enough for her. Foolish girl! she could not wait to see what I might live to do for her. She married—oh! so genteelly!—a young man, very well born, who had wooed her before my father died. He had the villany to remain constant when she had not a farthing, and he was dependent on distant relations and his own domains in Parnassus. The wretch was a poet! So they married. They spent their honeymoon genteelly, I daresay. His relations cut him. Parnassus paid no rents. He went abroad. Such heart-rending letters from her! They were destitute. How I worked! how I raged! But how could I maintain her and her husband too, mere child that I was? No matter. They are dead now, both;—all dead for whose sake I first ground colours and saved halfpence. And Frank Vance is a stingy, selfish bachelor. Never revive this dull subject again, or I shall borrow a crown from you, and cut you dead. Waiter, ho!—the bill. I'll just go round to the stables, and see the horse put to."

As the friends re-entered London, Vance said, "Set me down anywhere in Piccadilly; I will walk home. You, I suppose, of course, are staying with your mother in Gloucester Place?"

"No," said Lionel, rather embarrassed; "Colonel Morley, who acts for me as if he were my guardian, took a lodging for me in Chesterfield Street, Mayfair. My hours, I fear, would illsuit my dear mother. Only in town two days; and, thanks to Morley, my table is already covered with invitations."

"Yet you gave me one day, generous friend!"

"You the second day—my mother the first. But there are three balls before me to-night. Come home with me, and smoke your cigar while I dress."

"No; but I will at least light my cigar in your hall,—prodigal!"

Lionel now stopped at his lodging. The groom, who served him also as valet, was in waiting at the door. "A note for you, sir, from Colonel

Histories in the lives of many might be recorded within those walls. Lovers there had breathed their first vows; bridal feasts had been held; babes had crowed in the arms of proud young mothers; politicians there had been raised into ministers; ministers there had fallen back into independent members;" through those doors corpses had been borne forth to relentless vaults. For these races and their records what cared the owner? Their writing was not on the walls. Sponged out as from a slate, their reckonings with Time; leaving dim, here and there, some chance scratch of his own, blurred and bygone. Leaning against the mantelpiece, Darrell gazed round the room with a vague wistful look, as if seeking to conjure up associations that might link the present hour to that past life which had slipped away elsewhere; and his profile, reflected on the mirror behind, pale and mournful, seemed like that ghost of himself which his memory silently evoked.

The man is but little altered externally since we saw him last, however inly changed since he last stood on those unwelcoming floors; the form still retained the same vigour and symmetry—the same unspeakable dignity of mien and bearing—the same thoughtful bend of the proud neck—so distinct, in its elastic rebound, from the stoop of debility or age. Thick as ever the rich mass of dark-brown hair, though, when in the impatience of some painful thought his hand swept the loose curls from his forehead, the silver threads might now be seen shooting here and there—vanishing almost as soon as seen. No, whatever the baptismal register may say to the contrary, that man is not old—not even elderly; in the deep of that clear grey eye light may be calm, but in calm it is vivid; not a ray, sent from brain or from heart, is yet flickering down. On the whole, however, there is less composure than of old in his mien and bearing—less of that resignation which seemed to say, "I have done with the substances of life." Still there was gloom, but it was more broken and restless. Evidently that human breast was again admitting, or forcing itself to court, human hopes, human objects. Returning to the substances of life, their movement was seen in the shadows which, when they wrap us round at remoter distance, seem to lose their trouble as they gain their width. He broke from his musing attitude with an abrupt angry movement, as if shaking off thoughts which displeased him, and gathering his arms tightly to his breast, in a gesture peculiar to himself, walked to and fro the room, murmuring inaudibly. The door opened; he turned quickly, and with an evident sense of relief, for his face brightened. "Alban, my dear Alban."

"Darrell—old friend—old schoolfriend—dear, dear Guy Darrell!" The two Englishmen stood, hands tightly clasped in each other, in true English greeting—their eyes moistening with remembrances that carried them back to boyhood.

Alban was the first to recover self-possession; and when the friends had seated themselves, he surveyed Darrell's countenance deliberately, and said: "So little change!—wonderful! What is your secret?"

"Suspense from life—hybernating. But you beat me; you have been spending life, yet seem as rich in it as when we parted."

"No; I begin to decry the present and laud the past—to read with glasses, to decide from prejudice, to recoil from change, to find sense in

just in time to keep my appointment—reached Ouzelford early this morning, went through the ceremony, made a short speech, came on at once to London, not venturing to diverge to Fawley (which is not very far from Ouzelford), lest, once there again, I should not have strength to leave it—and here I am." Darrell paused, then repeated, in brisk emphatic tone: "Parliament? No. Labour? No. Fellowman. I am about to confess to you; I would snatch back some days of youth—a wintry likeness of youth—better than none. Old friend, let us amuse ourselves! When I was working hard—hard—hard—it was you who would say: 'Come forth, be amused'—you ! happy butterfly that you were! Now, I say to you: 'Show me this flaunting town that you know so well; initiate me into the joy of polite pleasures, social commune—

'Dulce mihi furere est amico.'

You have amusements, let me share them.'"

"Faith," quoth the Colonel, crossing his legs, "you come late in the day! Amusements cease to amuse at last. I have tried all, and begin to be tired. I have had my holiday, exhausted its sports; and you, coming from books and desk fresh into the playground, say, 'Football and leapfrog.' Alas! my poor friend, why did not you come sooner?"

DARRELL.—"One word, one question. You have made EASE a philosophy and a system; no man ever did so with more felicitous grace; nor, in following pleasure, have you parted company with conscience and shame. A fine gentleman ever, in honour as in elegance. Well, are you satisfied with your choice of life? Are you happy?"

"Happy—who is? Satisfied, perhaps!"

"Is there any one you envy—whose choice, other than your own, you would prefer?"

"Certainly."

"Who?"

"You."

"I!" said Darrell, opening his eyes with unaffected amaze. "I! envy me! prefer my choice!"

COLONEL MORLEY (peevishly).—"Without doubt. You have had gratified ambition—a great career. Envy you! who would not? Your own objects in life fulfilled; you coveted distinction—you won it; fortune—your wealth is immense; the restoration of your name and lineage from obscurity and humiliation—are not name and lineage again written in the *Libro d'oro?* What king would not hail you as his councillor? what senate not open its ranks to admit you as a chief? what house, though the haughtiest in the land, would not accept your alliance? And withal, you stand before me stalwart and unbowed, young blood still in your veins. Ungrateful man, who would not change lots with Guy Darrell? Fame, fortune, health, and, not to flatter you, a form and presence that would be remarked, though you stood in that black frock by the side of a monarch in his coronation robes."

DARRELL.—"You have turned my questions against myself with a kindliness of intention that makes me forgive your belief in my vanity. Pass on —or rather pass back; you say you have tried all in life that distracts or sweetens. Not so; lone bachelor; you have not tried wedlock. Has not that been your mistake?"

COLONEL MORLEY. — "Answer for yourself. You have tried it." The words were scarce out of his mouth ere he repented the retort. For Darrell started as if stung to the quick; and his brow, before serene,

warmth).—"In every case, I tell you, no widow shall doff her weeds for me. Did she love the first man? fickle is the woman who can love twice. Did she not love him? why did she marry him? perhaps she sold herself to a rent-roll? Shall she sell herself again to me, for a jointure? Heaven forbid! Talk not of widows. No dainty so flavourless as a heart warmed up again."

COLONEL MORLEY.—"Neither maids, be they old or young, nor widows. Possibly you want an angel. London is not the place for angels."

DARRELL.—"I grant that the choice seems involved in perplexity. How can it be otherwise if oneself is perplexed? And yet, Alban, I am serious; and I do not presume to be so exacting as my words have implied. I ask not fortune, nor rank beyond gentle blood, nor youth, nor beauty, nor accomplishments, nor fashion, but I do ask one thing, and one thing only."

COLONEL MORLEY.—"What is that? you have left nothing worth the having, to ask for."

DARRELL.—"Nothing! I have left all! I ask some one whom I can love; love better than all the world—not the *mariage de convenance*, not the *mariage de raison*, but the *mariage d'amour*. All other marriage, with vows of love so solemn, with intimacy of commune so close, all other marriage, in my eyes, is an acted falsehood—a varnished sin. Ah, if I had thought so always! But away regret and repentance! The Future alone is now before me! Alban Morley! I would sign away all I have in the world (save the old house at Fawley), ay, and after signing, cut off, to boot, this right hand, could I but once fall in love; love, and be loved again, as any two of heaven's simplest human creatures may love each other while life is fresh! Strange, strange—look out into the world; mark the man of our years who shall be most courted, most adulated, or admired. Give him all the attributes of power, wealth, royalty, genius, fame. See all the younger generations bow before him with hope or awe; his word can make their fortune; at his smile a reputation dawns. Well; now let that man say to the young, Room amongst yourselves—all that wins me this homage I would lay at the feet of Beauty. I enter the lists of love,' and straightway his power vanishes, the poorest booby of twenty-four can jostle him aside; before, the object of reverence, he is now the butt of ridicule. The instant he asks right to win the heart of woman, a boy whom, in all else, he could rule as a lackey, cries, 'Off, Greybeard, *that* realm at least is mine!'"

COLONEL MORLEY.—"This were but eloquent extravagance, even if your beard were grey. Men older than you, and with half your pretensions, even of outward form, have carried away hearts from boys like Adonis. Only choose well; that's the difficulty—if it was not difficult, who would be a bachelor!"

DARRELL.—"Guide my choice. Pilot me to the haven."

COLONEL MORLEY.—"Accepted! But you must remount a suitable establishment; reopen your way to the great world, and penetrate those sacred recesses where awaiting spinisters weave the fatal web. Leave all to me. Let Mills (I see you have him still) call on me tomorrow about your *ménage*. You will give dinners, of course?"

DARRELL.—"Oh, of course; must I dine at them myself?"

Morley laughed softly, and took up his hat.

"So soon!" cried Darrell. "If I

WHAT WILL HE DO WITH IT?

DARRELL.—"Was she with him at the time?"

COLONEL MORLEY.—"Lady Montfort?—No; they were very seldom together."

DARRELL.—"She is not married again yet?"

COLONEL MORLEY.—"No, but still young, and so beautiful, she will have many offers. I know those who are waiting to propose. Montfort has been only dead eighteen months—died just before young Carr's marriage. His widow lives, in complete seclusion, at her jointure-house near Twickenham. She has only seen even me once since her loss."

DARRELL.—"When was that?"

MORLEY.—"About six or seven months ago; she asked after you with much interest."

DARRELL.—"After me!"

COLONEL MORLEY.—"To be sure. Don't I remember how constantly she and her mother were at your house? Is it strange that she should ask after you? You ought to know her better—the most affectionate grateful character."

DARRELL.—"I dare say. But at the time you refer to, I was too occupied to acquire much accurate knowledge of a young lady's character. I should have known her mother's character better, yet I mistook even that."

COLONEL MORLEY.—"Mrs. Lyndsay's character you might well mistake,—charming but artificial: Lady Montfort is natural. Indeed, if you had not that illiberal prejudice against widows, she was the very person I was about to suggest to you."

DARRELL.—"A fashionable beauty! and young enough to be my daughter. Such is human friendship! So the marquesate is extinct, and Sir James Vipont, whom I remember in the House of Commons—respectable man—great authority on cattle—timid, and always saying, 'Did you read that article in to-day's paper?'—has the estates and the earldom."

COLONEL MORLEY.—"Yes. There was some fear of a disputed succession, but Sir James made his claim very clear. Between you and me, the change has been a serious affliction to the Viponts. The late Lord was not wise, but on State occasions he looked his part—*très Grand Seigneur*—and Carr managed the family influence with admirable tact. The present Lord has the habits of a yeoman; his wife shares his tastes. He has taken the management not only of the property, but of its influence, out of Carr's hands, and will make a sad mess of it, for he is an impracticable, obsolete politician. He will never keep the family together—impossible—a mad thing. I remember how our last muster, five years ago next Christmas, struck terror into Lord ——'s Cabinet; the mere report of it in the newspapers set all people talking and thinking. The result was, that, two weeks after, proper overtures were made to Carr—he consented to assist the ministers—and the country was saved! Now, thanks to this stupid new Earl, in eighteen months we have lost ground which it took at least a century and a half to gain. Our votes are divided, our influence frittered away; Montfort-house is shut up, and Carr, grown quite thin, says that in the coming 'Crisis' a Cabinet will not only be formed, but will also last—last time enough for irreparable mischief,—without a single Vipont in office."

Thus Colonel Morley continued in mournful strain, Darrell silent by his side, till the Colonel reached his own door. There, while applying

the desultory links of reverie suggested an object to his devious feet. He had but to follow that street to his right hand, to gain in a quarter of an hour a sight of the humble dwelling-house in which he had first settled down, after his early marriage, to the arid labours of the bar. He would go, now that, wealthy and renowned, he was revisiting the long-deserted focus of English energies, and contemplate the obscure abode in which his powers had been first concentrated on the pursuit of renown and wealth. Who among my readers that may have risen on the glittering steep ("Ah, who can tell how hard it is to climb!"*) has not been similarly attracted towards the roof at the craggy foot of the ascent, under which golden dreams refreshed his straining sinews? Somewhat quickening his steps, now that a bourne was assigned to them, the man growing old in years, but, unhappily for himself, too tenacious of youth in its grand discontent, and keen susceptibilities to pain, strode noiselessly on, under the gaslights, under the stars; gaslights primly marshalled at equidistance; stars that seem to the naked eye dotted over space without symmetry or method —Man's order, near and finite, is so distinct; the Maker's order, remote, infinite, is so beyond Man's comprehension even of *what* is order!

Darrell paused hesitating. He had now gained a spot in which improvement had altered the landmarks. The superb broad thoroughfare continued where once it had vanished abrupt in a labyrinth of courts and alleys. But the way was not hard to find. He turned a little towards the left, recognising, with admiring interest, in the gay white would-be Grecian edifice, with its French *grille*, bronzed, gilded, the transformed Museum in the still libraries of which he had sometimes snatched a brief and ghostly respite from books of law. Onwards yet through lifeless Bloomsbury, not so far towards the last bounds of Atlas as the desolation of Podden Place, but the solitude deepening as he passed. There it is, a quiet street indeed! not a soul on its gloomy pavements, not even a policeman's soul. Nought stirring save a stealthy, profligate, good-for-nothing cat, flitting fine through yon area bars. Down that street had he come, I trow, with a livelier, quicker step the day when, by the strange goodluck which had uniformly attended his wordly career of honours, he had been suddenly called upon to supply the place of an absent senior, and, in almost his earliest brief, the Courts of Westminster had recognised a master;—come, I trow, with a livelier step, knocked at that very door whereat he is halting now; entered the room where the young wife sat, and at sight of her querulous peevish face, and at sound of her unsympathising languid voice, fled into his cupboard-like back parlour—and muttered "courage—courage" to endure the home he had entered longing for a voice which should invite and respond to a cry of joy.

How closed up, dumb, and blind, looked the small mean house, with its small mean door, its small mean rayless windows. Yet a FAME had been born there! Who are the residents now? Buried in slumber, have *they* any "golden dreams?" Works therein any struggling brain, to which the prosperous man might whisper "courage;" or beats, there, any troubled heart to which faithful

---

* "Ah, who can tell how hard it is to climb
The steep where Fame's proud temple shines afar?"
 BEATTIE.

him: on the very brink of the last scandal, a cold, caught at some Vipont's ball, became fever; and so from that door the Black Horses bore away the Bloomsbury Dame, ere she was yet—the fashion! Happy in grief the widower who may, with confining hand, ransack the lost wife's harmless desk, sure that no thought concealed from him in life will rise accusing from the treasured papers. But that pale proud mourner, hurrying the eye over sweet-scented *billets*, compelled, in very justice to the dead, to convince himself that the mother of his children was corrupt only at heart—that the Black Horses had come to the door in time —and, wretchedly consoled by that niggardly conviction, flinging into the flames the last flimsy tatters on which his honour (rook-like in his own keeping) had been fluttering to and fro in the charge of a vain treacherous fool. Envy you *that* mourner? No! not even in his release. Memory is not nailed down in the velvet coffin; and to great loyal natures, less bitter is the memory of the lost when hallowed by tender sadness, than when coupled with scorn and shame.

The wife is dead. Dead, too, long years ago, the Lothario! The world has forgotten them; they fade out of this very record when ye turn the page; no influence, no bearing have they on such future events as may mark what yet rests of life to Guy Darrell. But as he there stands and gazes into space, the two forms are before his eye as distinct as if living still. Slowly, slowly he gazes them down; the false smiles flicker away from their feeble lineaments; woe and terror on their aspects— they sink, they shrivel, they dissolve!

CHAPTER V.

The wreck cast back from Charybdis.

Souviens-toi de la Gabrielle.

GUY DARRELL turned hurriedly from the large house in the great square, and, more and more absorbed in reverie, he wandered out of his direct way homeward, clear and broad though it was, and did not rouse himself till he felt, as it were, that the air had grown darker; and, looking vaguely round, he saw that he had strayed into a dim maze of lanes and passages. He paused under one of the rare lamp-posts, gathering up his recollections of the London he had so long quitted, and doubtful for a moment or two which turn to take. Just then, up from an alley fronting him at right angles, came sullenly, warily, a tall, sinewy, ill-boding tatterdemalion figure, and, seeing Darrell's face under the lamp, halted abrupt at the mouth of the narrow passage from which it had emerged — a dark form filling up the dark aperture. Does that ragged wayfarer recognise a foe by the imperfect ray of the lamplight? or is he a mere vulgar footpad, who is doubting whether he should spring upon a prey? Hostile his look—his gesture—the sudden cowering down of the strong frame, as if for a bound; but still he is irre-

which he stands. He looks round, the policeman is baffled, the coast clear. He steals forth, and pauses under the same gaslight as that under which Guy Darrell had paused before—under the same gaslight, under the same stars. From some recess in his rags he draws forth a large, distained, distended pocketbook — last relic of sprucer days — leather of dainty morocco, once elaborately tooled, patent springs, fairy lock, fit receptacle for bank-notes, *billets-doux*, memoranda of debts of honour, or pleasurable engagements. Now how worn, tarnished, greasy, rapscallion-like, the costly bauble! Filled with what motley unlovable contents — stale pawn-tickets of foreign *monts de piété*, pledges never henceforth to be redeemed; scrawls by villanous hands in thievish hieroglyphics; ugly implements replacing the malachite penknife, the golden tooth-pick, the jewelled pencil-case, once so neatly set within their satin lappets. Ugly implements, indeed— a file, a gimlet, loaded dice. Pellmell, with such more hideous and recent contents, dishonoured evidences of gaudier summer life — locks of ladies' hair, love-notes treasured mechanically, not from amorous sentiment, but perhaps from some vague idea that they might be of use if those who gave the locks or wrote the notes should be raised in fortune, and could buy back the memorials of shame. Diving amidst these miscellaneous documents and treasures, the prowler's hand rested on some old letters, in clerk-like fair caligraphy, tied round with a dirty string, and on them, in another and fresher writing, a scrap that contained an address—"Samuel Adolphus Poole, Esq., Alhambra Villa, Regent's Park." "To-morrow, Nix my Dolly; to-morrow," muttered the tatterdemalion; "but to-night;—plague on it, where is the other blackguard's direction? Ah, here—" And he extracted from the thievish scrawls a *peculiarly* thievish-looking hieroglyph. Now, as he lifts it up to read by the gaslight, survey him well. Do you not know him? Is it possible? What! the brilliant sharper! The ruffian exquisite! Jasper Losely! Can it be? Once before, in the fields of Fawley, we beheld him out at elbows, seedy, shabby, ragged. But then it was the decay of a foppish spendthrift— clothes distained, ill-assorted, yet, still of fine cloth; shoes in holes, yet still pearl-coloured brodequins. But now it is the decay of no foppish spendthrift; the rags are not of fine cloth; the tattered shoes are not brodequins. The man has fallen far below the politer grades of knavery, in which the sharper affects the beau. And the countenance, as we last saw it, if it had lost much of its earlier beauty, was still incontestably handsome. What with vigour, and health, and animal spirits, *then* on the aspect still lingered light; *now*, from corruption, the light itself was gone. In that herculean constitution excess of all kinds had at length forced its ravage, and the ravage was visible in the ruined face. The once sparkling eye was dull and bloodshot. The colours of the cheek, once clear and vivid, to which fiery drink had only sent the blood in a warmer glow, were now of a leaden dulness, relieved but by broken streaks of angry red—like gleams of flame struggling through gathered smoke. The profile, once sharp and delicate like Apollo's, was now confused in its swollen outline; a few years more, and it would be gross as that of Silenus—the nostrils, distended with incipient carbuncles, which betray the gnawing fang that alcohol fastens into the liver. Evil passions had destroyed the outline

run away from his face. Thin as he was, he looked all skin and no bones —a goblin of a man whom it would not astonish you to hear could creep through a keyhole. Seeming still more shadowy and impalpable by his slight, thin, sable dress, not of cloth, but a sort of stuff like alpaca. Nor was that dress ragged, nor, as seen but in starlight, did it look worn or shabby; still you had but to glance at the creature to feel that it was a child in the same Family of Night as the ragged felon that towered by its side. The two outlaws stared at each other. "Cutts!" said Losely, in the old rollicking voice, but in a hoarser, rougher key—" Cutts, my boy, here I am; welcome me!"

"What! General Jas.!" returned Cutts, in a tone which was not without a certain respectful awe, and then proceeded to pour out a series of questions in a mysterious language, which may be thus translated and abridged: "How long have you been in England? how has it fared with you? you seem very badly off? coming here to hide? nothing very bad, I hope? what is it?"

Jasper answered in the same language, though with less practised mastery of it—and with that constitutional levity which, whatever the time or circumstance, occasionally gave a strange sort of wit, or queer, uncanny, devil-me-care vein of drollery, to his modes of expression.

"Three months of the worst luck man ever had—a row with the gens-d'armes—long story—three of our pals seized—affair of the galleys for them, I suspect—French frogs can't seize me—fricasseed one or two of them—broke away—crossed the country—reached the coast—found an honest smuggler—landed off Sussex with a few other kegs of brandy—remembered you—preserved the address you gave me— and condescend to this rat-hole for a night or so. Let me in—knock up somebody—break open the larder—I want to eat—I am famished—I should have eaten you by this time, only there's nothing on your bones."

The little man opened the door—a passage black as Erebus. "Give me your hand, General." Jasper was led through the pitchy gloom for a few yards; then the guide found a gas-cock, and the place broke suddenly into light. A dirty narrow staircase on one side; facing it, a sort of lobby, in which an open door showed a long sanded parlour, like that in public-houses—several tables, benches, the walls whitewashed, but adorned with sundry ingenious designs made by charcoal or the smoked ends of clay-pipes. A strong smell of stale tobacco and of gin and rum. Another gaslight, swinging from the centre of the ceiling, sprang into light as Cutts touched the tap-cock.

"Wait here," said the guide. "I will go and get you some supper."

"And some brandy," said Jasper.

"Of course."

The bravo threw himself at length on one of the tables, and, closing his eyes, moaned. His vast strength had become acquainted with physical pain. In its stout knots and fibres, aches and sharp twinges, the dragon-teeth of which had been sown years ago in revels or brawls, which then seemed to bring but innocuous joy and easy triumph, now began to gnaw and grind. But when Cutts reappeared with coarse viands and the brandy bottle, Jasper shook off the sense of pain, as does a wounded wild beast that can still devour; and after regaling fast and ravenously, he emptied half the bottle at a draught, and felt himself restored and fresh.

"Shall you fling yourself amongst the swell fellows who hold their club here, General?" asked Cutts; "'tis

there went she. He might baffle the police, not her. Hunger had often forced him to accept her aid. As soon as he received it, he hid from her again, hurrying himself deeper and deeper in the mud, like a persecuted tench. He associated her idea with all the ill-luck that had befallen him. Several times some villanous scheme on which he had counted to make his fortune had been baffled in the most mysterious way; and just when baffled—and there seemed no choice but to cut his own throat or some one else's—up turned grim Arabella Crane, in the iron-grey gown, and with the iron-grey ringlets—hatefully, awfully beneficent—offering food, shelter, gold—and some demoniacal, honourable work. Often had he been in imminent peril from watchful law or treacherous accomplice. She had warned and saved him, as she had saved him from the fell Gabrielle Desmarets, who, unable to bear the sentence of penal servitude, after a long process, defended with astonishing skill, and enlisting the romantic sympathies of young France, had contrived to escape into another world by means of a subtle poison concealed about her *distinguée* person, and which she had prepared years ago with her own bloodless hands, and no doubt scientifically tested its effect on others. The cobra capella is gone at last! "*Souviens-toi de ta Gabrielle*," O Jasper Losely! But why Arabella Crane should thus continue to watch over him whom she no longer professed to love—how she should thus have acquired the gift of ubiquity and the power to save him—Jasper Losely could not conjecture. The whole thing seemed to him weird and supernatural. Most truly did he say that she had *cowed him*. He had often longed to strangle her; when absent from her, had often resolved upon that act of gratitude. The moment he came in sight of her stern, haggard face—her piercing lurid eyes—the moment he heard her slow, dry voice in some such sentences as these—"Again you come to me in your trouble, and ever shall. Am I not still as your mother, but with a wife's fidelity, till death us do part? There is the portrait of what you were—look at it, Jasper. Now turn to the glass—see what you are. Think of the fate of Gabrielle Desmarets! But for me, what, long since, had been your own? But I will save you—I have sworn it. You shall be wax in these hands at last;"—the moment that voice thus claimed and insisted on redeeming him, the ruffian felt a cold shudder — his courage oozed—he could no more have nerved his arm against her than a Thug would have lifted his against the dire goddess of his murderous superstition. Jasper could not resist a belief that the life of this dreadful protectress was, somehow or other, made essential to his —that, were she to die, he should perish in some ghastly and preternatural expiation. But for the last few months he had, at length, escaped from her—diving so low, so deep into the mud, that even her net could not mesh him. Hence, perhaps, the imminence of the perils from which he had so narrowly escaped—hence the utterness of his present destitution. But man, however vile, whatever his peril, whatever his destitution, was born free, and loves liberty. Liberty to go to Satan in his own way was to Jasper Losely a supreme blessing compared to that benignant compassionate *espionage*, with its relentless eye and restraining hand. Alas and alas! deem not this perversity unnatural in that headstrong self-destroyer! How many are there whom not a

all parties—when recognised leaders have contrived to damage themselves—when a Cabinet is shaking, and the public neither care to destroy nor to keep it;—a time, too, when the country seemed in some danger, and when, mere men of business held unequal to the emergency, whatever name suggested associations of vigour, eloquence, genius, rose to a premium above its market price in times of tranquillity and tape. Without effort of his own—by the mere force of the undercurrent—Guy Darrell was thrown up from oblivion into note. He could not form a cabinet—certainly not; but he might help to bring a cabinet together, reconcile jarring elements, adjust disputed questions, take in such government some high place, influence its councils, and delight a public weary of the oratory of the day, with the eloquence of a former race. For the public is ever a *laudator temporis acti*, and whatever the authors or the orators immediately before it, were those authors and orators Homers and Ciceros, would still shake a disparaging head, and talk of these degenerate days, as Homer himself talked ages before Leonidas stood in the pass of Thermopylæ, or Miltiades routed Asian armaments at Marathon. Guy Darrell belonged to a former race. The fathers of those young Members rising now into fame, had quoted to their sons his pithy sentences, his vivid images; and added, as Fox added when quoting Burke, "but you should have heard and seen the man!"

Heard and seen the man! But there he was again!—come up as from a grave—come up to the public just when such a man was wanted. Wanted how?—wanted where? Oh, somehow and somewhere! There he is! make the most of him.

The house in Carlton Gardens is prepared, the establishment mounted. Thither flock all the Viponts —nor they alone; all the chiefs of all parties—nor they alone; all the notabilities of our grand metropolis. Guy Darrell might be startled at his own position; but he comprehended its nature, and it did not discompose his nerves. He knew public life well enough to be aware how much the popular favour is the creature of an accident. By chance he had picked the time; had he thus come to town the season before, he might have continued obscure, a man like Guy Darrell not being wanted then. Whether with or without design, his bearing confirmed and extended the effect produced by his reappearance. Gracious, but modestly reserved— he spoke little, listened beautifully. Many of the questions which agitated all around him had grown up into importance since his day of action; nor in his retirement had he traced their progressive development, with their changeful effects upon men and parties. But a man who has once gone deeply into practical politics might sleep in the Cave of Trophonius for twenty years, and find, on waking, very little to learn. Darrell regained the level of the day, and seized upon all the strong points on which men were divided, with the rapidity of a prompt and comprehensive intellect—his judgment perhaps the clearer from the freshness of long repose, and the composure of dispassionate survey. When partisans wrangled as to what should have been done, Darrell was silent; when they asked what should *be* done, out came one of his terse sentences, and a knot was cut. Meanwhile it is true this man, round whom expectations grouped and rumour buzzed, was in neither House of Parliament; but that was

mournfulness in the retrospect? is their eagerness to renew the strife? Is that interest in the Hour's debate feigned or real? Impossible for him who gazed upon that face to say. And that eye would have seemed to the gazer to read himself through and through to the heart's core, long ere the gazer could hazard a single guess as to the thoughts beneath that marble forehead—as to the emotions within the heart over which, in old senatorial fashion, the arms were folded with so conventional an ease.

CHAPTER VII.

Darrell and Lionel.

DARRELL had received Lionel with some evident embarrassment, which soon yielded to affectionate warmth. He took to the young man whose fortunes he had so improved; he felt that with the improved fortunes the young man's whole being was improved;—assured position, early commune with the best social circles, in which the equality of fashion smooths away all disparities in rank, had softened in Lionel much of the wayward and morbid irritability of his boyish pride; but the high spirit, the generous love of independence, the scorn of mercenary calculation, were strong as ever; these were in the grain of his nature. In common with all who in youth aspire to be one day noted from "the undistinguishable many," Lionel had formed to himself a certain ideal standard, above the ordinary level of what the world is contented to call honest, or esteem clever. He admitted into his estimate of life the heroic element, not undesirable even in the most practical point of view, for the world is so in the habit of decrying—of disbelieving in high motives and pure emotions—of daguerreotyping itself with all its ugliest wrinkles, stripped of the true bloom that brightens, of the true expression that redeems, those defects which it invites the sun to limn, that we shall never judge human nature aright, if we do not set out in life with our gaze on its fairest beauties, and our belief in its latent good. In a word, we should begin with the Heroic, if we would learn the Human. But though to himself Lionel thus secretly prescribed a certain superiority of type, to be sedulously aimed at, even if never actually attained, he was wholly without pedantry and arrogance towards his own contemporaries. From this he was saved not only by good-nature, animal spirits, frank hardihood, but by the very affluence of ideas which animated his tongue, coloured his language, and, whether to young or old, wise or dull, made his conversation racy and original. He was a delightful companion; and if he had taken much instruction from those older and wiser than himself, he so bathed that instruction in the fresh fountain of his own lively intelligence, so warmed it at his own beating impulsive heart that he could make an old man's gleanings from experience seem a young

CHAPTER VIII

Saith a very homely proverb (pardon its vulgarity), "You cannot make a silk purse out of a sow's ear." But a sow's ear is a much finer work of art than a silk purse. And grand, indeed, the mechanician who could make a sow's ear out of a silk purse, or conjure into creatures of flesh and blood the sarcenet and tulle of a London drawing-room.

"MAMMA," asked Honoria Carr Vipont, "what sort of a person was Mrs. Darrell?"

"She was not in our set, my dear," answered Lady Selina. "The Vipont Crookes are just one of those connections with which, though, of course, one is civil to all connections, one is more or less intimate, according as they take after the Viponts or after the Crookes. Poor woman! she died just before Mr. Darrell entered Parliament and appeared in society. But I should say she was not an agreeable person. Not nice," added Lady Selina, after a pause, and conveying a world of meaning in that conventional monosyllable.

"I suppose she was very accomplished—very clever?"

"Quite the reverse, my dear. Mr. Darrell was exceedingly young when he married—scarcely of age. She was not the sort of woman to suit him."

"But at least she must have been very much attached to him—very proud of him?"

Lady Selina glanced aside from her work, and observed her daughter's face, which evinced an animation not usual to a young lady of a breeding so lofty, and a mind so well disciplined.

"I don't think," said Lady Selina, "that she was proud of him. She would have been proud of his station, or rather of that to which his fame and fortune would have raised her, had she lived to enjoy it. But for a few years after her marriage they were very poor; and though his rise at the bar was sudden and brilliant, he was long wholly absorbed in his profession, and lived in Bloomsbury. Mrs. Darrell was not proud of that. The Crookes are generally fine—give themselves airs—marry into great houses if they can—but we can't naturalise them—they always remain Crookes—useful connections, very! Carr says we have not a more useful—but third-rate, my dear. All the Crookes are bad wives, because they are never satisfied with their own homes, but are always trying to get into great people's homes. Not very long before she died, Mrs. Darrell took her friend and relation, Mrs. Lyndsay, to live with her. I suspect it was not from affection, or any great consideration for Mrs. Lyndsay's circumstances (which were indeed those of actual destitution, till—thanks to Mr. Darrell—she won her lawsuit), but simply because she looked to Mrs. Lyndsay to get her into our set. Mrs. Lyndsay was a great favourite with all of us, charming manners—perfectly correct, too—thorough Vipont—thorough gentlewoman—but artful! Oh, so artful! She humoured poor Mrs. Darrell's absurd vanity; but she took care not to injure herself. Of course, Darrell's wife, and a Vipont—though only a Vipont Crooke—had free passport into the outskirts of good society, the great par-

Guy Darrell was very pleasant at "the small family dinner-party." Carr was always popular in his manners—the true old House of Commons manner, which was very like that of a gentlemanlike public school. Lady Selina, as has been said before, in her own family circle was natural and genial. Young Carr, there, without his wife, more pretentious than his father—being a Lord of the Admiralty—felt a certain awe of Darrell, and spoke little, which was much to his own credit, and to the general conviviality. The other members of the symposium, besides Lady Selina, Honoria, and a younger sister, were but Darrell, Lionel, and Lady Selina's two cousins; elderly peers — one with the garter, the other in the cabinet—jovial men who had been wild fellows once in the same mess-room, and still joked at each other whenever they met as they met now. Lionel, who remembered Vance's description of Lady Selina, and who had since heard her spoken of in society as a female despot who carried to perfection the arts by which despots flourish, with majesty to impose, and caresses to deceive—an Aurungzebe in petticoats—was sadly at a loss to reconcile such portraiture with the good-humoured, motherly woman who talked to him of her home, her husband, her children, with open fondness and becoming pride, and who, far from being so formidably clever as the world cruelly gave out, seemed to Lionel rather below par in her understanding; strike from her talk its kindliness, and the residue was very like twaddle. After dinner, various members of the Vipont family dropped in—asked impromptu by Carr or by Lady Selina, in hasty three-cornered notes, to take that occasion of renewing their acquaintance with their distinguished connection. By some accident, amongst those invited there were but few young single ladies; and by some other accident, those few were all plain. Honoria Vipont was unequivocally the belle of the room. It could not but be observed that Darrell seemed struck with her—talked with her more than with any other lady; and when she went to the piano, and played that great air of Beethoven's, in which music seems to have got into a knot that only fingers the most artful can unravel, Darrell remained in his seat aloof and alone, listening, no doubt, with ravished attention. But just as the air ended, and Honoria turned round to look for him, he was gone.

Lionel did not linger long after him. The gay young man went, thence, to one of those vast crowds which seemed convened for a practical parody of Mr. Bentham's famous proposition—contriving the smallest happiness for the greatest number.

It was a very good house, belonging to a very great person. Colonel Morley had procured an invitation for Lionel, and said, "Go; you should be seen there." Colonel Morley had passed the age of growing into society —no such cares for the morrow could add a cubit to his conventional stature. One amongst a group of other young men by the doorway, Lionel beheld Darrell, who had arrived before him, listening to a very handsome young lady, with an attention quite as earnest as that which had gratified the superior mind of the well-educated Honoria. A very handsome young lady certainly, but not with a superior mind, nor supposed hitherto to have found young gentlemen "insipid." Doubtless she would henceforth do so. A few minutes after, Darrell was listening again—this time to another young

an author may feel who has been the rage, and without fault of his own is so no more. The rays that had gilt him had gone back to the orb that lent. And they who were most genial still to Lionel Haughton, were those who still most respected thirty-five thousand pounds a year—in Guy Darrell!

Lionel was angry with himself that he felt galled. But in his wounded pride there was no mercenary regret—only that sort of sickness which comes to youth when the hollowness of worldly life is first made clear to it. From the faces round him there fell that glamour by which the *amour propre* is held captive in large assemblies, where the *amour propre* is flattered. "Magnificent, intelligent audience," thinks the applauded actor. "Delightful party," murmurs the worshipped beauty. Glamour! glamour! Let the audience yawn while the actor mouths; let the party neglect the beauty to adore another, and straightway the "magnificent audience" is an "ignorant public," and the "delightful party" a "heartless world."

CHAPTER IX.

Escaped from a London Drawing-room, flesh once more tingles and blood flows—Guy Darrell explains to Lionel Haughton why he holds it a duty to be—an old fool.

LIONEL HAUGHTON glided through the disenchanted rooms, and breathed a long breath of relief when he found himself in the friendless streets.

As he walked slow and thoughtful on, he suddenly felt a hand upon his shoulder, turned, and saw Darrell.

"Give me your arm, my dear Lionel; I am tired out. What a lovely night! What sweet scorn in the eyes of those stars that we have neglected for yon flaring lights."

LIONEL.—"Is it scorn?—is it pity? Is it but serene indifference?"

DARRELL.—"As we ourselves interpret; if scorn be present in our own hearts, it will be seen in the disc of Jupiter. Man, egotist though he be, exacts sympathy from all the universe. Joyous, he says to the sun, 'Life-giver, rejoice with me.' Grieving, he says to the moon, 'Pensive one, thou sharest my sorrow.' Hope for fame; a star is its promise! Mourn for the dead; a star is the land of reunion! Say to earth, 'I have done with thee;' to Time, 'Thou hast nought to bestow;' and all Space cries aloud, 'The earth is a speck, thine inheritance infinity. Time melts while thou sighest. The discontent of a mortal is the instinct that proves thee immortal.' Thus construing Nature, Nature is our companion, our consoler. Benign as the playmate, she lends herself to our shifting humours. Serious as the teacher, she responds to the steadier inquiries of reason. Mystic and hallowed as the priestess, she keeps alive by dim oracles that spiritual yearning within us, in which, from savage to sage—through all dreams, through all creeds—thrills the sense of a link with Divinity. Never, therefore, while conferring with Nature, is Man wholly alone, nor is she a single companion with uniform shape. Ever new, ever various, she can pass from gay to severe—from fancy to

were to his eyes the moon-track in the ocean of history—light on the waves over which they had gleamed—all the ocean elsewhere dark! With him thought I; as my father spoke, his child believed. But what to the eyes of the world was this inheritor of a vaunted name?—a threadbare, slighted, rustic pedant—no station in the very province in which mouldered away the last lowly dwelling-place of his line. By lineage high above most nobles, in position below most yeomen. He had learning, he had genius; but the studies to which they were devoted only served yet more to impoverish his scanty means, and led rather to ridicule than to honour. Not a day but what I saw on his soft features the smart of a fresh sting, the gnawing of a new care. Thus, as a boy, feeling in myself a strength inspired by affection, I came to him, one day as he sate grieving, and kneeling to him, said, 'Father, courage yet a little while; I shall soon be man, and I swear to devote myself as man to revive the old fading race so prized by you; to rebuild the House that, by you so loved, is loftier in my eyes than all the heraldry of kings.' And my father's face brightened, and his voice blest me; and I rose up—ambitious!" Darrell paused, heaved a short, quick sigh, and then rapidly continued:—

"I was fortunate at the university. That was a day when chiefs of party looked for recruits amongst young men who had given the proofs and won the first-fruits of emulation and assiduity. For statesmanship then was deemed an art which, like that of war, needs early discipline. I had scarcely left college when I was offered a seat in Parliament, by the head of the Viponts, an old Lord Montfort. I was dazzled but for one moment—I declined the next. The fallen House of Darrell needed wealth, and Parliamentary success, in it higher honours, often require wealth—never gives it. It chanced that I had a college acquaintance with a young man named Vipont Crooke. His grandfather, one of the numberless Viponts, had been compelled to add the name of Crooke to his own, on succeeding to the property of some rich uncle, who was one of the numberless Crookes. I went with this college acquaintance to visit the old Lord Montfort, at his villa near London, and thence to the country-house of the Vipont Crookes. I staid at the last two or three weeks. While there, I received a letter from the elder Fairthorn, my father's bailiff, entreating me to come immediately to Fawley, hinting at some great calamity. On taking leave of my friend and his family, something in the manner of his sister startled and pained me—an evident confusion, a burst of tears—I know not what. I had never sought to win her affections. I had an ideal of the woman I could love. It did not resemble her. On reaching Fawley, conceive the shock that awaited me. My father was like one heart-stricken. The principal mortgagee was about to foreclose—Fawley about to pass for ever from the race of the Darrells. I saw that the day my father was driven from the old house would be his last on earth. What means to save him?—how raise the pitiful sum—but a few thousands—by which to release from the spoiler's gripe those barren acres which all the lands of the Seymour or the Gower could never replace in my poor father's eyes? My sole income was a college fellowship, adequate to all my wants, but useless for sale or loan. I spent the night in vain consultation with Fairthorn. There seemed not a hope. Next morning

not kept. No child of mine survives to be taught reverence to my father's grave. My wedded life was not happy: its record needs no words. Of two children born to me, both are gone. My son went first. I had thrown my life's life into him—a boy of energy, of noble promise. 'Twas for him I began to build that baffled fabric—'Sepulchri immemor.' For him I bought, acre on acre, all the land within reach of Fawley—lands twelve miles distant. I had meant to fill up the intervening space—to buy out a mushroom earl whose woods and cornfields lie between. I was scheming the purchase — scrawling on the county map — when they brought the news that the boy I had just taken back to school was dead—drowned bathing on a calm summer eve. No, Lionel. I must go on. That grief I have wrestled with—conquered. I was widowed then. A daughter still left—the first-born, whom my father had blest on his deathbed. I transferred all my love, all my hopes, to her. I had no vain preference for male heirs. Is a race less pure that runs on through the female line? Well, my son's death was merciful compared to——" Again Darrell stopped—again hurried on. "Enough! all is forgiven in the grave! I was then still in the noon of man's life, free to form new ties. Another grief that I cannot tell you; it is not all conquered yet. And by that grief the last verdure of existence was so blighted, that—that—in short, I had no heart for nuptial altars — for the social world. Years went by. Each year I said, 'Next year the wound will be healed; I have time yet.' Now age is near, the grave not far; now, if ever, I must fulfil the promise that cheered my father's deathbed. Nor does that duty comprise all my motives. If I would regain healthful thought, manly action, for my remaining years, I must feel that one haunting memory is exorcised, and for ever laid at rest. It can be so only—whatever my risk of new cares — whatever the folly of the hazard at my age—be so only by—by——" Once more Darrell paused, fixed his eyes steadily on Lionel, and, opening his arms, cried out, "Forgive me, my noble Lionel, that I am not contented with an heir like you; and do not you mock at the old man who dreams that woman may love him yet, and that his own children may inherit his father's home."

Lionel sprang to the breast that opened to him; and if Darrell had planned how best to remove from the young man's mind for ever the possibility of one selfish pang, no craft could have attained his object like that touching confidence before which the disparities between youth and age literally vanished. And, both made equal, both elevated alike, verily I know not which at the moment felt the elder or the younger! Two noble hearts, intermingled in one emotion, are set free from all time save the present; par each with each, they meet as brothers twin-born.

END OF VOL. I.

www.ingramcontent.com/pod-product-compliance
Lightning Source LLC
Chambersburg PA
CBHW030316170426
43202CB00009B/1020